Sanctions and Sanctuary

WOMEN IN CROSS-CULTURAL PERSPECTIVE

Sue-Ellen Jacobs, Series Editor

This series presents ethnographic case studies that address theoretical, methodological, and practical issues in basic and applied fieldwork; it also includes cross-cultural studies based on secondary sources. Edited by Sue-Ellen Jacobs, the series aims to broaden our knowledge about the varieties and commonalities of women's experiences. One important focus of the series is on women in development and the effects of the development process on women's roles and status. By considering women in the full context of their cultures, this series offers new insights on sociocultural, political, and economic change cross-culturally.

Sanctions and Sanctuary

Cultural Perspectives on the Beating of Wives

EDITED BY

Dorothy Ayers Counts, Judith K. Brown, and Jacquelyn C. Campbell

Westview Press

BOULDER • SAN FRANCISCO • OXFORD

Women in Cross-Cultural Perspective

Copyright © 1992 by Westview Press, Inc.

Published in 1992 in the United States of America by Westview Press, Inc., 5500 Central Avenue, Boulder, Colorado 80301-2847, and in the United Kingdom by Westview Press, 36 Lonsdale Road, Summertown, Oxford OX2 7EW

Library of Congress Cataloging-in-Publication Data
Sanctions and sanctuary : cultural perspectives on the beating of
  wives / edited by Dorothy Ayers Counts, Judith K. Brown, and
Jacquelyn C. Campbell.
    p.   cm.—(Women in cross-cultural perspective)
  Includes bibliographical references and index.
  ISBN 0-8133-7897-4
  1. Wife abuse—Cross-cultural studies. I. Counts, Dorothy Ayers.
II. Brown, Judith K.   III. Campbell, Jacquelyn.   IV. Series.
HV6626.S25   1992
362.82′92—dc20   90-23009
                                                                           CIP

Printed and bound in the United States of America

The paper used in this publication meets the requirements
(∞) of the American National Standard for Permanence of Paper
for Printed Library Materials Z39.48-1984.

10   9   8   7   6   5   4   3   2   1

To Beatrice B. Whiting, with admiration, gratitude, and friendship, and to those women around the world who are being beaten and those trying to help them

ERRATA SHEET FOR:

Sanctions and Sanctuary:
Cultural Perspectives
on the Beating of Wives

edited by
Dorothy Ayers Counts
Judith K. Brown
Jacquelyn C. Campbell

Please add the following lines to the top of page 38:

top crossing and I didn't know he had a beer. He was hiding it. And then
we got off and he told me, "I've got beer." "Well," I told him, "Don't drink,

Contents

Foreword

When Jacquelyn Campbell asked me to write this foreword, my first thought was, "I wish this collection had been published two years earlier." My wish for earlier publication was selfish, as two years ago I was churning through the ethnographic literature looking for information about spousal violence and detailed descriptions of wife-beating events in non-Western societies. Although I eventually found enough information to survey violence between spouses in ninety societies, it was obvious that spousal violence is a topic that is often ignored or given only passing attention by ethnographers. *Sanctions and Sanctuary: Cultural Perspectives on the Beating of Wives* is a significant step in filling this gap in the ethnographic record. Fourteen of the seventeen chapters provide overviews of wife-battering in different societies as well as detailed descriptions of wife-battering events and their social context in those societies (see Chapter 1 for the editors' distinction between wife-beating and battering). Although emphasis is placed on societies in Melanesia, there is also coverage on groups from Central America, South America, Taiwan, the Middle East, and Africa.

The value of this volume is not in a probability sampling of the world's societies but, rather, in the rich ethnographic descriptions that indicate the range and diversity of wife-battering and its contexts around the world. Thus, societies with frequent, less frequent, infrequent, and no wife-battering are included, as are societies in which wife-battering is linked to female suicide (a phenomenon largely ignored in Western-based research on family violence) and in which women have alternatives that allow them to escape batterings. These chapters give one a real sense of the surprising variation in the types and frequency of wife-battering around the world. In addition, they provide information that places wife-battering in the political, economic, and social contexts in which it occurs. This is important, as cross-cultural research consistently shows that individual behavior must be interpreted and explained within its broader cultural context. To go one step further, the descriptions here also support, though in an anecdotal way, previous cross-cultural findings on the relationship between battering and economic and political inequalities between men and women.

The detailed ethnographies are the major strength and contribution of this collection, yet it is far more than a compendium of descriptions. Chapters 1, 2, and 17 provide conceptual and theoretical contexts that place the descriptions in more general frameworks. Included are prior cross-cultural research, evolutionary biology, and Western-based research. Because the authors followed the same general approach in organizing their ethnographic information, the chapters tend to flow and to compliment one another — no mean achievement in an edited work such as this.

Beyond informing, this collection also stimulates the reader to think about and study topics and issues perhaps ignored in earlier cross-cultural and single-culture studies of family violence. For example, the authors illustrate what comes in the aftermath of family violence — the feelings and responses of the victims, the perpetrators, and the community; the distinction between socially acceptable and unacceptable violence in the family context; the role of social change both over time and over place; and the emotion anger seen from a cross-cultural perspective.

To sum up, this collection adds valuable information to the growing cross-cultural literature on family violence. These descriptions of wife-battering in fourteen cultures need to be considered by any serious student of family violence, whether his or her interests are descriptive, conceptual, theoretical, or applied. This book should serve as a model for collections on other topics, which would do well to emulate both the consistency in coverage from chapter to chapter and the integration of the data into broader perspectives.

David Levinson
Human Relations Area Files

Preface

The conversations and symposia resulting in this volume began in 1985 when I returned from Papua New Guinea newly aware of the problem of wife-beating there. In an effort to learn how other anthropologists had dealt with incidents of wife abuse and domestic violence in the societies they had studied, I looked for books and articles on the topic. When I found almost no anthropological discussion of wife-beating or battering, I called on Judy Brown for help. Because of her long interest and considerable expertise in women's issues, I knew that if anyone would be familiar with the anthropological literature on wife-beating and battering it would be Judy. Intrigued with the problem, Judy did her own search of the literature. Her research results were similar to mine; clearly anthropologists had ignored or had glossed over with throw-away one-liners a topic of serious dimensions and great importance to women. In an effort to bring the problem to the attention of other anthropologists, we called on our colleagues who had data on wife-beating and battering in societies where they had worked to share their experiences and insights with us. To this end, Judy and I co-organized a session on wife-beating at the 1987 meetings of the American Anthropological Association, and I organized a series of sessions and a symposium at the Association for Social Anthropology in Oceania (ASAO) meetings in 1986, 1987, and 1988. Many, but not all, of the chapters in this volume were presented at one or more of these sessions. Jacquelyn Campbell, who published one of the first cross-cultural studies on wife-beating and who has both conducted research on and had practical experience with shelters for battered women, participated in the American Anthropological Association meetings. Following the meetings she joined us as a co-editor of this volume; it was she who kept us going when we were discouraged, and it was Jackie who first contacted Westview Press and who negotiated with them during the earlier stages of publishing this volume.

The reactions of some of our colleagues when we began to discuss wife-beating and battering as a cross-cultural problem gave us insight into why anthropologists have until very recently either ignored domestic violence or given it only summary treatment. Some argued that we should not exploit our host's hospitality by exposing a dark side of their culture; others said that they would talk about the problem but would not publish it because they feared such publication would result in their being denied permission to return to the field; some were concerned that their informants might be punished if it were known that they had discussed the subject with an outsider. One woman told me that she was publishing, as fiction and under a pseudonym, a collection of accounts of wife-beating from the African society where she had worked for many years. She was publishing in this way because she believed that if she wrote under her own name her informants could be identified, and she feared for their lives. Others argued that if we raised the topic we would be imposing our political agenda on other societies with results that might be harmful to them. One colleague – an indigenous member of one of the societies being discussed – argued that the topic of domestic violence should not be examined. He feared that if women were encouraged to protest traditional gender roles in marriage – including the right of men to beat their wives – the institution of marriage would be destabilized and family life in his society would suffer.

These concerns point to a dilemma faced by anthropologists. On the one hand, the people of other cultures may use standards that are very different from ours to define what constitutes acceptable or unacceptable behavior. By the standards of some societies there may be no category of illegitimate wife-beating, and the people of that society – women as well as men – may reason that the stability of their society rests on the continuation of long-accepted practices grounded in the teachings of their ancestors or in religious doctrine. As anthropologists we must concede this, and most of us try not to judge other people by the values of our society or to suggest that they should conform to ideals that arise from our culture – ideals that we preach but may not practice. We respect the right of other peoples to hold values different from our own, and it is not our place to criticize them for behavior that is acceptable in their society but that is unacceptable and the subject of political agendas in our own. On the other hand, we are uncomfortable with analyses that are restricted to describing and explaining violence toward women and with explanations that seem almost to justify practices that we personally find abhorrent – practices that may result in the suffering, maiming, suicide, or murder of women who have befriended us and whom we care for and respect. We are caught between our own ethnocentrism on the one hand and the sterile aloofness of extreme relativism on the other.

There is no easy solution to this dilemma. It is, however, appropriate to note that while we must not apply our own values to and pass judgment on behavior that is not seen as deviant or abusive by the majority of the people of a community, many of the people – men as well as women – in the societies where anthropologists work do perceive domestic violence in general, and wife-beating and battering in particular, to be a problem. Leaders in these societies welcome discussion, for solutions to problems can be found only after those problems are publicly admitted and a dialogue begun. In Papua New Guinea, for example, the national government is aware of the personal, social, and economic costs of wife-beating and battering. Consequently, it has supported efforts by the Women and Law Committee, the Law Reform Commission of Papua New Guinea, and concerned private citizens to educate men and children about alternatives to violence and to make women aware of their rights if they are beaten. It is our hope that this volume will contribute in some small way to a search for successful sanctions against wife-beating and battering and the establishment of sanctuaries for abused women in our own societies and in the communities that have been our hosts.

We wish to express our thanks to all our colleagues who participated in the symposium on wife-beating at the American Anthropological Association meetings and in the ASAO sessions on domestic violence. My co-editors and I are particularly grateful to Virginia Kerns for suggesting the book's title. The chapters by Carucci, Lateef, McDowell, Nash, and Mitchell were previously published, in a slightly different form, in a special issue of *Pacific Studies* (Volume 13, July 1990) entitled "Domestic Violence in Oceania." That work is available as a separate volume from the University Press of Hawaii. Our thanks to Dale Robertson, editor of *Pacific Studies,* for permission to publish those papers here.

The editors are indebted to George Preisinger for creating the maps; to Jan Baker, Christina Campbell, and Marcie Propst for invaluable editorial assistance; and to Cheryl Smith for technical services and for greatly appreciated help and support. We also wish to thank Kellie Masterson and Ellen McCarthy of Westview Press for their interest in and support of this project and for their editorial assistance.

Dorothy Ayers Counts
Dundas, Ontario, Canada

Map of the World

TAIWAN

(See Enlarged
Map of
OCEANIA)

IRAN

INDIA

MAYOTTE

IKUNG

GARIFUNA

ECUADORIAN
VILLAGERS

Map of Oceania

1

Introduction: Definitions, Assumptions, Themes, and Issues

Judith K. Brown

Our purpose is to provide a unique and innovative perspective on a complex problem that has only recently generated public concern in Euro-American society: wife-beating. The present volume is the first collection of ethnographic explorations (largely first hand) devoted to the subject. The overview of customs in a variety of cultures is supplemented by evidence for analogous behavior among non-human primates. Descriptive information is drawn from societies that vary in the prevalence and severity of reported wife-beating; from societies that are located in widely scattered geographic areas; and from societies that range in complexity from hunter-gatherers, to horticulturalists (with special emphasis on Melanesia, a culture area in which wife-beating has been widely reported), to industrializing complex societies. All of those who have contributed to this volume hope that this new information and enlarged perspective will call attention to the worldwide plight of battered wives, promote their cause, and further the efforts of those working to eliminate the abuse of women.

This introduction will begin by providing some definitions and assumptions shared by the contributors. Next a brief review of previous cross-cultural studies will be presented and other promising areas of research will be suggested. The chapters will be introduced and a final section will identify the themes and issues raised by their authors.

DEFINITIONS AND ASSUMPTIONS

Most earlier cross-cultural studies have dealt with more than one type of family violence. The subject of this volume is restricted to wife-beating, which will be defined as a man intentionally inflicting pain on a woman, within a non-transient, male-female relationship, whether or not the partners are officially married. The subject is further restricted to physical aggression, because it can be identified unambiguously. Psychological abuse, verbal assault, threats, intimidation, calumny, humiliating ridicule, emotional blackmail and extortion are no doubt as pervasive, and may be as injurious as a physical attack. However, non-physical aggression is not as readily amenable to observation by an outsider, particularly by an ethnographer from another society.

Care must be exercised to distinguish between wife-beating and wife-battering.[1] This is an important difference, although an unfamiliar one in our own society, where almost all of what is labeled as "wife-beating" is actually wife-battering. The distinction had its beginning in an exchange between Erchak (1984) and Gibbs (1984), the first dialogue on husband-to-wife aggression to appear in a major anthropological journal. (For further elaboration of the difference, see Counts, in press a.)

In many non-industrial societies, husbands beat their wives in what Beatrice Whiting (personal communication) refers to as a "physical reprimand." Where such behavior is customary, it is viewed as unremarkable. The distinction between wife-beating and wife-battering is necessary to accommodate data from these societies, where men who beat their wives are not "abnormal" or deviant. Their conduct is culturally expected. The women in these societies are not meek and accepting. They are compelled to tolerate such treatment, but would decidedly prefer husbands who do not beat them (see Counts, Chapter 5 this volume). Wife-battering, on the other hand, is something extraordinary, possibly resulting in severe injury, incapacity or even death. In most instances, such behavior is not viewed as usual or acceptable by members of the society and elicits intervention by a third party or parties. The distinction does not depend entirely on the response of others to the assault, but also on the extent of the aggression, since in some instances even the murder of wives provokes no reaction.

A full explanation of aggression against wives must include not only sociocultural but also psychological variables. It must indicate whether the individual's behavior is the result of psycho-physical factors (such as alcoholism [Leonard and Jacob 1988] or neurological disorders [Elliott 1988]), or is the result of a particular life history. Psychological reasons for wife-beating and wife-battering are largely independent of cultural variables. Thus even societies in which wife-beating and wife-battering are reported as virtually absent and as strongly disapproved are not immune to the presence of the occasional brutal individual who ill treats his wife for idiosyncratic reasons. (The analysis of psychological variables is beyond the scope of this volume.) It is therefore assumed that wife-beating is universal, but its incidence in any particular society can range from being an extremely rare, individual matter to being a frequent and regular occurrence. And the severity can range from mild to actual murder. Frequency and severity of wife-beating vary independently (see Kerns, Chapter 10 this volume).

In our own society there is supposed disapproval of both wife-beating and wife-battering. However, this is no deterrent, since American men seem to perceive the sanctions as neither certain nor severe, according to a recent, chilling study by Carmody and Williams (1987). Some societies share our disapproval of both wife-beating and wife-battering and sanction both negatively. Other societies condone wife-beating and may even view it as necessary, but wife-battering is disapproved, rare or self-defeating. (This pattern is particularly appropriate for a society in which women make a major contribution to subsistence.[2] Husbands physically chastise women for poor work performance and other shortcomings, but a woman's injury or incapacitation would work a hardship on her kin, including the husband, whose physical survival depends on her productivity.) The third pattern is one in which neither wife-beating nor wife-battering is disapproved, and even the murder of a wife may go unpunished, as in the murders of wives in Brazil (60 Minutes, transcript 1988) and the dowry murders in India (Claireborne 1984; Bordewich 1986; Miller, Chapter 13 this volume). In a number of these societies, mothers-in-law instigate and take part in the aggression against young wives. Women contribute little to subsistence in such societies, but their vulnerability is not the result of economic factors alone. Wifely behavior that elicits a beating or battering can vary from the inadequate performance of duties, such as a late or poorly prepared meal; to practicing sorcery; to immodesty, suspected infidelity, and actual adultery; to the ill-treatment of a child, a co-wife, the children of a co-wife and insolence toward affines; to disobedience and insubordination. (Also see Counts 1990a and in press a; Lateef, Chapter 14 this volume.) The latter two wifely offenses are widely viewed as egregious and are punished with the extreme severity typical of righteous indignation (see Mushanga 1977–78). Surprisingly disproportionate vehemence and violent rage are seen as justified, because of the firm belief that the entire social fabric would unravel if such wifely behavior were countenanced. A wife's assertiveness or her flirtations with autonomy are viewed as equivalent to insurrection and as a threat against the sacred social order.

SOME PREVIOUS CROSS-CULTURAL STUDIES: A BRIEF REVIEW

For a variety of reasons, anthropologists typically strive to paint "their" village in a favorable light. (See Counts 1990a, 1990b.) The result is that the ethnographic literature provides scant data on unlovable behavior such as wife-beating (an imbalance this volume attempts to rectify). Nevertheless a number of cross-cultural studies have made use of the relative frequency of wife-beating as a variable, in testing hypotheses using a sample of non-industrial societies. (Cross-national studies, dealing with Euro-American in-

dustrialized societies, will not be reviewed here.) The validity of the conclusions of cross-cultural studies depends upon the statistical significance
of the findings, upon the appropriateness of the test statistic, upon the size
and selection of the sample societies, and ultimately upon the quality of the
ethnographic data reported for those societies on the variables under consideration. It is the latter factor most especially, which is open to question
in the studies to be reviewed below. This note of caution, concerning possible variation in the validity of the original data, should be kept in mind.

Early Correlational Studies Using a Worldwide Sample *assumptions*

As early as 1962, John W. M. Whiting and his co-workers at Harvard
University's Palfrey House had devised a set of codes for wife-beating, based
on data for 71 societies described in the Human Relations Area Files. Slater
and Slater (1965) and Lester (1980) utilized these ratings. For Slater and
Slater frequency of wife-beating was one of a series of variables which were
positively and significantly correlated with "narcissism," the subject of their
research. Lester's brief paper is one of several that seeks to find a relationship between the presence of wife-beating and other indices of aggression
at the societal level. He also examines the relationship of "the oppression
of women" and the frequency of divorce to wife-beating and concludes that
it is more prevalent where the divorce rate is high, women's status is inferior
and cruelty and aggression are more prevalent. The paper is extremely brief
and reports only the significance of various correlations. The sources of the
codes of the antecedent variables are not always given, nor is there information on the size and composition of the samples, for each of the reported
correlations. Like Lester, Masumura (1979) examined the relationship of
wife-beating to other forms of aggressive behavior such as homicide and personal crime. A much fuller account than Lester's, Masumura's article nevertheless does not identify his 86 sample societies. The author concludes that
the significant correlation between wife abuse and other forms of aggression
may be due to underlying factors such as sexual jealousy and the possibility
that certain societies are violence prone. For two other early cross-cultural
studies, Naroll (1969) and Schlegel (1972), wife-beating was not a central
focus, but was one of many variables in research concerned with aspects of
methodology and with "the sick society," in the case of Naroll and with
"female autonomy" in the case of Schlegel. Whiting and Whiting (1975) al-
lude to the Palfrey House ratings in their study of intimacy and aloofness in
marriage. These characteristics of marriage are unrelated to wife-beating.
However, the Whitings suggest a relationship between wife-beating and the
degree of isolation of the married pair. They note that "there is safety in
numbers," an important observation, to be discussed further below and confirmed in several of the chapters that follow.

Using a sub-sample of forty-six societies from the Human Relations Area Files Probability Sample Files, Levinson (1981) examined the correlation between the use of physical punishment to discipline children and wife-beating, testing one portion of the hypothesis suggested by Straus: "Violence in one family role is associated with violence in other family roles" (1977:721). Levinson's findings, though statistically significant, only partially support the hypothesis. Although both forms of intra-familial violence tend to be rare in some societies, the predicted relationship between frequent use of physical punishment and frequent wife-beating is not borne out. Most societies that scored as "common" or "frequent" on wife-beating scored "rare" or "infrequent" on physical punishment of children.

The last of the earlier cross-cultural studies using a worldwide sample coded for wife-beating was conducted by Broude and Greene (1983). Using Murdock and White's Standard Cross-Cultural Sample of 186 societies plus fifteen alternate societies, the authors were able to find information on wife-beating for only 71 cases, and in 57 wife-beating was coded as present. The study created seventeen scales to measure non-sexual aspects of the relationship between husbands and wives such as how marriages are arranged, customs pertaining to newlyweds, attitudes toward and ease of divorce. Of all these variables, only one, remarrying widows having their husbands chosen for them, was significantly related to wife-beating. This single finding could be the result of chance and suggests that wife-beating in many societies may have little to do with the non-sexual relationship between husbands and wives (as will be suggested below).

Previous Studies Using Anecdotal Cross-Cultural Evidence

Several earlier studies have used cross-cultural evidence concerning wife-beating in a less quantified and less systematic way. For example, Mushanga (1977–78) provides a descriptive study (to be considered more fully below) that presents data only from sub-Sahara Africa. Straus (1977) uses anecdotal anthropological evidence in support of his hypotheses concerning intra-familial violence. As noted above, Levinson (1981) tested one of these cross-culturally. Straus suggests "near universality" for intra-familial violence (which includes wife-beating), but cautions that its actual prevalence is not fully known. His basic conclusion is that "the level of physical aggression in the conjugal relationship tends to be isomorphic with the level of physical aggression in nonfamily spheres of life...." (1977:724). And the level of violence in the husband-wife relationship is "isomorphic" with the level of violence in the parent-child relationship. Straus's use of the ethnographic literature seems somewhat haphazard. He does not explain the basis for his choice of tribal examples, nor why he uses particular sources (for example, citing information on the !Kung from Eibl-Eibesfeldt, rather than from the classic works by Marshall, Draper or Lee). The ethnographic literature, vast and somewhat uncharted for the non-anthropologist, contains more and less reliable sources. Ethnographic examples are convincing only when their choice is explained and when sources are evaluated.

Steinmetz (1981) conducted a study using questionnaires on individuals from a sample of six societies, examining among other variables the frequency and severity of marital abuse. The questionnaire is described as "structured," and the brief paper does not include examples of the questions. The sample size for each society varies and there is no information on the conditions under which the tests were administered, how the subjects were chosen or how the protocols were scored. No tests of significance appear on the article's tables. The author rightly concludes that the study raises more questions than it answers. A three-way comparison among India, Ireland and the United States was conducted by Tellis-Nayak and Donoghue (1982), attempting to relate marital violence to the structuring of decision making authority. The research design, the quality of the data and the method of analysis are such as to render any of the conclusions tentative at best.

Recent Cross-Cultural Studies

Campbell's (1985) important exploratory research differs from all other cross-cultural studies of wife-beating because the author restricts her sample to societies described by female ethnographers working with female informants. The sample is small, the number of variables examined is extensive and the results are more suggestive than conclusive. Yet this study is significant because of the care with which ethnographic sources were selected and hence for the validity of the data.

Two recent works by Levinson are the most ambitious cross-cultural studies of various forms of family violence. The first (Levinson 1988), an anthropological chapter in a major new comprehensive handbook on family violence (Van Hasselt et al. 1988), provides an informed overview for the non-anthropologist. The second, Levinson's (1989) more technical, book-length cross-cultural study, is also based on his ongoing, long-range holocultural research. Two elaborate appendices provide information on methodology and coding. His sample of ninety societies, whose accounts are drawn from the Human Relations Area Files, are identified and the scales on which they were rated are reported. Some of his conclusions: wife-beating is more likely in societies in which men control the family wealth, in which conflicts are solved by means of physical violence and in which women do not have an equal right to obtain a divorce. One finding that invites further investigation: societies characterized by female work groups tend to have infrequent incidences of wife-beating. Is there a third variable responsible for this correlation? Are these work groups associated with matrilocal residence or are they the result of female domination of subsistence activities? Are there other manifestations of women's coalitions and solidarity that may serve as a deterrent to wife-beating?

OTHER LINES OF EVIDENCE

Anthropological and cross-cultural data provide only one of several approaches to the phenomenon of wife-beating. (The need to consider psychological variables has been noted above.) Three other promising areas of research, some of which have influenced several of the chapters that follow, will be briefly identified. The first is concerned with the psychophysiological aspect of male sexual arousal and response. In their pioneering cross-cultural study of sexual behavior, Ford and Beach (1951) suggested that male sexual excitement may actually be enhanced by aggression. (Also see Miller, Chapter 13 this volume.) Further research on the relation of sexual arousal and aggression has been provided by Tannenbaum and Zillmann (1975). More recently Zillmann (1984, 1986) has suggested there is a neurological reason for the connection between male sexual pleasure and aggression. (Alternatively, both sex and violence provide control over women. And this basically similar motivation may underlie both behaviors, whether or not there is a neurological explanation.) Zillmann's findings are troubling and unwelcome, but can not be ignored. They call attention to the interrelatedness of wife-beating, sexual activity and male sexual performance, a promising area for further research.

The possible relationship between male sexual behavior and wife-beating has been overlooked by anthropological research, with one exception: the study by Mushanga (1977–78), dealing with wife "victimization" (which appears to include the murder of wives) in sub-Sahara Africa. The beaten and murdered spouses were not only being insubordinate and untraditional, but they derogated their husband's sexual performance. Mushanga seems to suggest that the women had it coming.

A second area of promising related research is evolutionary biology. In a complex and wide-ranging chapter, Burgess and Draper (1989) consider a number of variables pertaining to family violence, and interpret these in terms of "inclusive fitness," "parental investment" and "paternal certainty." Among mammals, humans are unusual in combining an exclusive sexual partnership with life in heterosexual social groups, rendering paternal certainty problematical. The widespread cultural solutions are: the separation of the sexes in daily life, patriarchal rule (with men also controlling most forms of wealth), and patrilocal residence. In the non-industrial world, the latter two are far more usual than alternative arrangements. The authors note that in human social groups there is pervasive stress on patriarchal values and the sexual double standard, but Burgess and Draper do not regard these as inevitable, simply because they are in the service of paternal certainty. Although they regard marital violence as predictable from the point of view of evolutionary biology, the authors nevertheless take account of the modifying influence of culture, of social circumstances and of individual differences.

Daly and Wilson, who have also applied evolutionary biology to the data on wife-beating and the murder of wives (Daly, Wilson and Weghorst 1982; Daly and Wilson 1988a, 1988b), focus on male sexual jealousy, which in their view serves human adaptation by augmenting paternal certainty. The authors suggest that this explains why there is a qualitative difference between male and female jealousy, why male sexual jealousy is the predominant motive in violence against women and why male sexual jealousy is a cross-cultural universal. In support of the latter assertion, they re-examine previous cross-cultural studies dealing with sexual behavior and explain contradictory evidence as misinterpretations on the part of comparativists. Daly and Wilson did not engage in an independent search for ethnographic data. They might have discovered negative evidence from South America in Carneiro (1958) and from West Africa in Muller (1969), Netting (1969) and Smedley (1974). Male sexual jealousy appears not to be universal and does not provide the motive for a phenomenon like the notorious dowry murders (Claireborne 1984; Bordewich 1986; Miller, Chapter 13 this volume).[3] This is not to deny that in explaining violence against women, male sexual jealousy is indeed an important variable and may very well have originated in the service of human adaptation. However, the expression of male sexual jealousy is molded by culture, by social circumstances and by personal inclination. Foster's (1972) anthropological study of the related subject of envy suggests some of the complexities in the cross-cultural study of human motives. Daly and Wilson provide an intriguing hypothesis, which invites some modifications.

A third area of promising related research is the investigation of aggression against females among nonhuman primates. Both observational studies in the wild (see Tracy and Crawford, Chapter 2 this volume) and laboratory studies give evidence of primate behavior analogous to wife abuse in humans (Nadler 1988; Turkington 1987). Nadler reports that among the great apes, mating behavior in the wild follows three distinct patterns, none of which typically includes sexual aggression. However, in a laboratory situation that gave the great ape males free access to a female, sexual behavior did not follow the pattern seen in the wild, and there was pronounced sexual aggression. In a "limited access test" situation, in which the laboratory females were provided with the option to escape from the male, sexual activity became more like that displayed in the wild, and male sexual aggression was obviated. (Apparently in the wild, the female's smaller size gives her an advantage in speed and also makes possible the escape into loftier branches that will not hold the heavier male.) Data from non-human primates, even species related as closely to humans as the great apes, must be interpreted with caution, particularly when behavior is artificially induced in a laboratory setting. Nevertheless the importance of the option to escape from the male is pertinent to the practical need for sheltering among human subjects of male violence.

The evidence from studies of non-human primate male aggression, the alleged evolutionary significance of marital violence and of male "proprietary jealousy," and the possible neurological connection between male aggression and enhanced male sexual pleasure all raise troubling issues, but are not presented here to make aggression against women appear so deep-seated as to be inevitable and unalterable. The purpose is not to provide an apologia for violence against women, but rather to underscore the urgency of the world-wide problem of wife-beating and wife-battering, and to suggest that future research may have to encompass more than the traditional social sciences.

INTRODUCTORY COMMENT

Drawing on anthropological and ethological data, the ensuing chapters will present descriptions of primate behavior as well as ethnographic information from societies that vary in the incidence and in the severity of wife-beating and wife-battering. The collection begins with a chapter reporting observations of male to female aggression among non-human primates in the wild. These data, reported by Tracy and Crawford, in many instances appear strikingly analogous to human behavior. The next chapters are arranged according to societal complexity, beginning with hunter-gatherers, moving to horticulturalists, then to complex industrializing societies. The chapters dealing with rapidly changing hunter-gatherer societies focus on Australian Aborigines (Burbank) and the !Kung of southern Africa (Draper). Horticultural societies include four Melanesian societies, the Lusi speakers of Kaliai (Counts), the villagers of Bun on the Yuat River (McDowell), the Wape (Mitchell), and the Nagovisi (Nash). This over-representation of Melanesia is intentional, in order to afford the reader an opportunity for a within-region comparison between two negative instances, the Nagovisi and the Wape, with two more typical Melanesian cases in which wife-beating is prevalent, Bun and Kaliai.[4] Other horticultural societies include the Marshall Islanders of Micronesia (Carucci),[5] the Garifuna of Belize (Kerns), the mestizo villagers of Ecuador (McKee), and the Malagasy speakers of Mayotte, an island off the coast of east Africa (Lambek). Somewhat greater societal complexity is represented by the last group: industrializing, complex societies. These consist of India (Miller), its provincial counterpart among Indo-Fijians (Lateef), the villagers of Iran (Hegland), and Taiwanese villagers (Gallin). A final chapter by Campbell relates the ethological and ethnographic material to circumstances in our own society and notes implications for action as well as for further research.

THEMES AND ISSUES

In our own society, the ordinary citizen regards wife-beating as evidence that a marital relationship has gone deplorably awry, the result of a husband engaging in behavior that is brutal and unacceptable. But as the following chapters will demonstrate, and as suggested above, the perspective provided by ethology and anthropology suggests that matters are far more complicated and involve more than the relationship between spouses and the individual proclivities of the husband. (These two variables are not without importance and bear examination, but as psychological variables, they are beyond the scope of the present volume.)

Draper (Chapter 4 this volume) suggests that a potential for wife-beating inheres in the dimorphism of the sexes in humans, a potential that is modified by various cultural factors. Collier (1988) in a recent inquiry into the nature of inequality suggests that the right to beat a wife differentiates a woman's relationship to her husband from her relationship to her brother and to her lover. Both authors using very different types of anthropological evidence imply that the ubiquity of wife-beating should be regarded as less remarkable than its infrequency or near absence in some societies. What emerges from the material about to be presented suggests that the prevalence or relative absence of wife-beating in any particular society is predictable when certain factors are known. These can be categorized as follows: those that deal with aspects of womanhood, those that deal with the relationship of men to men and women to women, those that deal with the isolation of wives and those that deal with sanctions and sanctuary. Of these, the latter are the most important determinants of the frequency and the severity of wife-beating and wife-battering.

Aspects of Womanhood

In every society, the treatment women receive depends in large part upon their age, their economic role and their acknowledged or denied adulthood. First, older women, although not immune from ill treatment (see Draper, Chapter 4 this volume), are less likely to be beaten than younger wives (see Kerns, Chapter 10, and McKee, Chapter 11, this volume). And older wives are less likely to be the victims of spousal homicide in Euro-American society, according to Daly and Wilson (1988a and 1988b). In part, this is the result of the greater extra-domestic support an older woman can muster. She will have established coalitions within her community, even if she had been an outsider, when she moved there as a young bride. Also, she is likely to have grown children, particularly sons, who will come to her aid. And in part, this is because her old or middle-aged husband, with lessened energies at his disposal, will be preoccupied with other matters, such as arranging marriages, dealing in politics, accumulating wealth and gaining supernatural power (see Counts, in press b). Second, societies in which women have an important economic role may approve physical reprimand, but will not condone the abusive treatment permitted in those societies in which women are viewed as more expendable. Third, women are less likely to be beaten in societies in which they are regarded as autonomous adults (see Kerns, Chapter 10, and Lambek, Chapter 12, this volume).

Relationships of Women to Women and Men to Men

In many societies, the prevalence of wife-beating has less to do with the relationship between the partners than with the relationship among a society's women, or the position of the husband in the dominance hierarchy of the male peer group or the standing of the husband's kinship group in the community. On the one hand, the relationship among women can exert a positive influence on how wives are treated. Research as diverse as Levinson's (1989) cross-cultural study, the non-human primate evidence reported by Tracy and Crawford (Chapter 2), and Mitchell's study of the Wape (Chapter 7) suggests that the presence of coalitions of females can reduce male to female aggression. Furthermore, in some societies older women have the role of peacemakers and are expected to intervene in marital disputes and to prevent serious injury (see Kerns, Chapter 10).

On the other hand, quite the opposite may be the case, and elder women in their roles as senior wives (see Counts, Chapter 5) or as mothers-in-law (see Miller, Chapter 13; Lateef, Chapter 14; and Gallin, Chapter 16) may actually instigate or participate in the ill-treatment of young wives. Is it possible to predict which of these opposite roles older women will fulfill in any particular society? Brown (in press) suggests that post-marital residence, descent, and the contribution women make to subsistence determine the relationship between a society's matrons and their younger female kin. Taking a Marxist feminist view, Sacks (in press) suggests that antagonism between mothers-in-law and brides, particularly among agrarian peasants, functions to preserve patriarchal power. If the antagonism did not exist and if mothers-in-law and brides were in a position to collude, their "enormous economically destructive potential" would seriously threaten patriarchal power.

In some societies, a man may feel compelled to beat his wife in order to establish and assure his position within the male peer group. The beating has little to do with the husband-wife relationship, but a great deal to do with a man's avoidance of ridicule and his position as "a man among men." Thus in the well-known case of the Yanomamo, a man must appear fierce and can do so convincingly by beating his wife (Chagnon 1968; also see Gelber 1986; Counts 1990a; Draper, Chapter 4; and McKee, Chapter 11, this volume). Or a man may assert physical control over "his" women-folk to insure the standing of his kin group within the community. In many societies, particularly those in the circum-Mediterranean region, the respectability accorded a household is proportional to the imposed virtue and modesty of its women (also see Papanek 1979; Lateef, Chapter 14 this volume). This in turn has economic implications for the group, and hence explains in part the ready willingness of the older, more integrated women of the household to help chaperon, chastise and confine the younger female members.

There's Safety in Numbers

In our own society, the recent notorious wife abuse cases reported in the media called attention to the remarkable physical and psychological isolation imposed upon the women victims by their abusive partners. Tracy and Crawford (Chapter 2 this volume) note analogous behavior reported for non-human primates. Several of the chapters for example, (see Chapters 3, 7, and 10 by Burbank, Mitchell, and Kerns) stress the importance of community intervention in preventing serious harm and note the potential danger for isolated wives.

In many societies, the isolation of a wife, particularly a young wife, is the result of the rules for post-marital residence. The crucial factor is not which spouse moves at marriage, but the proximity of the wife's kin to the newly established household. A wife has the support of her kin not only in matrilocal societies (see Chapter 8 by Nash on the Nagovisi), which are few in number worldwide, but in all societies that do not practice community exogamy. As a rule, when a wife's kin are nearby, their presence provides a deterrent against wife-battering. But on occasion, if a woman's behavior is viewed as truly infuriating, her brothers (see McDowell, Chapter 6) and her father (see Gallin, Chapter 16) may actually join a husband in beating her. However, a wife is in a much more vulnerable position and there is a far greater likelihood that she will be ill-treated, if she is isolated from her family by rules for post-marital residence that compel her to move to her husband's distant community at marriage. (See Burgess and Draper 1989 for an extensive examination of the relationship of various forms of social structure and marital violence; also see Counts 1990 a.)

The isolation of a wife is also determined by the degree of privacy a society traditionally assigns to the domestic sphere. In general, when domestic activities take place almost entirely out of doors and in full view of the rest of the community, or when domestic activity is audible through thin house walls, it is less likely that women will be battered because others will step in (see Chapters 3 and 4 by Burbank and Draper). There is greater danger that wives will be abused when the domestic sphere is veiled in privacy. This is more typical of complex societies, in which, however, some protection may be afforded through a wife's recourse to law enforcement agencies and the courts. In some societies, women's access to these institutions is made very difficult (see Counts, in press a), or it may be illegal for any agency to intervene in domestic matters. Such circumstances serve to isolate women and to place them in great jeopardy. In addition, as Counts (in press a), among others, has pointed out for Melanesia, when the authorities themselves beat their wives, they are unlikely to prosecute other men for doing so.

Sanctions and Sanctuary

Not only is there cross-cultural variation from society to society, in the amount, frequency and severity of aggression against women, and in what is condoned or disapproved, but also in the sanctions that apply and in the availability of sanctuary for beaten wives. In our own society, the question is frequently asked about a battered wife, "Why does she stay?" The answer is that she stays because she is terrified, because leaving will mean separation from her children, because she does not have the resources to manage without her partner, and, above all, because our society provides no easy solutions to the immediate problem of where to go. (Also see Chapters 4 and 10 by Draper and Kerns.) Effective sanctuary must provide the guarantee of safety to the woman (without imposing the penalty of separation from her children), as well as to those who provide her with a refuge. It must provide the wife with the possibility of prolonged support, whether by her own labors or by the generosity of others. And sanctuary must be available at the very moment when it is needed, no matter what hour of day or night. Generally, in those societies in which a woman remains in or near the community of her own family after marriage, such sanctuary is readily available. But there are exceptions (see Hegland, Chapter 15 this volume), if the family lacks the socially recognized authority or the resources to take her in. In some instances sanctuary may be provided by neighbors, elders, community leaders, and, in complex societies, by specialized shelters. As Kerns (Chapter 10 this volume) points out for the Garifuna, because the women are able to leave a partner who beats them, they are never battered. However, in other societies, sanctuary is as problematical as in the United States, and women are compelled to remain with their abusive spouses (see Lateef, Chapter 14 this volume).

Sanctions imposed by a society may be informal or formal, negative or positive. Informal negative sanctions include gossip about a wife beater or expressions of open disdain by his family and neighbors. Formal negative sanctions can take the form of court-ordered punishment. Whether aggression toward a wife results in wrath and retribution from the spirits of her ancestors (see Chapter 7 by Mitchell) or in retaliation from her living kin, or in incarceration and fines imposed by a law enforcement agency, whenever sanctions are certain, immediate and severe, the incidence of wife-beating is reduced.

But a society may also provide inducements of a positive kind to encourage alternatives to wife-beating. Informal positive sanctions include the community's admiration for a man who can keep peace among his wives without the use of force, whose wife performs her duties willingly, or who commands domestic respect without having to impose it. Formal positive sanctions include the political power that derives from the support of a wife's kin. But perhaps the greatest reward is a harmonious marriage, which appears to be a universal ideal.

Evening the Score

The extent of wife-beating in any particular society can be predicted in large part from the certainty, immediacy and severity of the sanctions that apply and from the sanctuary that is available to wives; both of these in turn depend to a large degree upon the customary post-marital residential arrangements. Of course matters are never quite this simple and there are other factors that must be taken into account, as noted above. There is, however, one additional deterrent to wife-beating: the means at a woman's disposal for getting even. Some wives may strike back, and do so with a weapon (see McDowell, Chapter 6). They may leave a partner to return to their own kin. They may resort to shaming an abusive husband publicly and noisily or they may attempt suicide. They may invoke supernatural revenge (see Chapter 9 by Carucci) or poison a husband's food. They may mobilize public opinion against the husband and cause problems in his relationship with their own kin group (a particularly troublesome matter where marriages are arranged by an exchange of sisters). They may allow gardening or cooking or child care to lapse below standard. They may shamelessly flaunt the relationship with a lover, or assert their autonomy by pointedly engaging in other interdicted behavior. Any one of these counter measures may result in a Pyrrhic victory, when the suicide attempt succeeds (see Counts, in press a; Mitchell, Chapter 7), when leaving a husband means giving up one's children (see Counts, in press a) or when the male retaliates with even greater violence and brutality (Counts, in press a). Nevertheless the ethnographic record suggests that women in non-industrial societies have found a great many ways to even the score.

NOTES

An earlier version of this paper was read at the 1987 Meeting of the American Anthropological Association. My thanks to all who participated in the original symposium and to the authors who have contributed chapters to this book.

This chapter has benefited from discussions I have had with Beatrice B. Whiting, and from suggestions and comments by many of the contributors to this volume, particularly Victoria Burbank, Charles Crawford, Patricia Draper, Virginia Kerns, Lauris McKee and Karen Tracy as well as my colleagues Peter Bertocci, Pauline Kolenda, Denise Schmandt-Besserat and Sylvia Yanagisako. Above all I am indebted to Jacquelyn Campbell and Dorothy Counts, for sharing insights and ideas and for their patience, grace and good humor.

1. Beatrice Whiting first alerted me to the importance of this distinction.
2. The fact that the abuse by a husband may be limited to injuries that do not interfere with a woman's subsistence activities and child bearing capacities was first suggested to me by Patricia Draper.
3. Pauline Kolenda (personal communication) has pointed out that these murders are an urban phenomenon in India.
4. Data compiled by Gelber (1986) for the New Guinea Highlands suggest that physical violence against women is widespread.
5. The Marshall Islanders are reluctant cultivators who gather and fish.

REFERENCES CITED

Bordewich, Fergus M. 1986. Dowry Murders. Atlantic Monthly 250 (1): 21—27.

Broude, Gwen J., and Sarah J. Greene. 1983. Cross-Cultural Codes on Husband-Wife Relationships. Ethnology 22: 263—280.

Brown, Judith K. In press. Addendum to the Second Edition. *In* In Her Prime: New Views of Middle-Aged Women. Second Edition. Virginia Kerns and Judith K. Brown, eds. Urbana, Ill: University of Illinois Press.

Burgess, Robert L., and Patricia Draper. 1989. The Explanation of Family Violence: The Role of Biological, Behavioral, and Cultural Selection. *In* Family Violence. Lloyd Ohlin and Michael Tonry, eds. Pp. 59—116. Chicago: University of Chicago Press.

Campbell, Jacquelyn. 1985. Beating of Wives: A Cross-Cultural Perspective. Victimology: An International Journal 10 (1—4): 174—185.

Carmody, Dianne C., and Kirk R. Williams. 1987. Wife Assault and Perception of Sanctions. Violence and Victims 2 (1): 25—38.

Carneiro, Robert L. 1958. Extra-Marital Freedom among the Kuikuru Indians of Mato Grosso. Revista do Museu Paulista. n.s. 10: 135—142.

Chagnon, Napoleon. 1968. Yanomamo: The Fierce People. New York: Holt, Rinehart and Winston.

Claireborne, William. 1984. Dowry Killings Show Social Stress in India. Washington Post September 22: 1—3.

Collier, Jane F. 1988. Marriage and Inequality in Classless Societies. Stanford, Cal.: Stanford University Press.

Counts, Dorothy A. 1990a. Domestic Violence in the Pacific: Conclusion. Pacific Studies 13(3):225—254. Special Issue: Domestic Violence in Oceania. Dorothy A. Counts, ed.

———. 1990b. Domestic Violence in the Pacific: Introduction. Pacific Studies 13(3):1—6. Special Issue: Domestic Violence in Oceania. Dorothy A. Counts, ed.

———. In press a. The Fist, the Stick and the Bottle of Bleach: Wife Bashing and Female Suicide in a Papua New Guinea Society *In* Contemporary Pacific Societies. V. Lockwood, T. Harding and B. Wallace, eds. Honolulu: University of Hawaii Press.

———. In press b. *Tamparonga:* "The Big Women" of Kaliai (Papua New Guinea). *In* In Her Prime: New Views of Middle-Aged Women. Second Edition. Virginia Kerns and Judith K. Brown, eds. Urbana, Ill: University of Illinois Press.

Daly, Martin, and Margo Wilson. 1988a. Evolutionary Social Psychology and Family Homicide. Science 242: 519—524.

———. 1988b. Homicide. New York: Aldine De Gruyter.

Daly, Martin, Margo Wilson, and Suzanne J. Weghorst. 1982. Male Sexual Jealousy. Ethology and Sociobiology 3: 11—27.

Elliott, Frank A. 1988. Neurological Factors. *In* Handbook of Family Violence. Vincent Van Hasselt, Randall L. Morrison, Alan S. Bellack and Michel Hersen, eds. Pp. 359—382. New York: Plenum.

Erchak, Gerald M. 1984. Cultural Anthropology and Spouse Abuse. Current Anthropology 25(3): 331—332.

Ford, Clellan S., and Frank A. Beach. 1951. Patterns of Sexual Behavior. New York: Harper & Row.

Foster, George M. 1972. The Anatomy of Envy: A Study in Symbolic Behavior. Current Anthropology 13(2): 165—202.

Gelber, Marilyn G. 1986. Gender and Society in the New Guinea Highlands: An Anthropological Perspective on Antagonism toward Women. Boulder, Colo: Westview.

Gibbs, James L. 1984. On Cultural Anthropology and Spouse Abuse. Current Anthropology 25(4):533.

Leonard, Kenneth E., and Theodore Jacob. 1988. Alcohol, Alcoholism, and Family Violence. *In* Handbook of Family Violence. Vincent Van Hasselt, Randall L. Morrison, Alan S. Bellack and Michel Hersen, eds. Pp. 383—406. New York: Plenum.

Lester, David. 1980. A Cross-Cultural Study of Wife-Abuse. Aggressive Behavior 6:361—364.

Levinson, David. 1981. Physical Punishment of Children and Wifebeating in Cross-Cultural Perspective. Child Abuse and Neglect 5: 193—195.

———. 1988. Family Violence in Cross-Cultural Perspective. *In* Handbook of Family Violence. Vincent Van Hasselt, Randall L. Morrison, Alan S. Bellack and Michel Hersen, eds. Pp. 435—455. New York: Plenum.

———. 1989. Family Violence in Cross-Cultural Perspective. Newbury Park, Cal.: Sage.

Masumura, Wilfred T. 1979. Wife Abuse and Other Forms of Aggression. Victimology: An International Journal 4(1):46—59.

Muller, Jean-Claude. 1969. Preferential Marriage Among the Rukuba of Benue-Plateau State, Nigeria. American Anthropologist 71(6):1057—1061.

Mushanga, Tibamanya Mwene. 1977—78. Wife Victimization in East and Central Africa. Victimology: An International Journal 2(3—4):479—485.

Nadler, Ronald. 1988. Sexual Aggression in the Great Apes. *In* Human Sexual Aggression: Current Perspectives. Annals of the New York Academy of Sciences, Vol. 528. Robert A. Prentky and Vernon L. Quinsey, eds. Pp. 154—162. New York: The New York Academy of Sciences.

Naroll, Raoul. 1969. Cultural Determinants and the Concept of the Sick Society. *In* Changing Perspectives in Mental Illness. S.C. Plog and R.G. Edgerton, eds. Pp. 128—155. New York: Holt, Rinehart and Winston.

Netting, Robert McC. 1969. Women's Weapons: The Politics of Domesticity Among the Kofyar. American Anthropologist 71(6):1037—1046.

Papanek, Hanna. 1979. Family Status Production: The "Work" and "Non-Work" of Women. Signs 4(4):775—781.

Sacks, Karen Brodkin. In press. Dirty Old Ladies: Age and Gender in Cultural and Biological Perspectives. *In* In Her Prime: New Views of Middle-Aged Women. Second Edition. Virginia Kerns and Judith K. Brown, eds. Urbana, Ill: University of Illinois Press.

Schlegel, Alice. 1972. Male Dominance and Female Autonomy. New Haven, Conn.: HRAF Press.

60 Minutes, transcript. 1988. Machismo. Produced by John Tiffin. Feb. 21. CBS News 20 (23):2—5.

Slater, Philip, and Dori A. Slater. 1965. Maternal Ambivalence and Narcissism: A Cross-Cultural Study. Merrill-Palmer Quarterly 11(3):241—259.

Smedley, Audrey. 1974. Women of Udu: Survival in a Harsh Land. *In* Many Sisters: Women in Cross-Cultural Perspective. Carolyn Matthiasson, ed. Pp. 205—228. New York: Free Press.

Steinmetz, Suzanne. 1981. A Cross-Cultural Comparison of Marital Abuse. Journal of Sociology and Social Welfare 8(2): 404—414.

Straus, Murray A. 1977. Societal Morphogenesis and Intrafamily Violence in Cross-Cultural Perspective. *In* Issues in Cross-Cultural Research. Annals of the New York Academy of Sciences, Vol. 285. Leonore L. Adler, ed. Pp. 717—730. New York: The New York Academy of Sciences.

Tannenbaum, Percy, and Dolf Zillmann. 1975. Emotional Arousal in the Facilitation of Aggression Through Communication. *In* Advances in Experimental Social Psychology, Vol. 8. Leonard Berkowitz, ed. Pp. 149—192. New York: Academic Press.

Tellis-Nayak, V., and Gearoid O. Donoghue. 1982. Conjugal Egalitarianism and Violence Across Cultures. Journal of Comparative Family Studies 13 (3):277—289.

Turkington, Carol. 1987. Male Apes Show Aggressive Mating Behavior. The Monitor of the American Psychological Association 18(3):16.

Van Hasselt, Vincent, R. L. Morrison, A. S. Bellack and Michael Hersen, eds. 1988. Handbook of Family Violence. New York: Plenum.

Whiting, John W.M., and Beatrice B. Whiting. 1975. Aloofness and Intimacy of Husbands and Wives: A Cross-Cultural Study, Ethos, 3(2):183—207.

Zillman, Dolf. 1984. Connections Between Sex and Aggression. Hillsdale, N.J.: Lawrence Erlbaum.

———. 1986. Sex-Aggression Linkages. Paper presented at the Invited Symposium in Social Psychophysiology, 94th Annual Meeting of the American Psychological Association. Washington.

2

Wife Abuse:
Does It Have an Evolutionary Origin?

Karen Keljo Tracy and Charles B. Crawford

Wife-beating is a form of male violence towards women that has received much attention in American social science literature in the last two decades. Although the literature has been very useful in bringing the issue to public awareness and in generating legislation to make wife-beating a criminal matter, it has not been very effective in theory building. It has been described largely in terms of social and psychological pathology, as a "dysfunctional behavior," a rather bizarre occurrence outside of normal human experience. As writer Katha Pollitt recently observed, "We need to stop thinking of male violence as some kind of freak of nature, like a tornado. Because the thing about tornadoes is, you can't do anything about them." (Pollitt 1989:20).

The ubiquity of wife abuse, both within and across cultures, suggests that it could have its origin in our evolutionary past. Recent evidence, including much of the data reported in other chapters in this book, indicates that wife-beating may be a cross-cultural behavioral universal, despite its wide variety in terms of frequency and severity across cultures. As such, it may indicate underlying biological predispositions congruent with, but not necessarily proving, the mechanism of natural selection (Barash 1978:276–308). Darwin's theory of evolution through natural selection is that living organisms have been formed over long periods of time by a continuous process involving differential survival and reproduction. It should be mentioned here that in the usage of modern evolutionary theory, natural selection pertains to individuals, not groups or species. It favors those who optimize the number of surviving offspring.

From an evolutionary perspective a behavior is either (a) the result of an adaptation, a behavior that was shaped by differential reproduction in an ancestral population, (b) a "beneficial effect," a behavior that currently contributes to fitness, but that did not contribute to fitness in an ancestral population, and therefore was not shaped by natural selection, or (c) a behavior that was adaptive in an ancestral population but that no longer contributes to biological fitness. In essence, adaptations have evolved to help animals deal with the contingencies of their environments and favor those individuals that optimize their number of surviving offspring.

Behavioral traits are only adaptive for a specific environment in a particular context. Since less than 1 percent of human ancestral heritage has occurred outside the context of hunting and gathering bands (Symons 1981:35), most of our current behavioral predispositions evolved to suit the conditions in that particular environment. However, genetic predispositions that were functional in that environment may not be suitable for other environmental conditions. Therefore, in this paper wife abuse will be discussed in an evolutionary psychological context.

Since adaptations evolved to help ancestral organisms deal with environmental conditions, it may well be that by altering certain aspects of the environment, abusive behaviors can be decreased or eliminated. However, it is important to understand the evolutionary basis for such behavior in order to know what types of environmental changes would be the most effective. Because we can only speculate about spouse abuse in human ancestral history, we have chosen to focus on "wife abuse-like" behavior that has recently been observed in non-human primates; however, let it be noted that such behaviors are prevalent in a large number of species and are not by any means the exclusive domain of the primate order. Although we are fully aware that these cases can only serve as analogues to the human case, we believe that studying the behaviors of those species that most resemble our own could be useful in understanding the dynamics involved in the human situation.

In studying the primate literature, we have selected three areas that relate to an evolutionary psychological view on wife abuse. The first involves sexual dimorphism between male and female of a given species and incorporates Darwin's theory of sexual selection. The second comprises the arena of mate retention, which includes such behaviors as mate guarding, sexual jealousy, and sequestration. The third area comprises social interactions between male and female partners in which real or perceived non-reciprocation can generate aggressive responses.

ULTIMATE CAUSATION AND WIFE-BEATING

According to modern evolutionary theorists, the ultimate goal of an animal's behavior is to perpetuate its own individual genes; this goal is referred to as "reproductive fitness." The assumption is not that the organism is driven to produce lots of offspring. It is rather that natural selection has shaped behavioral mechanisms, motives, cognitive biases, etc., that resulted in ancestral organisms producing more offspring than those who did not have these behaviors. The behavior of a given individual is thus ultimately self-interested by nature. Let it be emphasized, however, that this goal is not a conscious one; neither humans nor animals behave in a volitional, deliberate way in order to maximize their reproductive fitness.

In evolutionary terminology, trying to interpret behavior from an "ultimate" causal perspective is to understand why a given individual behaves in a particular way, specifically, how behavior enhances reproductive fitness. "Proximate" causal analysis, by contrast, focuses on how an individual acquires and displays certain behaviors. To this point, most of the social science literature on wife-beating has centered on proximate rather than ultimate causes of the behavior. Research centering on proximate causes is indeed useful to behavioral science. However, if we do not also understand the ultimate cause of this behavior, we have no solid theoretical base from which to work.

Evolutionary psychology focuses on ultimate cause. It is concerned with: (a) the conditions in ancestral populations that rendered some behaviors adaptive and others maladaptive; (b) the mechanisms that evolved to produce adaptive behaviors; and (c) the way the mechanisms that evolved to produce the adaptive behaviors function in contemporary environments. Thus evolutionary psychology provides a paradigm for understanding how variations in environmental conditions can lead to conflict, violence, and pathological behaviors, perhaps eventually leading to an understanding of how environmental conditions can be modified to change troublesome behaviors.

For an individual of any primate species, including Homo sapiens, the most direct path to this ultimate goal of "reproductive fitness" requires mating with an animal of the opposite sex and generating offspring, which must be protected and tended until they are capable of surviving and mating on their own. However, it would also include behaviors (labeled "inclusive fitness") designed to ensure the survival of blood kin, who share the individual's genes. If this theory is correct, then one would expect little violence, especially of a life-threatening kind, towards kin. Indeed, a vast body of literature has been built and continues to expand in support of this idea of non-violence towards blood relatives throughout the animal kingdom (Symons 1981:51–58; Trivers 1985:118–121; Wilson 1980:55–63). Thus it is posited that some sort of innate mechanisms exist to inhibit violence between individuals related by blood.

Because of incest avoidance in mating behaviors in most primates, mates are generally not related by blood. Thus a possible mechanism that would inhibit violence between blood relations will not obtain in this specific situation. Indeed, Daly and Wilson (1987:302–303) have demonstrated that in human populations, domestic violence culminating in death significantly more often involves non-blood-related kin than blood relatives.

Because mates are necessary to produce progeny and provide resources to rear them, they have a high value for an animal's reproductive fitness. All primate species have had to develop mechanisms to attract and mate with typically non-related opposite-sexed individuals. Although most of these mechanisms involve consensual, cooperative behaviors, some rely on coercion and aggression. Because of the high valence attached to a mate, behaviors directed towards that mate are often highly emotionally charged. Since mating relationships are so vital for reproductive fitness, any indication of disruption of that relationship can evoke a powerful emotional and behavioral response in the animal.

While Darwin's concept of natural selection involves the relative capability of organisms to adapt to their surroundings, Darwin posited another construct, which he called "sexual selection," to describe males' and females' differential ability to attract sexual partners and pursue their goal of reproductive fitness. Sexual selection involves both intersexual selection and intrasexual selection (Kevles 1986:4–14; Symons 1981:22; Trivers 1985:15). Intersexual selection is founded on the choice of mate by the sex making the higher minimal parental investment (usually females). Intrasexual selection involves competition between the members of the sex making the lower minimal parental investment (usually males) for access and control of the sex making the greater minimal parental investment (usually females). It results in sexual dimorphism in size, physical aggressiveness, and the production of organs of threat. Reproductive strategies differ between males and females; thus, some authors believe that some amount of conflict is inherent in male-female relationships. Catton and Gray summarize these differences in strategies as follows:

> In the battle of the sexes the males have most of the weapons, and whenever they can avoid looking after the young they will use every possible means to try and fertilize more females. In the females' armoury there is often only one defence against the male onslaught, but its effect is devastating. Females can say no (Catton and Gray 1985:152).

It is clear that female consent delimits the male's ability to reproduce. In order to win this consent, the male employs many strategies, which may include fighting off competing males, preventing females from mating with other males, and providing resources that the female can use in maintaining herself and caring for her young. The female, who must bear and generally also provide most of the rearing of the young, uses the strategy of choosing the male who can best provide her and her progeny with resources, such as food, protection, and assistance in rearing her young. Although animal data is not always pertinent to the human case, writers such as David Buss (1989:735–736), who studies human mate retention, believe that differential means of reproduction lead men and women to pursue different strategies in securing and retaining mates. Whenever these strategies clash, conflict should be anticipated.

SEXUAL DIMORPHISM

One of the results of sexual selection is sexual dimorphism. In most primate species, as well as our own, males are bigger in size and musculature than are females; in many species males also have bigger canines than females and thus are more likely to inflict serious injury than are females. Although the size and strength difference may have evolved primarily due to intrasexual competition among males, this difference may also have had the "beneficial effect" of allowing the males dominance over the females in many species. In general, the greater the sexual dimorphism, the more the male is apt to be clearly dominant over the female, the more likely the mating pattern is to be polygamous and the less the male is apt to be involved in parental care of the young.

Although there is not currently much data regarding male-female violence in the wild, what evidence there is points to more male-to-female violence in sexually dimorphic species than in those in which male and female are physically similar in strength and size. For example, in Hamadryas baboons, in which the male is twice as large as the female, males hold harems of females. If a female should stray, he threatens her or bites her neck until she stays close to him (Kummer 1985:374–375). Similarly, when an unfamiliar human approaches a group of mountain gorillas, the male cuffs the females in his harem, succeeding in getting them to flee with him; again the male is twice the size of the female (Nichols 1989:83). Fossey reported an incident in which a male, apparently unprovoked, attacked a female and beat her to death, returning again and again to savage the body even after she was dead (Fossey 1981:508–511).

Goodall has also recorded many acts of male-female violence among common chimpanzees, in which the female weighs about 75 percent as much as the male (Hrdy 1981:175), in the wild. She observed that a male would attack a female in several different kinds of situations. Some of the more common situations involved a female's refusal to mate with a male, the refusal of a female to accompany a male on a "consortship" journey, the approach of another male when a more dominant male was dominating a female during her fertile period, the approach of an unfamiliar female, and a "spillover" effect of aggression from a male who had engaged in fighting other males. Since the first three situations relate to mate retention, they will be discussed in that section. However, the "spillover effect" seems to be purely a function of the size and power advantage of the male over the female (Goodall 1986:313–341).

Goodall reported that females tended to flee with their infants whenever male-male violence erupted, as the loser(s) would often attack a female or her infant after such a battle, with no provocation whatsoever from the victim (Goodall 1986:482). De Waal (1989:150,248) also reported similar unprovoked aggression of males towards females in several sexually dimorphic species of primates. Both Goodall and de Waal emphasized, however, that male violence severe enough to cause injury to a female was exceedingly rare (Goodall 1986:313; de Waal 1989:77) in part due to the female's efforts at peacemaking when males became angry and, when appropriate, female avoidance of angered males. Incidents resulting in severe injury to the females tended to erupt only when the male dominance hierarchy was in flux, thus causing much intrasexual aggression, which then spilled over on the females. Despite the rarity of severe male aggression towards females, minor aggression and threats were commonplace. However, a lone adult female attacked an adult male only in one specific type of situation, that is, when that male was threatening her young.

Evidence from laboratory studies reported by Nadler (1988:160) suggests that the female's smaller size may allow her to avoid male aggression by being able to evade the larger male, particularly in arboreal species. Thus, the female's smaller size may be a "beneficial effect" for her in that she can more easily escape injury or forcible copulation by a substantially larger male, thereby enhancing her ability to exercise mating choice. In orangutans, when an adult male and an adult female animal were placed in a zoo cage and allowed free access to each other, the male immediately chased and caught the female, wrestled her down to the floor, and copulated with her. Although she struggled at first, he was able by his greater size and strength to subdue her and engage in forcible copulation. However, if the cage was modified so that the female could escape through a door that was too small to accommodate the male, the male soon changed his behavior to perform a display for the female and wait immobile until she initiated the copulation. Nadler concluded that perhaps the reason that forcible copulations in the wild almost always are perpetrated by subadult males rather than by mature males is that the latter's larger size precludes them from catching the lighter, more mobile females.

There is almost no intersexual violence in species for which little sexual dimorphism exists, such as the tamarin and the gibbon. When such violence erupts, there is no sex difference regarding the initiation of the fight. The male and the female tend to form monogamous pair bonds, with no clear dominance pattern of one above the other, and they share the chores of caregiving for their offspring. Of course, biology is not entirely destiny when it comes to primates. In some species with little dimorphism, such as spider monkeys, males tend to dominate and aggress against females. There is no species with substantial sexual dimorphism, however, in which females display equal or more aggression towards the males than do the males towards them. Goodall (1986:482) suggests that this is due in part to the healthy respect given males by females as they will necessarily lose to the male's superior size and strength. Thus they tend to prevent aggressive incidents by deferring to dominant males and, in addition, acting as peacemakers to reduce male-male aggression (Goodall 1986:585–586), in order to diminish the possibility of its overflowing onto themselves and their offspring.

What of the human case? Humans are judged to be mildly sexually dimorphic, with males about 5 percent to 12 percent taller (Hrdy 1981:175) and 20 percent to 30 percent (Mitchell 1981:10) heavier than women, with significantly greater upper body strength. Reviewing wife-beating in the U.S., Saunders (1986:49) states that while battering husbands tend to be average in height and weight, their battered wives tend to be below the norm in both. However, unlike other animals, humans have access to lethal weapons; use of weapons such as guns can exacerbate or override differences in size and strength.

Authors such as de Waal believe that wife-beating in human societies is an ever present danger given the average superiority in strength of the husband:

> Nonhuman primates are endowed with particularly highly developed checks on escalated fighting. Some of these are innate, others seem publicly enforced. Severe attacks by young adult males on females, for example, are often stopped by other members of the group. Older males have learned to control their aggression against females. . . . In human social life . . . male aggression may tip over into violent crime if the appropriate balancing mechanisms and social controls are lacking (de Waal 1989:11).

While the appropriate balancing mechanisms and social controls to check the aggression of husbands towards their wives may have been present in the tightly knit context of the ancestral hunting and gathering band, they are apt to be less reliably present in the context of modern urban societies. There the anomic conditions of large cities and fluctuating populations may result in individuals living hundreds of miles from their extended families. De Waal considers the lack of respect for women by men to be a dangerous situation in modern times and sees education and the social example set for young boys as the key to preventing wife-beating.

MATE GUARDING

As was mentioned earlier, the reproductive interests of males are not necessarily congruent with those of females. It is unlikely that wife abuse has ever been in the reproductive interest of women. However, it might in some cases have been advantageous for men in ancestral populations in that wife abuse may have represented one tactic used by a man to control the reproductive behavior of his wife.

Sexual reproduction necessitates locating and retaining a mate for at least as long as it takes the male to copulate with a female. Money and Tucker wrote: "When it comes down to the biological imperatives that are laid down for all men and women, there are only four: Only a man can impregnate; only a woman can menstruate, gestate, and lactate" (Money and Tucker 1975:38). These differences have implications for optimal reproductive strategies for each sex. Since men need only inseminate in order to reproduce, the use of deviousness and coercion in attracting and retaining a mate might have made sense in an ancestral population. Since women invest not only in fertilization, but also in pregnancy and lactation, it would have behooved them to exercise careful choice before permitting sexual intercourse.

For primates, females bear the young and have no doubt as to the maternity of their infants. Since the female invests more directly in offspring, it is to her advantage to exercise choice in her selection of a mate and to select a male who is physically healthy with sound genes and other resources to invest in mate and offspring. After she has been impregnated and has garnered whatever resources she can from one male, it might benefit her to attract several other males in order to amass resources for rearing her offspring and to ensure male protection from predators and other males for herself and her young.

Male primates, however, have no guarantee of paternity and are not necessarily involved in the rearing of offspring. Males of many species, therefore, have developed strategies for enticing females to mate with them and for guarding against cuckolding. Mate retention behaviors aimed at ensuring exclusive sexual access include several different tactics. One such tactic is "mate guarding," exemplified in behaviors such as "herding" in the Hamadryas baboon (Cosmides and Tooby 1989:64–65). If a female in the harem of the male Hamadryas strays too far from him, he threatens and, if necessary, bites her. This action will cause the female Hamadryas baboon to stay close to him. Interestingly, however, if a male Hamadryas should try the same technique on a female Savannah baboon, which is physiologically very similar to the Hamadryas baboon, she will flee him and not allow him to approach her in the future.

Another male mate retention tactic is exemplified by the "consortship journeys" (Goodall 1986:457–465) undertaken by male common chimps in which a female is singled out from the troop and coaxed into accompanying the male alone into a spot in the forest — well-isolated from the other chimps. If she tries to call out to alert others of her whereabouts or tries to flee, the male will forcibly cover her mouth or strike and bite her to bring her into compliance. On this journey, the male has exclusive sexual access to the female, and sometimes is successful in impregnating her.

While "consortships" are sometimes successful in perpetuating an individual male's genes, they are riskier than staying with the troop and claiming exclusive rights to a fertile female. Therefore the most dominant male in a troop will instead monopolize the sexual access to a female during her four fertile days (Goodall 1986:450–453). Because this male has already established dominance, most of the time other males will not even approach his consort. If another male does approach, however, the dominant male will typically attack the female. This strategy is more beneficial for him than attacking the other male for many reasons:

1. While the dominant male fights the intruder, a third male could slip in and copulate with the fertile female;
2. The dominant male is unlikely to receive any injury from attacking the female, but is at risk from another male;
3. By attacking the female, he discourages her from accepting the advances of other males in the future.

Although rape is rare in common chimps, Goodall (1986:466–469) witnessed female chimps refusing the sexual advances of a son or a brother. In such cases, the male often beat her severely and forcibly copulated with her. Also, she sometimes saw a situation in which a male tried to initiate copulation with a female only to have her refuse to get into a copulatory crouch position. The male was then observed to whip the female with a branch. Such incidents were rare, as females typically readily complied with requests for copulation. Nadler also cited an example in which male chimps were observed trapping females in trees from which escape was impossible and forcibly copulating with them. He concluded that "some degree of male aggressivity is inherent in the species-typical mating pattern of chimpanzees." (Nadler 1988:158). Nadler argues that female compliance in copulatory activities initiated by the male does not necessarily imply receptivity but rather reflects an attempt to appease a potentially hostile male to avoid injury to herself.

Some authors believe that human wife-beating stems from sexual jealousy and the need for mate retention. Carlson (1987:19) found that the best predictor of male-female violence in dating couples was sexual involvement. Daly and Wilson have written, "intensive studies . . . are unanimous in suggesting that male sexual proprietariness constitutes the dangerous issue in marriage" (Daly and Wilson 1988:200). These authors cite studies from several different cultures (although their literature review is not exhaustive) demonstrating that husbands who killed their wives generally did so for one of three reasons, all having to do with their retention and sexual control over their wives:

1. Their wives had left them or threatened to end the relationship;
2. They suspected or knew that their wives were being unfaithful;
3. Their wives refused their sexual advances.

Daly and Wilson concluded, "Men . . . strive to control women . . . women struggle to resist coercion and to maintain their choices" (Daly and Wilson, 1988:205).

RECIPROCITY

Most primates, including humans, are social animals; it is to their advantage to cooperate and live together harmoniously in order to survive and reproduce. One type of cooperation feasible between two individuals, such as a mating pair, is "reciprocal altruism," defined as "the trading of altruistic acts in which benefit is larger than cost so that over a period of time both enjoy a net gain" (Trivers 1985:361). The problem with this system is that one of the individuals may not reciprocate, thus leaving the other with a net loss rather than a net gain. An unwary altruist, therefore, would ultimately lose in reproductive fitness. In primate literature, there is evidence that failure to reciprocate engenders fiercer attacks than other types of irritating behaviors. Trivers (1985:377) used anthropomorphic language to describe such intense reactions in common chimps; he termed it "moralistic aggression." Researchers such as Cosmides and Tooby (1989:86–92) present evidence that the human brain is preprogrammed with a propensity to "detect cheaters" (non-reciprocators). It must be emphasized here that what is important is the perception of non-reciprocation by a particular individual in a given relationship, not what an impartial judge might decide is a fair amount of give and take. While norms of reciprocity between husband and wife may have been relatively simple and clear to both spouses in the context of the ancestral hunter-gatherer band, these norms are not always clear in more modern settings. In modern technologically advanced societies, cultural diversity is so great and cultural change is so rapid that individual husbands and wives may frequently hold different expectations about what behaviors are appropriate for themselves and their partners in order to maintain an equitable situation within a marriage.

Reciprocal systems involve a rather delicate balance; if there is a power disparity in a relationship, the possibilities of altruistic exchanges are diminished. Several authorities on wife abuse in North America have indicated that a status inconsistency between partners is associated with a higher risk of wife-beating (Gelles and Cornell 1985:75; Shields, McCall and Hannecke 1988:94; Tavris and Wade 1984:288.) Although many authors do not specify the direction of this inconsistency, Walker (1984:11) found that a sample of battered American women had significantly higher educational levels and higher social class backgrounds than their husbands as compared to non-violent control couples. The same pattern was found by Browne (1987:20–21) in her sample of American battered women who ultimately killed their husbands. In a similar vein, Okun (1986:48–49) concluded from his search of North American wife-beating literature that there was a consistent tendency for wife-abuse to be more severe in couples in which the wife had a higher educational or occupational level than did the husband. Thus such a husband may feel "one down" in the relationship and believe that he is at risk for being cheated in some way by his wife. He may thus resort to violence in order to tip the scales in his own favor. As Saunders wrote, " . . . one episode of violence of any intensity may shift the power balance in the relationship by making the woman more passive" (Saunders 1986:48). Once this power has shifted, it may be increasingly easier for the husband to obtain what he wants by violent means, and increasingly harder for the wife to resist.

RECONCILIATION

More powerful than the need to dominate and aggress among social primates is the need to maintain harmonious social relationships. Researchers studying the common chimp (de Waal 1989:48; Goodall 1986:357–361; Trivers 1985:377) believe that these animals may consider interruptions in relationships more potentially threatening than the physical harm done by aggression. De Waal cited an example of a female who, after being severely bitten by a male, reconciled and chose to sleep close to him for the night. Goodall (1986:361) also reported that after a male has attacked a female very severely, he will often attempt to reconcile with her immediately, hugging and patting her. More commonly, the female will seek post-fight reassurance from the male.

CONCLUSION

Recent observational studies of primate behavior demonstrate that wife-abuse-like behavior is found in a number of species close to Homo sapiens on the phylogenetic scale. The variety of situations evoking male aggression towards females are many, and the responses of individual animals to this aggression is also diverse. We need a much broader research base before we can begin to understand the causes of and solutions for wife-beating. One strategy used by female primates to combat male aggression was to form a coalition with other females or with a male animal (de Waal 1989; Goodall 1986:573; Mitchell 1981:105). Another was to flee, a strategy facilitated by the female's smaller size and mobility. Still another was for the female to appease a male before he became aggressive or for her to initiate reconciliation immediately following a fight. Because males more frequently attack females after fighting with other males, Goodall (1986:571) observed females actively taking a peacemaking role to get two males to reconcile after a fight as a preventative measure.

Solutions to wife-beating will not be simple, and perhaps wife-beating will never totally be eliminated on a worldwide basis, but it can certainly be reduced and its severity alleviated. Gelles and Straus state, "We believe that human beings are less fearful of violence and injury than the violation of social order" (Gelles and Straus 1988:19). Thus, perhaps on both an individual and a societal level, spouse abuse, which is a potential threat to such order, is hushed up, glossed over. Those individuals who violate societal norms to such an extent as to bring such abuse to the attention of society are often stigmatized. Such abuse as comes to the attention of the public is seen as "unnatural," "sick." As long as wife-beating is viewed as a bizarre event, with blame cast upon both batterer and victim, it will continue to occur. Effective remedies cannot be undertaken at the individual level unless societies choose to censure wife-beating.

The evidence we have cited from the area of sexual dimorphism suggests that the average male has enough strength advantage over the average female to allow men to use physical means to control their wives unless society exacts penalties for wife-beating. As Gelles and Straus (1988:32) note, wife-beating quickly rewards the aggressor by allowing him to work off anger, see immediate compliance by his victim, and by giving him an increased amount of control over her. Once begun, it tends to be habit-forming. A popular misconception is that the wife must have provoked the beating and thus is to be held accountable for her own abuse. The primate literature on male attacks on females tends to support Angela Browne's observation on the immediate antecedents of an attack:

> In most cases, although the violence may have been preceded by verbal abuse or other signs of difficulty, the actual assault was triggered by a seemingly minor occurrence or seemed to have no trigger at all (Browne 1987:51).

One way to combat wife-beating is therefore to condemn interpersonal violence in general.

One principle which is evident from the literature that we have cited under the topic of mate-guarding is that the common-sense notion that an abused female should simply leave a battering spouse is misguided. The act of leaving or of threatening to leave may put the wife and, in some cases her children, at more jeopardy than any other act. This danger is especially acute in the time immediately following a woman's flight in which emotions are particularly high and tend to cloud judgment. Therefore, the availability of a safe place to which the woman may flee with her children during volatile episodes enhances her ability to escape continued violence. Over the past two decades, in North America, battered women's shelters have been formally established to serve this vital function and to provide guidance for such families to halt future violence.

The concept of social reciprocity is useful in explaining why habitual abusers feel justified in beating their wives. Many report that their wives deserved their battering. Angela Browne suggests:

> Most strong emotions, particularly unpleasant ones, become translated into anger and then externalized as somebody's 'fault.' The 'offender' is labeled and punished, and the abusive man becomes the victim and, therefore, is 'justified' in his aggression (Browne 1987:83).

Once a husband has thus cognitively justified his use of force against his wife, a cycle is set up whereby any behavior by her which is "disobedient" by his subjective standards is seen as justification for a beating. Such incidents seem to arouse an emotion akin to what Trivers (1985:377) calls "moralistic aggression" in primates, aggression that appears to be vastly disproportionate to the "offense" which is committed.

A common fallacy is to assume that what is natural is necessarily good. Even if it were proven unequivocally that wife-beating is a "natural tendency," that does not mean that it is either good or inevitable. It can be prevented to a large extent by human laws and cultural practices (Catton and Gray 1985:212–213). Although our biological nature may set limits and predispositions on our behavior, it cannot inexorably determine how we are capable of acting nor does it address the moral issue of how we should act.

REFERENCES CITED

Barash, David P. 1978. Sociobiology and Behavior. New York: Elsevier.

Browne, Angela. 1987. When Battered Women Kill. New York: The Free Press.

Buss, David. 1989. Conflict Between the Sexes: Strategic Interference and the Evocation of Anger and Upset. Journal of Personality and Social Psychology 56(5):735—747.

Carlson, Bonnie E. 1987. Dating Violence: A Research Review and Comparison with Spouse Abuse. Social Casework 68(1):16—23.

Catton, Chris, and James Gray. 1985. Sex in Nature. New York: Facts on File Publications.

Cosmides, Leda, and John Tooby. 1989. Evolutionary Psychology and the Generation of Culture, Part II. Ethology and Sociobiology 10:51—97.

Daly, Martin, and Margo Wilson. 1987. Evolutionary Psychology and Family Violence. In Sociobiology and Psychology. Charles Crawford, M. Smith, and D. Krebs, eds. Pp. 293—309. Hillsdale, NJ: Lawrence Erlbaum Associates.

———. 1988. Homicide. New York: Aldine de Gruyter.

de Waal, Frans. 1989. Peacemaking Among Primates. Cambridge, MA: Harvard University Press.

Fossey, Dian. 1981. The Imperiled Mountain Gorilla. National Geographic 159(4):500—523.

Gelles, Richard J., and C. P. Cornell. 1985. Intimate Violence in Families. Beverly Hills, CA: Sage.

Gelles, Richard J., and Murray A. Straus. 1988. Intimate Violence. New York: Simon and Schuster.

Goodall, Jane. 1986. The Chimpanzees of Gombe. Cambridge, MA: Belknap Press of Harvard University Press.

Hrdy, Sarah Blaffer. 1981. The Woman that Never Evolved. Cambridge, MA: Harvard University Press.

Kevles, Bettyann. 1986. Females of the Species. Cambridge, MA: Harvard University Press.

Kummer, Hans. 1985. A Male-dominated Society. *In* The Encyclopedia of Mammals. David Whyte and David Macdonald, eds. Pp. 374—375. New York: Facts on File Publications.

Mitchell, G. 1981. Human Sex Differences. New York: Van Nostrand Reinhold.

Money, John, and Patricia Tucker. 1975. Sexual Signatures. Boston: Little, Brown.

Nadler, Ronald D. 1988. Sexual Aggression in the Great Apes. *In* Human Sexual Aggression: Current Perspectives. Robert A. Prentky and Vernon L. Quinsey, eds. Annals of the New York Academy of Sciences 528:154—162.

Nichols, M. 1989. Gorilla: A Struggle for Survival in the Virungas. New York: Aperture Foundation.

Okun, Lewis. 1986. Woman Abuse. Albany, N.Y.: State University of New York Press.

Pollitt, Katha. 1989. Hers. The New York Times Magazine. June 18:18—20.

Saunders, D. G. 1986. When Battered Women use Violence: Husband-abuse or Self-defense. Victims and Violence 1(1): 47—60.

Shields, Nancy, George McCall, and Christine Hanneke. 1988. Patterns of Family and Nonfamily Violence: Violent Husbands and Violent Men. Violence and Victims 3(2):83—97.

Symons, Donald. 1981. The Evolution of Human Sexuality. New York: Oxford University Press.

Tavris, Carol, and Carole Wade. 1984. The Longest War. New York: Harcourt Brace Jovanovich.

Trivers, Robert. 1985. Social Evolution. Menlo Park, CA: Benjamin Cummings.

Walker, Lenore E. 1984. The Battered Woman Syndrome. New York: Springer.

Wilson, Edward O. 1980. Sociobiology. (Abridged ed.) Cambridge, MA: The Belknap Press of Harvard University.

3

Fight! Fight!: Men, Women, and Interpersonal Aggression in an Australian Aboriginal Community

Victoria K. Burbank

Addressing the question of how male aggression affects relations between men and women, this discussion of fighting between men and women in the Australian Aboriginal community of Mangrove[1] develops the theme that the manifestation of male aggression does not inevitably lead to asymmetries in gender relations.

Mangrove was established in the early 1950s. Situated on an approximate half square mile of coast in southeast Arnhem Land, this settlement was the home of about 400 Aborigines in 1977. By 1988 the population had grown to about 575. During these years the people of Mangrove lived in the midst of houses, trucks, pots and pans, processed food, toilets, showers, clothes, laundry detergent, tape recorders, cards, and videos. They were, to varying degrees, engaged in and dependent on such introduced institutions as Western-styled forms of education, medicine, government, religion, a money economy, and wage labor. Still much of their behavior was informed by distinctively Aboriginal models of etiquette, religion, kinship, and marriage (for a detailed discussion of Mangrove and the changes it represents for Aborigines in the area see Burbank 1988). It is difficult, if not impossible, to ascertain whether the amount of aggression present on the settlement represents levels that might have been present in nomadic times (for a discussion of this issue see Burbank 1989).

Between 1977 and 1988 I visited this southeast Arnhem Land community on three occasions; for 18 months in 1977 and 1978, for nine months in 1981, and for seven months in 1988. On each trip I recorded cases of aggressive behavior; some of these I observed, and many more were recounted by Aboriginal people, usually women. Although I cannot know for sure, the public nature of aggression on the settlement and the interest that people demonstrate in talking and hearing about it, suggest that I may have been able to record the majority of acts of physical aggression that occurred during my visits.

Elsewhere I present a detailed quantitative analysis of these cases (Burbank 1989). Here, in this limited space, let it suffice to say that aggressive interactions between men and women are not uncommon. For example, of the 101 fights recorded for a 19.5 month period in 1977 and 1978,[2] 58 were between men and women. Women were not merely the recipients of male aggression. In the case of 37 fights it was possible to ascertain who initiated the physical aggression of the encounter—that is, the first person reported to have picked up a weapon, destroyed an object, or physically attacked their opponent.[3] Women initiated physical aggression in 17 cases; men initiated physical aggression in 20 cases. Male aggression, however, appears to be more injurious. Men reportedly struck or injured women more than twice as often as women struck or injured men. For the most part, these were battles between members of the immediate family, often husbands and wives. And, in general, these were fights precipitated by family issues such as sexual jealousy or the infidelity of a spouse, use of household resources, or, sometimes, a man's intoxication (Burbank 1980a, 1980b). As such, these fights might be compared with incidents called "domestic violence" by police and social agencies in this country. However, it should be noted that the distinction between "domestic" and "political" issues in this Aboriginal community is not always clear-cut (Burbank 1989; cf. Collier 1974; Lamphere 1974).

Physical aggression hurts. It can incapacitate or kill. When its use parallels conflicting desires or interests, it can be seen as an attempt to coerce, intimidate, or dominate. It is in this guise that male aggression has been nominated as a foundation stone of gender asymmetry (e.g., Maccoby and Jacklin 1974; Mukhopadhyay and Higgins 1988; Quinn 1977; Rosaldo 1980). The proposition that a male potential for aggressive behavior may limit women's power or autonomy does not require that male aggression toward women be manifest. It is necessary, however, to demonstrate that women perceive the potential for male aggression, and perceive it as a danger to be avoided.

The women of Mangrove are certainly aware of the possibility that a man may attack a woman. They see or hear of these attacks if they don't actually experience them themselves. Indeed, when they speak about women and aggression they often speak about male attack. For example, in 1988 I asked six women to visualize a fight in which an adolescent girl was being beaten and asked who they thought might be doing this. Three of the women answered, "young boy" (i.e., adolescent boy), "[lover]," or "boyfriend." I also asked these six women if they could tell me about a fight that they had been in. Two chose to tell me about fights with their husbands. A third woman, the only woman who said she had never been in a fight, attributed this, among other things, to the fact that she had followed the advice of the "European" minister who married her. This is her account of what he said:

> Love your husband, take care of your husband; if your husband says anything to you, do it. And don't go running around with anyone, mind your husband as long as you live.

The following account of an Aboriginal practice at one time current for the people of Mangrove indicates that at least some women anticipate a greater male potential for aggressive behavior:

> Emu and bush turkey have strong power. If you eat them and somebody is fighting, the spear will come to you. They make you deaf and you fight. Younger boys can eat and women can always eat, but when a man is young neither he nor his mother will eat things like emu, turkey or fat from the dugong and turtle. . . . If he does eat emu, when somebody throws a spear he won't run away. He will throw back and kill that man. When a man becomes old, gets gray hair or has children, then he can eat.

> The women do this because this is the Law; they help the boy. If a boy eats, he will be cranky and fighting. If his mother eats, she won't get cranky, but he will.

At least some women also see male aggression as more dangerous than female aggression. For example, I asked four women who would get "really hurt" in a fight between men and women. "The woman," answered all four. It is not clear, however, that all women see men as more aggressive than women. For example, in 1978 and 1988 I asked women if they thought men or women were more "cheeky" (i.e., aggressive). Men are more "cheeky" according to six women. For example:

> Men are more cheeky than women, because men get spears and want to kill men. Women only get sticks and pull each other's hair. Women never murder their husbands, only men murder their wives.

> Men get more angry than women. They have lots of muscle, they are stronger than women. They get spears [metal spears, and spear throwers].

But one group of at least five women said that "Some women are cheeky, just like men." Three other women also thought that men and women were both "cheeky." I asked this question of one woman, the first quoted above, again in 1988. In the intervening years she had changed her mind or was thinking of "cheeky" in a different way. Women, she said this time, are more cheeky—they start the fights.

Short of death or permanent incapacitation, the power of aggressive behavior to intimidate, coerce, or dominate depends on how it is experienced by its target. A man may literally try to beat a woman into submission, but submission is not an inevitable response to aggression. In this regard, bruises and wounds need be viewed as no more than a potential cost of a chosen course of action.

How do the women of Mangrove experience male aggression? Some of these women talk about male aggression as though it were a means of dominating them. For example: "Some women are frightened of cheeky men. When women are married to a cheeky man they know they had better be careful." And, "George's wife is running off to another man, I don't know why, her husband is a young man. She keeps running around because he doesn't hit her. If he did, she would stop."

But while women may experience male aggression as a form of attempted domination, at least some women may also see male aggression as a rather ineffective means of trying to dominate them. For example, one woman told me about a married woman who ran off with a boyfriend on a number of occasions; the woman's husband would beat her, but following a trip to the clinic, she would run off again. Pursuing this theme in women's discourse, I asked six women in 1988 the following question: "A married woman got a hiding from her husband because he heard she has a friend [lover]. Should she go meet her friend again?"

Only two answered that she should not. Two of the remaining four urged caution. For example, one woman said that she should wait until her husband left the settlement and another suggested that she wait a few months before resuming her affair. But none of the four thought that a "hiding" would deter a woman from meeting her lover.

Women make many statements about male aggression as a response to women's behavior. For example: "A woman sleeps with her husband. If she didn't he would chase her with a [metal] spear." And, "Those men don't drink, fight, steal for nothing. They want women. Mothers might even get speared by them if they don't give their daughters in marriage."

It is clear that women think that men may act aggressively when women frustrate their desires. It is not clear that these speakers see dominance as the motive behind male aggression. On the basis of these statements alone, one could as easily say that male aggression is seen only as an expression of anger (cf. Myers 1986:161–162).

I suggest that at Mangrove male aggression is relatively ineffectual in changing women's attitudes and behavior because women do not see that as its primary goal. They see it instead largely as a means by which men display and express their anger. And they see male aggression this way not because the men of Mangrove do not attempt to dominate women through aggression (though I don't know that they do), but because of a cultural emphasis on aggression as an expression of anger (Burbank 1980a, 1989).

That women of Mangrove are not intimidated by male aggression is suggested by the apparent willingness with which women attack men thus inviting male attack:

> Last night Hetty and her husband had a fight over Brenda. He has been running around with her. Hetty was very angry and got a [metal spear] and speared her husband in the leg. Then he took the spear and speared her in the hand.

The women of Mangrove see men as stronger than themselves and if not more aggressive, then at least more dangerously so. These perceptions are undoubtedly created and reinforced by the greater amount of injury that they suffer at the hands of men. Why then do they fight with men?

I suggest that women at Mangrove initiate aggression against men because the norms of their community permit and encourage such behavior. Women, like men, have learned that anger is appropriately expressed through aggressive behavior (see also Straus 1980). They know that women are sometimes hurt or even killed by men, but they perceive that they themselves are unlikely to be seriously injured. Hence, when they get angry at men, they attack them.

Fighting at Mangrove is a structured activity, largely patterned by, and predicted by, cultural rules (see also Fox 1968). Although the following is a case in which a man attacks a woman, it illustrates the sociocultural context in which women dare attack men.

Sunny is a woman who was in her early 30s in 1988. She was married, had three children, and like many of the women at Mangrove today, lived with her mother and married sisters and brothers. This account is somewhat atypical insofar as the incident took place when Sunny was living away from Mangrove, her husband was drinking if not intoxicated, and the injury she suffered was more severe than that which is usually inflicted, though she is not the first woman at Mangrove to be stabbed. This is a part of her account of the incident[4]:

> When I was married, not to this husband, to the other one, when he was drunk, he always fought and argued with me. One day, Sunday afternoon, we went to the beach. He was drinking. We went crabbing and fishing and got a lot of fish. After we went out fishing, we came back home and we went down to the river and we were swimming but he was still drunk. I was carrying my son Timmy. My husband went and asked one of his cousins for a car, a white Falcon. And they gave him the key and then we went down to the

you might hit me and Timmy." He had a gun but that gun didn't have any
bullets. "I'll hit you," he said to me. "No."

"I'll hit you."

"No."

And we ran away and we were walking down by the side of the river, and
he was following us with the car, but he didn't walk down by the river side.
He was driving on the road, looking for our tracks but he didn't find us.

He got home first and we came last. The door was wide open and we went
inside. I was carrying Timmy and I put him on the bed. Timmy was crying
and my husband woke up and shut the door and he said, "I'll stab you with
the knife." He was coming closer and closer and I was shouting and screaming and I opened the door and took Timmy outside and my husband's cousin's
son heard us and went and got Timmy and said, "I'll take Timmy to my
father's house. I'll take him." "OK," I said, "He's full drunk, he might hit
him." After I gave Timmy to his cousin's son, I went back inside. My husband told me to shut the door. I wouldn't shut it so he did. I sat down on
the bed. He started arguing more and got a knife and stabbed me. [Here
Sunny shows me six scars on her arms and two on her legs.] And I was crying
and I started to bleed, blood was all over the floor, bed, I was jumping,
screaming, crying. My blood was on the wall. I ran outside now screaming
and crying and his cousin's wife saw me.

"What's wrong?"

"He stabbed me with the knife."

And he was fighting with his [other] cousin now and her husband. And
they started arguing about me and I was running and I saw him chasing me
with that same knife. His cousin was there and she asked her husband,
"What's wrong?" They looked down the road and they saw him chasing me.
I ran to my uncle's house. I saw my uncle there. He said, "You stand behind my back" and he said to my husband, "You come close, I'll hit you."
But my husband didn't listen. He came forward and punched me and when
he punched me I bled more. My uncle told his eldest sister, my sister-in-law,
"Take her to the hospital" and she did. First he told her to wash me and she
washed me, but the blood was still running and after that we went. And he
had a fight, my uncle hit my husband from the step, and my husband fell
down and he was bleeding then and my uncle's two wives talked for their
cousin, growled at my uncle, but my uncle said, "He is wrong, he stabbed
her."

I was in hospital and we rang the police and the police came there and
checked up. They didn't fix me at the mission, they fixed me at the town.
My sister-in-law and I were in the front of the police car and my husband was
in the back of the same car and we went to the hospital and the [nursing] sister
fixed me and did the stitches. The police took me to the police station to put
the statement and I put the statement and I didn't go to court. He went to
trial for stabbing me and they gave him one more chance.[5]

Closing the door clearly was an act of significance in the attack on Sunny.
Fights are public events in the village of Mangrove. Everyone knows when

a fight is taking place. Adults and children stop whatever they are doing and turn in the direction of the altercation. Cries of "fight, fight" can be heard as can the raised voices of participants and the barking of excited dogs. Life at Mangrove is spent outside; most activities are performed in public. Even the enclosed Western-style houses of the settlement do not interfere with open-air living for they are used primarily for sleeping and storage. Cooking, eating, work, and play take place out-of-doors within view and earshot of other people. So too fighting is largely a public event and thus easily monitored by neighbors and kin.

Women recognize that the public nature of fighting provides an important safeguard (see also Burgess and Draper 1989; Draper 1975; Erchak 1984). As knowledge of its occurrence is almost instantaneous, steps can be taken to minimize the effects of aggressive behavior. Comparing wife-beating in America and at Mangrove, a woman pointed out that, on the settlement where people fight "outside," there is always somebody to stop a fight. When a woman in a nearby community was fatally stabbed by her husband, another women explained how this was possible:

> That man and woman were fighting in front of everybody on Monday and she was alright. But yesterday when they were alone, he stabbed her. He locked the door of the house and then stabbed her with a spear.

A third woman, recounting her husband's aggressive displays of jealousy, was advised by her neighbor not to "go bush" with him. "By and by he'll strike you." A man, this advisor explained further, who wishes to give his wife a beating without interference may attempt to isolate her. One means of doing so is on the pretext of a hunting or fishing trip.

It is probably not just Sunny's good fortune that so many people protected her from the worst effects of her husband's aggression. Like the people at Mangrove, they undoubtedly recognize rules that specify appropriate behavior for assisting or otherwise intervening in fights and act accordingly [6]. One such rule may be stated as follows: If a member of my kindred is attacked I should come to his or her assistance. This rule may be modified by the reason attributed to the attack. If, for example, it is understood that a man is beating his wife for her infidelity, her kin will refrain from interfering, but only to a certain point. If they perceive that her injury is imminent they will come to her assistance, regardless of the reason for the attack: "If her husband is too rough, marking her, making her sick, making her dead, then we take partner."

Similarly, rules that specify that attackers should be stopped are also recognized. The general rule may be stated as follows: I should stop a member of my kindred if he or she is about to seriously injure someone in a fight. It is in the interest of members of a kindred to see that an aggressive act on the part of a family member does not result in the serious injury or death of another person, male or female, for it is said that aggression provoked by aggression can travel, so to speak, from one member of a kindred to another:

> When a man [kills or injures] somebody [trouble] will come to his family, everybody, father, mother, mother's sister, mother's brother, mother's father, everybody, the family. At [a nearby settlement] a man killed a woman. His father, sisters, uncles, his two old mothers were taken away to keep them from the trouble.

Even Sunny's husband may have acted to protect her. According to her account, he was alone with her in a house with a closed door, he had a knife, and he was drunk. Yet he did not stab her in any vital spot; he chose instead to strike at her arms and legs, areas of the body which are prescribed targets according to the rules of fighting (Burbank 1980a, 1989). Even though he had been drinking and had no one to remind or restrain him, Sunny's husband followed the rules.

Mangrove is a community like any other insofar as it is made up of diverse individuals with their own unique motives, needs, strengths, weaknesses, and powers of understanding. Some women, at least during some periods in their lives, may be more intimidated by male aggression than others. But the willingness of at least some of the women of Mangrove to attack men on occasion indicates that some of the women in this community are willing to risk male attack. This brief examination of rules surrounding fighting suggests that this willingness is based on women's realistic evaluation of their social circumstances. Men have killed women and the women of Mangrove know this. But the frequent help and protection that women see or receive from neighbors and kin is likely to have more salience than two deaths that occurred many years ago. These experiences remind them that people will attempt to prevent serious injury to a woman who is fighting with a man. Male aggression is seen as potentially dangerous but rarely so in actuality. It is not an experience to be avoided at any cost:

> I used to have fights with my husband, before we had our children. He used to think about other men staring at me and he used to see them and get jealous and we used to fight inside the house. He used to hit me and I used to grab him by the hair or sometimes scratch his face, sometimes hit him with a stick, not a [woman's fighting stick], but just any stick. He used to lock me up in the house, tell me not to come out. These days I have free time and go out with other girls, talk, tell stories. Before he used to never let me go with other girls.
> Why is he not locking you up now?
> Maybe he's giving up. He knows I know how to fight back. When I get a stick I just go ahead, I don't pull back, I just let go.

If the women of Mangrove do not always do what they want, it is likely for reasons other than a fear of physical aggression.

NOTES

Funds for research and analysis of data presented in this paper were provided by the Australian Institute of Aboriginal Studies, the Harry Frank Guggenheim Foundation, and the National Institute of Mental Health. An earlier version of this paper was presented at the Second International Conference on Hunting and Gathering Societies, Quebec, 1980. I wish to thank Drs. Lila Abu-Lughod, Patricia Draper, and Beatrice Whiting for their very helpful comments. I also want to thank Drs. Judith Brown and James Chisholm for help and encouragement while I was writing this paper.

1. This is a pseudonym, as are all personal names used in this paper.

2. I include here the 18 months of fieldwork and a six week break taken during 1977 and 1978 as at least some fights occurring during the latter period were reported.

3. It is, of course, quite possible that some actions were left out of these accounts. In the telling, a man's more dramatic attack on a woman might eclipse her milder attack on him, and vice versa.

4. In 1988 I asked Sunny, along with seven other women, to respond to a series of questions about aggressive behavior at Mangrove. I explained to each woman that I wanted this information for a book that I was writing about "fighting" on the settlement, that I would not use her name in the book, and that she could refuse to answer any of my questions. While I attempted to write down their answers verbatim, it should be noted that the statements presented here have been translated and edited. Although I tried to remember comments made in casual conversation word for word, they were usually recorded some time afterwards and thus can be regarded only as approximations of what people said.

5. Unlike the "European" police, Sunny's relatives did not give her husband "one more chance." The day after the incident, two of her classificatory "fathers" sent a chartered plane to bring Sunny and her son back to Mangrove. Back on the settlement, they advised her not to return to her husband.

6. At the time of the stabbing, Sunny was residing on a neighboring settlement. People from this settlement and Mangrove often move between the two villages. Some of the people living around Sunny and her husband might well have been people who normally reside at Mangrove. Whoever they were, their response to her need suggests that they recognize rules very similar to those recognized at Mangrove.

REFERENCES CITED

Burbank, Victoria. 1980a. Expression of Anger and Aggression in an Australian Aboriginal Community. Ph. D. dissertation, Rutgers University.

————. 1980b. Male Aggression and Female Autonomy: A Case from Aboriginal Australia. Paper presented at the Second International Conference on Hunting and Gathering Societies. Quebec.

————. 1988. Aboriginal Adolescence: Maidenhood in an Australian Community. New Brunswick: Rutgers University Press.

————. 1989. Fighting Sticks and Spears: Women and Aggression — An Exploration. Unpublished manuscript.

Burgess, Robert, and Patricia Draper. 1989. The Explanation of Family Violence: The Role of Biological, Behavioral, and Cultural Selection. *In* Family Violence: Crime and Justice — A Review of Research. Michael Tonry and Norval Morris, eds. Pp. 59—116. Chicago: University of Chicago Press.

Collier, Jane F. 1974. Women in Politics. *In* Woman, Culture and Society. Michelle Z. Rosaldo and Louise Lamphere, eds. Pp. 89—96. Stanford: Stanford University Press.

Draper, Patricia. 1975. !Kung Women: Contrasts in Sexual Egalitarianism in Foraging and Sedentary Contexts. *In* Towards an Anthropology of Women. Rayna Reiter, ed. Pp. 77—109. New York: Monthly Review Press.

Erchak, Gerald. 1984. Cultural Anthropology and Spouse Abuse. Current Anthropology 25:330—332.

Fox, Robin. 1968. Encounter with Anthropology. New York: Harcourt and Brace.

Lamphere, Louise. 1974. Strategies, Cooperation, and Conflict Among Women in Domestic Groups. *In* Women, Culture and Society. Michelle Z. Rosaldo and Louise Lamphere, eds. Pp. 97—112. Stanford: Stanford University Press.

Maccoby, Eleanor and Carol Jacklin. 1974. The Psychology of Sex Differences. Stanford: Stanford University Press.

Mukhopadhyay, Carol and Patricia Higgins. 1988. Anthropological Studies of Women's Status Revisited. Annual Review of Anthropology 17:461—495.

Myers, Fred. 1986. Pintupi Country, Pintupi Self: Sentiment, Place, and Politics Among Western Desert Aborigines. Washington: Smithsonian Institution Press.

Quinn, Naomi. 1977. Anthropological Studies on Women's Status. Annual Review of Anthropology 61:181—225.

Rosaldo, Michelle Z. 1980. The Use and Abuse of Anthropology: Feminism and Cross-Cultural Understanding. Signs 5:389—417.

Straus, Murray. 1980. Victims and Aggressors in Marital Violence. American Behavioral Scientist 23:681—704.

4

Room to Maneuver:
!Kung Women Cope with Men

Patricia Draper

INTRODUCTION

Among the !Kung San of Botswana, women are sometimes beaten by their husbands and coerced by other men, particularly their fathers. The factors that contribute to this form of aggression are various and are changing in recent years as a consequence of new economic and residential practices now seen among the !Kung as they have transformed themselves from mobile foragers to primarily sedentary food producers. The responses of women and their supporters to incidents of wife abuse are also changing. In this paper several episodes of wife-beating that came to my attention during recent field work among the !Kung will be reported and discussed in terms of the cultural values relevant to their former nomadic life and in terms of the realities of current life styles in the 1980s.[1] In a concluding section, the prospects for future patterns in wife abuse will be discussed. Before proceeding, a few words are in order regarding the general phenomenon of wife-beating in society and regarding the particular subject of wife-beating among the !Kung.

THE BIOSOCIAL BACKGROUND OF SEXUAL ASYMMETRY

The reality is that in human societies all women must face at least the prospect of being beaten by their husbands. This unhappy circumstance is not a simple matter of social or political inequality (Burgess and Draper 1989). The human male is larger and more aggressive than the female; around the world positions of authority are almost exclusively monopolized by men (Martin and Voorhies 1975). The tools of force are overwhelmingly the province of male interest and training, a situation which exacerbates the inequality between the sexes. The fact that sometimes individual women, by virtue of their kinship position or inherited power, come to stand in positions of power normally allocated to males only does not discredit the empirical association between male physiological sex and masculine gender role, on the one hand, and the use of force, whether legitimately conferred by the group or illegitimately seized by the individual, on the other hand.

The size difference between men and women is observed generally among mammals (with a few interesting exceptions) and is an outcome of mammalian reproductive physiology (Alexander et al. 1979). The "reasons" why dimorphisms of size and behavior run deep in our phylogeny have to do with the reproductive specializations of the sexes. Many aeons ago, when our primitive reptilian ancestors developed the capacity to retain fertilized eggs, the stage was set for the reproductive asymmetry now seen in mammals, one which is carried out in extreme form among the primates. This transformation required a long time to reach its current stage of elaboration and involved not only retained fertilized eggs but also lengthy internal gestation and postnatal nourishment and prolonged maternal care. In this way, some populations of organisms developed an alternate means of reproducing, one in which the sexes contributed unequally to the nurturing of the young.

Once a female developmental specialization in reproduction and parenting was established, the way was opened for males to become more specialized in directing effort toward finding access to mates and toward somatic developments that would favor successful competition with other males also seeking mating opportunity with the reproductive monopolists—females (Clutton-Brock et al. 1981; Trivers 1972). In non-social species in which males play no parental role in provisioning the mother or in defending the young, the reproductive specialization of the sexes and the dimorphism in size has no necessary implications for the ability of one sex to coerce the other. However, in humans and in the few other mammalian species in which the male parental role is critical to the survival of young, the "price" that females pay for gaining the economic cooperation of their mates is male sexual jealousy (Daly and Wilson 1988).

Humans carry the mammalian specialization to an extreme by producing only a few offspring who mature slowly and who require large amounts of parental care in order to survive. Women are committed to a disproportionate amount of this parental work since, unlike males, they cannot recoup one or a few infant or child deaths by finding another mate (Lancaster 1985). A woman who loses a child has lost not only that individual with whom she has personal ties, but she has lost irreplaceable reproductive time. A man who loses even all his children may experience an acute sense of personal loss, but he can replace them by establishing one or more additional mating relationships with other women. The reproductive inequality between the sexes gives rise, of course, both to the behavioral and somatic dimorphisms between the sexes and to the differing reproductive potentials of the sexes.[2]

There are at least three elements to consider in understanding the unique encumberment of the human female. These elements play a central role in her victimization.

1. Because of the extremely dependent state in which young are born and because of their slow development, any roles that conflict with her reproductive ones are generally avoided by her as an individual or denied her by other interested parties, especially her kin and her mates.

2. Unlike other primate females who terminate care of the next oldest offspring when a new infant is born, a woman maintains not one but several dependent offspring, albeit at different stages of dependence (Lancaster 1985). With each new child she adds to her encumberment and goes farther and farther into "debt" in the sense that her dependents multiply but her own physical reservoir of energies remain the same.

3. In order to rear offspring a woman must have help. Some aid comes from her kin but nearly all human groups attempt to regulate access to the reproductive capabilities of women by designating a mate (husband) and making him share in the work of rearing or defending the children.

Unlike most non-human social species, humans live in groups that include numerous other individuals who are eligible as mates. As a result, the sexual contract (paternal certainty in exchange for protection and economic resources) has consequences for other male-female relationships besides marital ones. Daughters and sisters of men, for example, have a vested interest in maintaining alliances with their male consanguines, not only because they benefit from men's labor but because these men protect them from other men. A woman's mate, if she has children by him, is also more likely to benefit her and her children than are foreign, unrelated men. It is probably true to say that in the past environments of evolutionary adaptation in which human social, psychological and sexual behavior has been molded by natural selection, a woman has had few degrees of freedom. The fitness penalties for a woman's error in judging economic or social support have been too severe. This fundamental and rather dismal picture (from the point of view of modern individualistic and humanitarian values) should be kept in mind by those who claim not to understand why so many women remain for so long in abusive environments.

An extremely interesting aspect of cultural variability is the extent to which the underlying reproductive asymmetry of men and women is institutionalized. Any circumstance in which fertility is low and monogamy is imposed, either as a result of ecological constraints or social conventions, is a good place to look for restraints on the ability of males to coerce females. The reason is that in this situation, the reproductive interests of the sexes are the same (Alexander et al. 1979:256–259; Alexander 1987:71–73) or more nearly identical than in other human groups (as, for example, among the !Kung). In technologically more advanced societies that have surpluses in the form of stored grains or herds of domestic animals, the fitness interests of the sexes are not the same. Men can advance their own fitness at the expense of other men by competing for access to more than one mate. Under the ecological conditions in which most (but not all) recent hunter gatherers have lived, the requirements for male labor are sufficiently high that most men can only support one mate and her children at a time. Where resources are potentially abundant and can be disproportionately controlled by a single man or alliances of men, male-male competition has direct consequences for male fitness (Dickemann 1979). In such social systems the variance in male reproductive success is high.

THE CASE OF THE !KUNG BUSHMEN: THE ETHNOGRAPHIC BACKGROUND

The !Kung of the Kalahari Desert in Namibia and Botswana, particularly when they were living as hunter gatherers, provided valuable data enabling scholars to look at relationships between ecological factors, mating behavior and male-female relationships. The !Kung have been well described in the anthropological literature and numerous field researchers have worked among them (Howell 1979; Lee and DeVore 1976; Marshall 1976). Until recent decades the !Kung have lived primarily as hunter gatherers.[3]

By the late 1980s when the field research for this chapter was conducted, all the !Kung of Western Botswana were settled around permanent sources of water. They were no longer full-time hunter-gathers; instead they lived in villages ranging in size from twenty to forty people. They kept small stock, a few cattle, and tended gardens while continuing to obtain a portion of their livelihood from the bush supplemented by a periodic government dole of maize meal and cooking oil.[4]

Hunter Gatherer Days: Prospects for the Coercion of Women

In the past, there were undoubtedly times when women were physically compelled and beaten by their husbands and others.[5] Yet there would have been many economic and practical restraints on the intimidations of women. Because of the arid and harsh environment in which they lived, and the simple technology, and probably also due to competition from numerous other predatory species in the environment, the ability of men to compete with other men was limited. Resources in the form of game and wild vegetable food were widely scattered and unpredictable in a terrain only sparsely inhabited. Regular and daily work by husband and wife was necessary to support their children. Further, more efficient forms of labor organization (involving larger, cooperative groups) were apparently not feasible because during most times of the year, local food and water supplies would not support large aggregates of people. In this sense there were strong ecological inhibitions on various forms of more hierarchical social relations and more highly rationalized forms of economy.

Polygyny was rare, chiefly because both men and women had to work regularly to provide enough food for themselves and the numbers of old and young who also lived in the bands. Polygyny remains common elsewhere in Africa in agricultural and pastoral communities largely because of the disproportionate subsistence load carried by women (Boserup 1970; Burton and White 1984; White et al. 1981). In this case, given the agricultural technology, women can work to feed themselves and their children without compromising the welfare of their children. Men, especially middle-aged and older men, are relieved of the necessity of producing food (Draper 1989) and can turn their attention to acquiring multiple wives, whose labor underwrites their high levels of leisure.

In subsistence-level societies women are valuable not only for their economic labor but for their reproductive labor. !Kung women, when they were living in hunting and gathering groups, were no exception. However, it appears that women were shielded from exploitation by a number of factors. The work of women was sufficiently taxing and incompatible with child care that increased work by women was harmful to their children (Blurton Jones et al. 1978) and therefore harmful to the fitness interests of their husbands. For example, gathering required that women travel so far from base camp that it was impractical for them to carry children as well as the gathered food (Draper 1978; Draper and Cashdan 1988). As a consequence, all children but nursing infants and toddlers were left at the base camp, under the care of other women and men. Hierarchical relations did not appear among !Kung men, apparently because the continuous economic need for cooperation undermined the expression of most forms of male-male competition. Kinship was bilateral and reports by various scholars confirm a long tradition of bilateral post-marital residence practices (Harpending and Wandsnider 1982:42; Lee 1982:43). The availability of kin, together with the small size of the foraging groups, meant there were few if any occasions when women were outside the ubiquitous, if informal, influence of public surveillance (Draper 1975).

Perhaps one of the most important safeguards against the physical harm of women came from the pervasive !Kung values condemning aggression.

!Kung strongly discouraged physical aggression as well as milder forms of interpersonal dominance. !Kung values opposed physical punishment for children and, indeed, any form of harsh treatment more severe than an occasional scolding (Draper 1976, 1978; Konner 1976). Husbands had no social entitlement to physically chastise wives; when spouses fought it was looked upon as shameful and stopped as quickly as possible.

During my recent field work, I talked to elderly !Kung in the context of collecting life history narratives. In the men's narratives, the theme of masculine anger, and particularly the poorly controlled anger of young men, was mentioned frequently.

> Gau, a man in his late 60s, while deploring an episode of recent wife-beating by a young man in a nearby village said, "These young men have too much anger. They don't know how to hold themselves back. In the old days, young men like this one (the wife beater) would never have been given a wife. In those days there were no Bantu and no police. When a man beat a woman her kinsmen would jump up and go at him with spears. They would even come from far away. People knew about this and were afraid of the anger and fighting that would follow. They wouldn't give a woman to such men."

While in former times women enjoyed the protection of their kin from abuse by husbands, it is interesting to note that many elderly women's recollections of their girlhood stressed the trauma they felt at their first marriages. In the past, when !Kung spent months at a time in the bush and had no regular contact with cattle people, !Kung parents arranged for their daughters to marry young, at around the age of menarche but sometimes before. Parents believed it was essential for a daughter to have a husband who would hunt and provide meat for her and her kin. Girls typically married men about ten years older than themselves (Howell 1979).

By being married at a young age and to men much older than themselves, and in circumstances in which the elders were making the decisions for them, !Kung women began their marital careers with little power in the relationship. Given the physical mobility of bands in the hunting and gathering days, together with the frequent movement of families in and out of bands, young brides could expect to be separated from their parents and siblings at least some of the time. Of the eight elderly women I interviewed, half indicated that one of their parents had already died by the time they married. These women stated that the death of one parent was used by their remaining elders as a reason for hastening negotiations for their husbands.

Many elderly women depicted their early years of marriage as stressful and coercive, more often blaming their parents than their husbands. Women stated that their fathers were severe and sometimes physically coercive in insisting that they stay with their husbands (Shostak 1981). Women claimed that as girls they were afraid of their husbands, whom they regarded as foreign, unwelcome interlopers. Not all women recall being physically beaten by their husbands or fathers, but their recollections emphasize their insecurity and their fearfulness and dread of being separated from their own families. The intensity of these emotions about separation from their parents is somewhat surprising, given that the !Kung custom of groom service meant that !Kung husbands often joined their brides as live-in sons-in-law.

> N!uhka, aged fifty-five, and old enough herself to have grown up living near Bantu, remembered from her childhood the terrible ordeal of her older sister whom their father insisted should marry a Bantu man. The father (without support from his wife, the mother of the girl) forced the girl to stay in the Bantu village with her mother-in-law and, according to the informant, beat her when she returned to her mother. One night the girl ran away, intending to find sanctuary in a distant village. The next morning she was discovered missing and a search party was launched. In this case, as she had been staying at a cattle post, her tracks were destroyed by the hooves of domestic stock as they left the kraals in the morning. Though search parties sought her for days she was never found. N!uhka flatly stated that her sister must have been eaten by wild animals.

This story clearly illustrates coercion of young !Kung women, not in this case by the husband, but by the wife's kin, on behalf of the husband. ≠isa, a woman in her fifties, remembers her marriage to her husband (fifteen years her senior) with a story that is both humorous and stark.

> My mother and father wanted me to marry Bo (her present husband). But I refused all talk of this marriage. The trouble went on for months and months. My parents insisted that I was married to him and that I must stay at the hut I had with my husband. I couldn't bear it. I kept coming back to where my mother and father lived but they drove me back. I wouldn't do anything for my husband! I didn't look at him, I didn't cook for him. When he brought me food I wouldn't eat it. If he gave me food, I just threw it around in the dirt. I sneaked away at night and slept in the bush. Even though I was so scared I wouldn't stay with that man. I searched in the bush for guinea fowl eggs and smeared them all over my body to make myself ugly and so I would smell bad. But it had no effect. He became angry that I wouldn't live peacefully with him and wouldn't prepare food but he didn't give up. One day he grabbed me and pushed me in the hut and forced me to have intercourse with him.

The !Kung of Today: Transition to Settled Life and Food Producing

In the last twenty years, the !Kung of western Botswana have settled around sources of permanent water and are becoming food producers. This transformation is extremely interesting on a number of grounds but particularly for the opportunity it offers for studying the dynamic interaction between changes in resources and technology and the social and sexual relations between men and women.

Although the economic practices have changed dramatically, and the continual reshuffling of people by inter-band mobility has ceased, in other ways the everyday tenor of social and emotional life of people does not seem drastically different. The local residential unit is a small village composed of about 15–30 people related to each other by bilateral ties of kinship and marriage. Most !Kung are monogamous, and marriages tend to be durable once they are well established. Fertility remains low, although there is some indication that younger cohorts of women have somewhat higher fertility.[6] Cohorts of women aged 60 years and over, 45–59 years, 30–44 years and 19–29 years average 3.6, 4.9, 3.8, and 2.5 live births, respectively.

These data suggest that whatever combination of nutritional, environmental, epidemiological and hormonal influences may have operated in the past to keep !Kung fertility low, they are still influential for sedentary !Kung in recent times (Harpending and Draper 1990; Harpending and Wandsnider 1982; Konner and Worthman 1980).

One might predict that the position of !Kung women has worsened along with the recent shift to sedentism and that they have become more vulnerable to domination by their husbands. This prediction would be based on other social structural factors that are often associated with food-producing techniques such as increased material wealth (especially in the form of livestock), the increased division of labor by sex, and the increased tendency for production to be organized in multi-generational family units with authority vested in senior males. Contemporary !Kung explicitly model themselves after the economic practices of nearby Bantu-speaking peoples (Tswana and Herero) and it would not be unusual to find that !Kung have also adopted Bantu cultural values which stress patriarchal authority and explicitly give men control over women. In fact, in the late 1980s it was not evident that recent economic changes had unambiguously worsened the position of women.

When a people experience cultural change, some customs change markedly, whereas other practices persist in the new setting. In the !Kung case, there are elements of their former life style (such as availability of kin) which are preserved in the modern, sedentary setting and which continue to offer a degree of protection of women from physical assaults by their husbands. Other practices, such as the early marriage of girls, are no longer followed so scrupulously. As a consequence adolescent girls are less subject to manipulation by kin and husbands. On the negative side, other changes, such as consumption of alcoholic drinks and the ability of people to gather in social settings that are beyond the influence of close kin, lead to increased incidents of violence.[7]

In spite of their changed economy, !Kung have retained many of their former customs which gave women some immunity from coercion their husbands when they lived as hunter gatherers. In other cultures women can be subject to mistreatment, not only from their husbands, but from their husband's kin, particularly when they come as wives from outside their husband's community (Brown, Chapter 1 this volume; Burgess and Draper 1989; Levinson 1989). Contemporary !Kung adults continue to stress bilateral ties in choosing with whom to reside and cooperate. For example, 59 percent of !Kung women lived with a father, 52 percent with a mother. Of !Kung men, 54 percent lived with a father, 59 percent lived with a mother. These data collected in 1987–1988 replicate findings based on !Kung residence patterns in 1968 (Harpending and Wandsnider 1982). The traditional practice whereby girls married in their early teens (or younger) is disappearing. Increasingly girls in the 15–20 year age range remain unmarried and continue to live with their parents. They frequently have children, sometimes with Herero and Tswana men, but these are informal liaisons, not marriages. The inter-ethnic children are retained by the mother and her kin (Draper and Kranichfeld 1990; Draper and Buchanan, in press). Whereas women aged 60 years and over report 6 percent of their children as fathered by Bantu, the percentages of mixed ethnicity children rise with younger cohorts of women: 45–59 years (18 percent); 30–44 years (16 percent) and 19–29 years (27 percent).

The delayed age of marriage and increased numbers of out-matings are related to at least two new conditions of modern life. First, the value of young men as hunters is much reduced due to the scarcity of game. These youths, who earlier would have been sought as sons-in-law, are now less essential. Many men of the 25–35 year age range are unmarried and without good prospects for finding wives. Some of these men are a concern for their elders as they get into fights and drink excessively. Second, young women marry later and spend more of their adult years as free agents. In the new settled economy, parents do not believe that early marriages for daughters are essential; they do not seem to think that sons-in-law are critical sources of labor.

Especially if they have cattle and goats, the parents or grandparents of young women willingly keep them at home. Their work is useful in the settled villages where labor is more intensive than among the foragers. Their children are also welcomed. Many middle-aged !Kung parents appear to find daughters and grandchildren more readily incorporated into the new economy than sons-in-law. Of course, the sedentary economy requires work from men: watering stock from deep wells, driving cattle to distant grazing, cutting thorn brush for stock enclosures, and hunting are key masculine tasks. However, it appears that for routine purposes these activities can be done relatively efficiently by a few conscientious men. Even though women's time is more or less co-opted by child care and they combine gardening, milking, water and fuel collecting with their maternal roles, some young men do not accommodate themselves to the new subsistence routines. They are idle and restless and are resented by older, harder working men.

In this transitional setting it is easy to understand how the marriage age of girls is delayed, how unmarried daughters and their children are readily absorbed into what is becoming a residentially localized, multi-generational, extended family, and how increasingly these young women form informal unions – not with young men of their own age and ethnic group – but with Tswana or Herero men whose superior social status and wealth gives them an advantage over !Kung youths. In sum, and at this particular point in the !Kung transition to sedentary, food producing economy, young !Kung women appear to be free of coercion at the hands of parents who formerly insisted on the early marriages of daughters to men in their twenties. Those girls who today remain unmarried in the settled villages are likewise not subject to potential mistreatment by inexperienced and poorly self-controlled husbands.

In an earlier paper, based on research in the late 1960s among those !Kung who were already sedentary, I described trends that I predicted would lead to decreased autonomy for !Kung women (Draper 1975). At that time my field work included two populations of !Kung, some who hunted and gathered, others who were settled. I was struck by a number of contrasting practices in the two groups. In comparison with the foraging !Kung, sedentary villages were smaller and less heterogeneous in their groupings of kin. !Kung of the settled villages accumulated more material wealth in the form of stock, larger and more durable houses, more clothing, and household implements. In comparison with women of the mobile groups who were frequently out of camp, ranging far on their own in their gathering expeditions, settled women appeared home-bound, concerned only with local domestic tasks and more deferent to men.

In terms of settlement pattern and architectural features, it seemed that a number of steps were being taken in the settled villages (erecting of fences around homesteads and visual barriers around individual houses, more distant spacing of houses) that taken together would lead to women spending more time alone, isolated from potential supporters and unable to protect themselves from abusive husbands. In other respects, the egalitarian style of interaction between the sexes that existed in the foraging groups appeared to be on the wane among the settled !Kung. Men were named as household heads; men, not women, were learning Bantu languages and entering into contractual relations with Bantu cattle owners. Whereas in the bush setting men and women exchanged tasks normally associated with one or the other sex, the sedentary people had a narrower tolerance for crossing sex roles. In particular, women's tasks, such as collecting water and cutting thatching grasses were scorned by men.

In fact, twenty years later, these tendencies have not coalesced in ways that promote violence against women. There are episodes of violence against women living in the settled groups (as there were undoubtedly among the foraging !Kung) and these will be detailed below. The precipitating circumstances and the social settings of violence have changed somewhat as have the types of responses women and their supporters can make.

In their new life style, !Kung continue to live in small villages in which individual household buildings associated with different families are placed close together. While the placement of individual huts is no longer as close as has been reported for !Kung living in mobile camps (Draper 1973), the various structures are within easy sight and sound of the residents. Further, the !Kung continue their habit of living primarily out of doors in the full view of other village residents and visitors. True, !Kung no longer live in temporary grass shelters; instead they build the more typical southern African mud hut or rondavel. However, few !Kung structures match those of the neighboring Herero. Their mudded rondavels are comparatively insubstantial and have poorly fitted doors that cannot be locked or barred from the inside. This means that a violent man cannot isolate his wife and beat her while holding outside people who would help her. The lack of visual privacy, coupled with the physical proximity of others, means that an attack upon a woman by her husband will be observed and stopped.

FOUR CASE HISTORIES:
WIFE-BEATING IN THE MODERN SETTING

Four episodes of wife-beating came to my attention during 1987–1988. While I did not observe any of these events personally, I was able to interview close kin of the victims in the days following the events and these discussions revealed some common patterns. The episodes differ in such factors as the setting of the violence, the ages and childbearing histories of the victims, the decisions by the wives whether to remain with the husbands, and the role of the wife's kin as interveners following the attacks.

Two of the beatings took place at !Angwa, the administrative center of western Ngamiland. !Angwa, a village of about 180 people, is unusual for having several discrete "neighborhoods." Other villages in !Kung territory are not only much smaller in total area but more homogeneous being, essentially, the linked compounds of closely related families. At the center of !Angwa are several small government-built structures, a clinic, a small store, a police station and the headman's office. Nearby are several compounds where beer is brewed and sold for about five cents per cup. Radiating out in various directions from !Angwa center, at a distance of one-half to one kilometre, are separate compounds where Tswana, Herero and !Kung live in family groupings.

Two of the four wife-beatings took place in !Angwa and not at the domestic, residential compounds of the principals.

In the first case, N/ahka, a middle aged woman, was attacked by her husband. His assault resulted in injuries to her face, head and lips. Her husband accused her of sleeping with another man, in this case a Tswana. N/ahka and her husband had been married for many years but had no children together. Her only child was a girl of about fourteen years whose father was a Herero, and to whom N/ahka had not been married. The father had never contributed to his daughter's support, and for many years the child had been reared by N/ahka's parents who lived at a different village. When N/ahka's parents heard about the beating, they made plans to lodge a formal complaint with the headman at !Angwa against their son-in-law. Other people, not close relatives of N/ahka or her husband, claimed that the couple had a long history of discord, allegedly because the wife liked to sleep with Bantu men.

In another case, also at !Angwa, Kwoba, a woman aged about forty-five years, was beaten by her husband. Kwoba and her husband had a home village elsewhere but had come to !Angwa to visit relatives who lived there. One evening the husband and wife were drinking at one of the open air taverns. On the way home they began to argue, and her husband beat Kwoba with his fists and a walking cane. People said later they had heard screaming, but they claimed that because the crowds at the tavern were often raucous, no one paid attention. I saw Kwoba two days following the beating. Both her eyes were blackened and swollen nearly shut; her lips were raised with scabs; her upper arm bore long, linear bruises, presumably from being struck by the husband with his cane.

The beatings of N/ahka and Kwoba occurred at locations that, compared to other villages, were comparatively free of the restraints of kin and long-term village mates. Informal social controls are also weakened at !Angwa due to the ethnic heterogeneity of the population and the availability of alcohol. Another factor undoubtedly exacerbates sexual tensions at !Angwa and that is the attractions, described above, that !Kung women find in Tswana and Herero men. When !Kung men and women mix with other ethnic groups in the context of the disinhibiting effects of alcohol, flirtations between !Kung women and Bantu men will be resented by !Kung men who have claims on particular women. Being not only physically smaller but judged socially inferior to Bantu as well, a !Kung man, faced with direct sexual competition by Bantu men and "emboldened" by alcohol, will probably retaliate violently against a woman he perceives to be straying, rather than attack her Bantu suitor.

After being beaten, neither N/ahka nor Kwoba left her husband, perhaps because neither of these middle-aged women had adult children who maintained independent households. Although N/ahka's parents threatened to take their son-in-law to the headman and to lodge formal charges against him, they spoke of winning damage payments from the husband, not of ending the marriage. N/ahka did not try to join her parents following the beating, though they lived less than a day's walk away from !Angwa. Her parents were among the more impoverished !Kung of the area and were already supporting N/ahka's daughter (mentioned above) and her aged and decrepit grandmother.

When I saw the second victim, Kwoba, two days after her beating, she was sitting at her home village in an apparently harmonious family grouping composed of her husband, her co-wife, and her co-wife's children and grandchildren. Kwoba herself had no surviving children. More than twenty years earlier her only child had died as an infant. Both of Kwoba's parents were dead. Her adult half-siblings already lived in the same village and so could not (or did not) give her sanctuary in the usual sense of the term. Like N/ahka, Kwoba was middle-aged and without grown children to whom she might turn. It is likely that the decisions by N/ahka and Kwoba to remain with their husbands were influenced by the fact that they had no where else to go.

The two remaining cases of wife-beating concern young women, both in their late teens.

Kxaru, about sixteen years, had been married for two years to a man, Kumsa, about thirty-three years old. As yet Kxaru had no children. Her husband, Kumsa, had a reputation for being sullen and angry and given to drink. The second time he beat his young wife while in a drunken state, he bruised her face and split her lip, making a scar still visible many months later. At that time Kxaru had been living with her husband and his family, whereas her own parents and adult siblings lived about fifty kilometres away. Kxaru's maternal grandparents, however, lived in a nearby village and were well acquainted with her husband and his kin. Upon hearing about the attack, the grandmother went to Kxaru's hut and led her away. She kept Kxaru at her own village until she recovered, later sending her back to her parents. Kxaru's parents were economically better off than many !Kung. They owned cattle and also herded cattle belonging to a wealthy Herero family. Therefore they had a better and more predictable supply of milk than many !Kung. Even months later, the grandmother and grandfather were visibly indignant about the beating of Kxaru and declared that they personally had annulled the marriage. The union, in fact, appeared to be over; Kxaru remained living with her parents and was being sought by another suitor. Kumsa continued to live at home with his parents, sleeping frequently during the daytime and generally behaving like a lout.

/Asa, aged nineteen, had been living at Chum!kwe, Namibia, a regional administrative center about seventy kilometres from where her parents lived in Botswana. Her husband was a man about twenty-seven years old and who was unusual among !Kung men for being literate and having a regular wage-earning job at Chum!kwe. /Asa's husband beat her, striking her on the head and laying open her scalp. Fortunately for /Asa, there was a medical clinic at Chum!Kwe where the laceration was stitched together. I saw the wound several weeks later; the scar was about three inches long across the top of her head. /Asa's father arranged for his nephew (also living at Chum!kwe) to bring /Asa and her year-old child back to her parents' village. They declared the marriage ended and helped her build a permanent mud hut in their own village. The father said he expected her to stay with them. He pointed to the nearby huts of his other grown children and the kraals that held the family's goats and few cattle as evidence of material wealth and kin support sufficient to incorporate his returned daughter.

The cases of Kxaru and /Asa (but not the cases of N/ahka and Kwoba) illustrate the continued power of a woman's kin group and the willingness of people to unilaterally intervene on behalf of the injured wife. Whereas in former times assaults on women reputedly led to counter violence directed at the husband or some one in his kin group, no such action was taken in the case of any of the four victimized women. !Kung know that the old days of self-help and blood feud are over since the Tswana have imposed their own system of law on the area.

Implicit in the contrast between the first and second pair of cases are the ages of the wives. Both Kxaru and /Asa were young and had their full reproductive careers ahead of them. Their youth benefited them in several ways. Because they were young, they stood a better probability of having two living parents and living siblings to act on their behalf. In addition their parents were prosperous enough to take them back.

In the cases of the two older abuse victims, several factors appear to be implicated in the lack of action being taken by the victims themselves: their age, their numbers of children, their ability to call on their parents and the economic resources available to their kin. N/ahka and Kwoba were at least twenty-five years older than the younger women. As such their reproductive value to their husbands and to their kin was diminished. Further, both were of low proven fertility (both had one child in the young adult years but no further births in the last fifteen years). Not only did they have no grown children to act on their behalf, they had no support group of descendant kin whose existence as tacit symbols of support might hold aggression by the husband in check. Although N/ahka had two younger, adult brothers of marriageable age, neither had found wives, nor were they living in independent households, both circumstances a testament to the family's poor prospects. Kwoba, as stated above, had adult half-siblings but they were already living in her village. Presumably, had she been beaten by her husband while in her own compound, they would have intervened.

Finally, as older women, the probability was small that either of them had living parents who could take their part. Kwoba's parents were long dead, and N/ahka's parents were alive but in such poor economic straits that they were apparently unable to act. Among the !Kung, generally, mortality rates are high with the result that as adults age there is a steep decline in the probability a person will have a living parent. For example, the percentages of adults of varying cohorts whose fathers and mothers were alive are: 60 years and over (2 percent fathers, 5 percent mothers) 45–59 (13 percent fathers, 25 percent mothers); 30–44 (41 percent fathers, 47 percent mothers); 19–29 years (73 percent fathers, 72 percent mothers).

A sample of four cases is insufficient to speak to the issue of wife-beating in !Kung society. These few case histories suggest that future, more ambitious studies of violence against wives should pay close attention to the woman's age and reproductive status, the numbers, ages and availability of her kin, as well as to the economic resources of her potential supporters.

CONCLUSION

This paper has described the social and economic conditions that influence the coercion of women by husbands in !Kung society. Past and contemporary lifestyles of !Kung have been contrasted. The transition from a foraging and hunting economy to a subsistence based on settled food producing has not led, in any simple fashion, to increased physical coercion of women. The cultural changes !Kung have experienced in the last two decades have not transformed all areas of life equally. Economic practices and former patterns of spatial mobility have changed drastically, as have the marriage customs in favor of early marriages for girls. On the other hand, the bilateral residence arrangements, the physical and social intimacy of everyday village life and the strong ties maintained between a woman and her kin group have been brought from the bush and installed in the permanent settlements with little if any change.

The fact that !Kung are not only changing their subsistence base, but entering into regular association with other ethnic groups of Botswana, must also be taken into account. The accumulation of external stresses are known in other cultural settings to promote pathological behaviors within families. The Bantu speakers constitute an economic threat as they and their domestic stock move in increasing numbers into an area of western Botswana that was previously occupied primarily by !Kung. Many !Kung are as yet inexperienced with the demands of a more complex economy and are struggling simultaneously to make a livelihood and to win political recognition of their claims to land and water rights in what they conceive to be their traditional territory.

An added irritant to fundamental conflicts of interest that affect !Kung men and women in the modern setting is the increased frequency with which Bushmen women make informal unions with non-!Kung men. A consequence has been an increased number of half-Bantu children born to !Kung mothers. At present it appears that the children themselves are not disadvantaged. On the other hand, each half-Bantu child represents lost mating opportunity to !Kung men. Perhaps young !Kung men who succeed in finding wives will be less willing to invest in women who already have children by other men (particularly if they are half-Bantu) and in women whose behavior suggests poor certainty of paternity. It will be ironic if the temporary gains realized by women (delayed age of marriage and reduced dependence upon husbands) turn out to be the flip side of family disorganization and increasingly hostile relations between the sexes.

In future decades, if !Kung succeed in increasing their ownership of stock, they may adopt more patriarchal values and patrilocal forms of residence as is common among the neighboring Bantu groups of Botswana. These developments could undermine women's autonomy and make them more vulnerable to coercion by husbands. In the meantime, !Kung retain many customs that in the mobile economy promoted the welfare of wives. At this point in their transition to stable food production, there are numerous possible outcomes and many suggestions that their cultural transformation will carry the strong stamp of their former traditions.

NOTES

1. I have done field work with !Kung in 1968—1969, 1975, 1978, 1987—1988. The most recent research was supported by the National Institute of Aging Grant No. P01AG03110.

2. For alternate views see Leacock (1978); Maccoby and Jacklin (1974:368—369); Mukhopadhyay and Higgins (1988:469).

3. See Yellen (1977) contrasted with Denbow and Wilmsen (1986) and Wilmsen (1989) on !Kung culture history.

4. About eight years ago, in response to a severe drought that lasted until 1987, the Botswana government began a food distribution program directed at poor people living in remote areas.

5. See reports by Howell (1979); Lee (1982:44, 1979); Marshall (1976:282); Shostak (1981:231—233).

6. Data are based on reproductive interviews with over 300 !Kung collected in 1987 and 1988.

7. See Colson and Scudder (1988).

REFERENCES CITED

Alexander, Richard D. 1987. The Biology of Moral Systems. New York: Aldine De Gruyter.

Alexander, Richard D., R. D. Hoogland, K. M. Howard, and P. W. Sherman. 1979. Sexual Dimorphisms and Breeding Systems in Pinnipeds, Ungulates, Primates, and Humans. *In* Evolutionary Biology and Human Social Behavior: An Anthropological Perspective. Napoleon Chagnon and W. G. Irons, eds. Pp. 902—935. North Scituate, Mass.: Duxbury Press.

Blurton Jones, G. Nicholas, and R. M. Sibly. 1978. Testing Adaptiveness of Culturally Determined Behavior: Do Bushmen Women Maximize Their Reproductive Success by Spacing Births Widely and Foraging Seldom? *In* Human Behavior and Adaptation, Symposium No. 18. Nicholas G. Blurton Jones and V. Reynolds, eds. Pp. 135—157. Society for Study of Human Biology. London: Taylor and Francis.

Boserup, Esther. 1970. Woman's Role in Economic Development. London: Allen and Unwin.

Burgess, Richard, and Patricia Draper. 1989. The Explanation of Family Violence: The Role of Biological, Behavioral, and Cultural Selection. *In* Crime and Justice: A Review of Research, Volume 11. Michael Tonry and Norval Morris, eds. Pp. 59—116. Chicago: University of Chicago Press.

Burton, M. L., and Douglas R. White. 1984. Sexual Division of Labor in Agriculture. American Anthropologist 86:568—83.

Clutton-Brock, T. H., S. D. Albon, and F. E. Guiness. 1981. Parental Investment in Male and Female Mammals. Nature 289:487—489.

Colson, Elizabeth, and Thayer Scudder. 1988. For Prayer and Profit: The Ritual, Economic, and Social Importance of Beer in Gwembe District, Zambia, 1950—1982. Stanford, California: Standford University Press.

Daly, Martin, and Margo Wilson. 1988. Evolutionary Social Psychology and Family Homicide. Science 242:519—524.

Denbow, J., and Edwin Wilmsen. 1986. The Advent and Course of Pastoralism in the Kalahari. Science 234:1509—15.

Dickemann, M. 1979. The Reproductive Structure of Stratified Societies: A Preliminary Model. *In* Evolutionary Biology and Human Social Organization: An Anthropological Perspective. Napoleon A. Chagnon and W. Irons eds. Pp. 331—367. North Scituate, Mass.: Duxbury Press.

Draper, Patricia. 1973. Crowding Among Hunter Gatherers: The !Kung Bushmen. Science 182:301—303.

―――. 1975. !Kung Women: Contrasts in Sexual Egalitarianism in Foraging and Sedentary Contexts. *In* Toward an Anthropology of Women. Rayna Reiter, ed. Pp. 77—109. New York: Monthly Review Press.

————. 1976. Social and Economic Constraints on !Kung Childhood. *In* Kalahari Hunter Gatherers. R. B. Lee and I. DeVore, eds. Pp. 200—217 Cambridge, Mass.: Harvard University Press.

————. 1978. The Learning Environment for Aggression and Anti-Social Behavior among the !Kung. *In* Learning non-Aggression. Ashley Montagu, ed. Pp. 31—53. New York: Oxford University Press.

————. 1989. African Marriage Systems: Perspectives from Evolutionary Ecology. Ethology and Sociobiology 10(1):145—169.

Draper, Patricia, and Anne Buchanan. In press. If You Have a Child You Have A Life: Demographic and Cultural Insights into Fathering in !Kung Life. *In* The Father-Child Relationship: Developmental, Symbolic and Evolutionary Perspectives. Barry Hewlett, ed. New York: Aldine de Gruyter.

Draper, Patricia, and Elizabeth Cashdan. 1988. Technological Change and Child Behavior among the !Kung. Ethnology 27(4):339—365.

Draper, Patricia, and M. Kranichfeld. 1990. Coming in from the Bush: The Significance of Household and Village Organization in Economic Change. Human Ecology 18 (4).

Harpending, Henry, and Patricia Draper. 1990. Estimating Parity of Parents: An Application to the History of Infertility Among the !Kung of Southern Africa. Human Biology 62(2):195—203.

Harpending, Henry, and L. Wandsnider. 1982. Population Structures of Ghanzi and Hgamiland !Kung. *In* Current Developments in Anthropological Genetics, II. Michael Crawford, ed. Pp. 29—49. New York: Plenum Press.

Howell, Nancy. 1979. Demography of the Dobe Area !Kung. New York: Academic Press.

Konner, M. J. 1976. Maternal Care, Infant Behavior and Development Among the !Kung. Kalahari Hunter-Gatherers. R. B. Lee and I. DeVore, eds. Pp. 218—245. Cambridge, Mass.: Harvard University Press.

Konner, M. J., and C. Worthman. 1980. Nursing Frequency, Gonadal Function and Birth Spacing Among !Kung Hunter-Gatherers. Science 207:788—791.

Lancaster, Jane B. 1985. Evolutionary Perspectives on Sex Differences in the Higher Primates. Gender and the Life Course. Alice S. Rossi, ed. Pp. 3—28. New York: Aldine.

Leacock, Eleanor. 1978. Women's Status in Egalitarian Society: Implications for Social Evolution. Current Anthropology 19:247—55.

Lee, Richard B. 1979. The !Kung San: Men, Women and Work in a Foraging Society. Cambridge: Cambridge University Press.

————. 1982. Politics, Sexual and Nonsexual, in an Egalitarian Society: The !Kung San. *In* Politics and History in Band Societies. Eleanor Leacock and Richard Lee, eds. Pp. 37—59. Cambridge: Cambridge University Press.

Lee, Richard, and I. DeVore, eds. 1976. Kalahari Hunter Gatherers. Cambridge, Mass.: Harvard University Press.

Levinson, David. 1989. Family Violence in Cross-Cultural Perspective. Frontiers Newbury Park, CA: Sage Publications.

Maccoby, Eleanor, and Carol Jacklin. 1974. The Psychology of Sex Differences. Palo Alto, California: Stanford University Press.

Marshall, Lorna. 1976. The !Kung of Nyae Nyae. Cambridge, Mass.: Harvard University Press.

Martin, M. Kay, and Barbara Voorhies. 1975. The Female of the Species. New York: Columbia University Press.

Mukhopadhyay, Carol C., and Patricia J. Higgins. 1988. Anthropological Studies of Women's Status Revisited: 1977—1987. Annual Review of Anthropology 17:161—95.

Shostak, Marjorie. 1981. Nisa: The Life and Words of a !Kung Woman. New York: Vintage.

Trivers, R. 1972. Parental Investment and Sexual election. *In* Sexual Selection and the Descent of Man: 1871—1971. Bernard Campbell ed. Pp. 136—179. Chicago: Aldine Publishing Company.

White, Douglas R., M. L. Burton, and M. M. Dow. 1981. Sexual Division of Labor in African Agriculture: A Network Autocorrelation Analysis. American Anthropologist 83: 824—49.

Wilmsen, Edwin. 1989. Land Filled with Flies. Chicago: Chicago University Press.

Yellen, John. 1977. Archaeological Approaches to the Present. Orlando, Fla.: Academic Press.

5

"All Men Do It": Wife-Beating in Kaliai, Papua New Guinea

Dorothy Ayers Counts

Look, gentlemen, we've all done it. . . . But I will not stand for it any longer. We've got to stop beating our wives.

> Police commissioner David Tasion to a gathering of provincial police commanders, Port Moresby, Papua New Guinea. *Pacific Islands Monthly* 1987 58(4):48.

The Lusi-Kaliai people of coastal West New Britain Province, Papua New Guinea, tell a story about an aggressive (and ugly) woman named Silimala who harasses and forces herself on a young man — Akono — until he marries her. In an attempt to discourage her attentions, Akono beats Silimala to death. But this being a folk tale (and a comedy at that), Silimala is not daunted. She persists until he agrees to marry her, and she accompanies Akono home as his second wife. There she behaves obnoxiously. She is lazy, she takes over the house that is occupied by Akono's first wife Galiki and tosses Galiki and her belongings out the door, and she burns, strikes and otherwise torments Galiki who endures the abuse passively, as a good woman should. Akono, she explains, must have desired this woman or he would not have brought her home. It is, therefore, her lot to accept whatever Silimala does, for it must be her husband's will. Finally, shamed by Silimala's treatment of Galiki, Akono conspires with Galiki and her mother to trick Silimala into committing suicide.

When I have heard this story told I have been impressed by several things.

- Silimala is an assertive, aggressive, stubborn woman who persists — in spite of violent punishment — until she has what she wants.
- Galiki's passive behavior allows her to overcome adversity and eventually to win the struggle with the support of her husband.

- Co-wife violence is taken for granted as an aspect of polygynous marriage, although the usual pattern of co-wife violence is reversed in the story. Commonly the second, new spouse is the one cherished by the husband and is attacked by the first, jealous wife.
- Everybody loathes Silimala. She deserves to be beaten. She even deserves to die. Both women and men laugh with approval when Silimala is fooled into killing herself. Furthermore, it is not unusual for a male member of the audience — overcome by his anger at Silimala's intransigence — to break into the narration and urge Akono to "hit her again."

The story of Silimala and the audience's response to the tale express a number of the assumptions and stereotypes that underlie domestic violence in Kaliai: the male should be the master in male-female interactions; a woman should not push herself onto a man and if she is rejected she should withdraw quietly; an assertive, aggressive, lazy woman who insists on having her way in spite of obvious male displeasure is an object of contempt and rage; it is correct for a man to do physical violence to such a woman.

Violence does not dominate family relationships or community life in Kaliai. Personal interactions are marked more by laughter, helpfulness, and cooperation than by anger and hostility. Ordinarily a Kaliai village is a cheerful and pleasant place to live, both for its residents and for a visiting anthropologist. Nevertheless violence is a component of Lusi-Kaliai family life. Adults laugh approvingly when toddlers hit older children, and children are expected to fight with one another. Wife-beating is common, and village women say that nearly all women may expect to be beaten by their husbands sometime during their marriage. Women strike their children, fight with their co-wives, and hit their sexual partners. The co-wife relationship is a particularly stressful one and has the potential for attempted murder or suicide, either by the first wife or by the husband who is shamed by his inability to control his wives. I am aware of four unsuccessful suicide or homicide attempts (three by women and one by a man) and two successful suicides (both by men) arising directly from the strife in a polygynous marriage.

The Lusi-Kaliai are not unusual, for domestic violence is common in Papua New Guinea. Nearly 75 percent of the women murdered in the country are killed by their husbands (Law Reform Commission of Papua New Guinea 1987:4). The national government has recognized that domestic violence is a serious problem. Consequently the Law Reform Commission of Papua New Guinea (LRC) has initiated a program of research to understand the causes of domestic violence and to design and implement reforms to reduce it (Toft 1985, 1986; Toft and Bonnell 1985). Among its findings is that violence is so embedded in the marital relationship that people often do not see it as a problem unless it exceeds the society's norms of acceptability or unless it becomes the basis of conflict between men (Law Reform Commission of Papua New Guinea 1987).

The Commission does not distinguish between acceptable and unacceptable violence, nor does it emphasize the alternatives that are available to women in isolated rural areas. In this chapter on wife-beating in Kaliai I will focus on these topics. I also raise the question, implicit in Silimala's story, of why Lusi-Kaliai women sometimes behave in ways that they know will result in their being beaten. What does their behavior, in the face of violent retribution, suggest about male-female relationships and gender roles in Kaliai?

DOMESTIC VIOLENCE IN KALIAI

The Lusi-Kaliai live in five villages located along the northwest coast of West New Britain. They are slash-and-burn horticulturalists who earn most of their cash income by producing copra, the primary commercial crop of the area. Their social organization is patrilineal and residence is ideally virilocal. In the past most marriages have been between people of the same or neighboring villages, so that wives usually reside no more than two or three hours travel time from their natal families. Nowadays this pattern is often broken by educated young people who choose mates from among friends in high school or town. In these cases, young wives may live many hours, or even days, away from their families.

Authority in both household and community affairs is based on sex and age. There is a political ideal of equality for males, and of the right of men to hold authority over women and younger men, but this right may be overridden by the force of an individual's personality. Although it is not the rule, a strong-willed and intelligent woman may boss her younger relatives and achieve a reputation as a skilled manipulator of the exchange system. These women are called *tamine ra tamone* "manly women," but, although they are respected by both women and men, they do not become political leaders.

Political leaders, or *maroni,* achieve their position by the conspicuous distribution of wealth items that include shell money, pigs, and pandanus mats made by women. These distributions occur when children are acknowledged as members of their fathers' lineages, when people marry, and during mortuary celebrations. Marriages are formalized by bridewealth and divorce is not difficult, but when a marriage ends custody of the children usually remains with their father. This creates an emotional hardship for the mother if her natal home is far from her ex-husband's residence.

It is my impression that domestic violence is less prevalent among the Lusi-Kaliai than among some of their neighbors where it is reported to be "particularly common and severe" (Chowning 1985:72). It is difficult to estimate accurately how often wife-beating occurs in rural communities for, as one of my consultants observed, most of it occurs at night or when the couple is alone in their gardens and unobserved by others. It is almost never a daily occurrence in any one family because the relatives of a woman whose husband beat her every day or several times a week would soon interfere to stop the violence. Nevertheless it is not uncommon in village life. During the four months of my research in 1985 there were, in the community of about 350 people where I lived, two episodes of wife-beating severe enough to lead others to interfere as well as a number of others which did not merit outside intervention. Incidents of domestic violence do not usually result in serious physical injury or bloodshed, for onlookers readily intervene to prevent these. While it is rare, a woman may attack her husband if she believes that he is having an affair or is planning to take a second wife. A woman who explodes in violent anger for these reasons generally has the sympathy of onlookers. If she leaves him, however, she may lose public support, and she jeopardizes her rights in her children who belong to their father and his kin group.

It is much more common for husbands to strike their wives. My consultants, female as well as male, generalize that "all" men hit their wives at one time or the other, but this is a normative rather than a statistical statement for, in fact, some do not. Women from the community where I did research name a half-dozen men (out of approximately 80 male householders) who either never strike their wives or who have not done so in many years, and an equal number who "don't just slap, they hit to 'kill'" — that is, to inflict real pain or injury. Women who are married to gentle men say their husbands are exceptional and consider themselves to be fortunate.

Just as public opinion supports the violent anger (but not the desertion) of a woman whose husband has taken a new sexual partner, both women and men uphold the right of a husband to hit his wife for cause. The justifications for wife-beating in Kaliai are similar to those discussed by the Law Reform Commission of Papua New Guinea (Toft 1985). A husband has the right (even the duty) to strike his wife if she flirts with other men or commits adultery; if she draws blood in punishing their children; if she fails to meet her domestic obligations such as preparing meals, caring for their children, keeping their house and its grounds clean and tidy, or working in the gardens; if she behaves in a way that publicly shames or insults her husband or his kin; if she fails to assist her husband in meeting his ceremonial obligations; if she fights with her co-wives or abuses his children by another woman. I have heard women comment critically that a male relative who failed to punish his wife for carelessness in her domestic chores was himself responsible for the dishevelled state of their household because he did not discipline her for neglecting her duties.

Although both women and men accept wife-beating in principle, and there is a strong feeling that others should not interfere in marital conflict, there is a point beyond which violence ceases to be acceptable and becomes abusive. Lusi-Kaliai willingly offer opinions as to whether a woman's behavior in a specific case merited a beating, and whether the punishment she received was too severe. Nevertheless, abuse is situationally defined in each case according to the perceived offense of the wife, the degree of punishment given by the husband, the circumstances in which the beating took place, and by the willingness of her kin to support her. The response to a beating — by the woman herself, by her relatives, or by witnesses not related to her — provides the best indication of when an "acceptable" level of punishment becomes abuse.

Abuse has occurred when the wife's kin support her effort to take the matter outside the domestic realm for redress or when others (usually, but not always, her relatives) interfere on her behalf. A woman's relatives will usually intervene if the beating is prolonged or if her husband publicly exposes her genitals, kicks her as though she were a dog, draws blood, or strikes her with a weapon larger than a small stick. Others, even the husband's relatives, may try to stop the beating if they fear that it is life-threatening or if it seems likely that the victim will be maimed or her bones broken. If a woman's natal family lives far away, a person of high standing in the community will likely intervene to stop the abuse because the reputation of the group will suffer when others learn that community members stood aside while she was injured or unjustly beaten. Furthermore, the husband's group will be required to pay compensation when her relatives learn of her mistreatment.

Regardless of the severity of the punishment, however, a major factor in their decision to interfere in a beating is whether others consider the wife to be guilty of the offense for which she is beaten. Although I know of no instance in which an offending woman's relatives helped her husband to beat her for her misbehaviour, her kin may refuse to help her escape from a violent husband, even one who is dangerously so. In one instance, for example, the relatives of a woman whose husband attempted to kill her for suspected adultery agreed with his assessment of her behavior. Consequently, they not only failed to interfere on her behalf but refused her requests for help in leaving the community and her violent husband.

Strategies Available to Beaten Women

When a woman considers herself to have been beaten unjustly or excessively, a number of strategies are available. Many require the support of her family and all have serious limitations.

1. *She may fight back.* This option is sometimes chosen by women in other Papua New Guinea societies. In fact, when Papua New Guinea women

commit murder their victims are almost always their husbands whom they kill in retaliation for long term abuse (Pacific Islands Monthly 1987:48).

Lusi-Kaliai women do not often fight back because they fear more severe punishment or public shaming in return. If a woman who is severely or unjustly beaten passively accepts abuse, her kin may feel anger or pity for her plight, as did Galiki's husband. In this case they can be expected to do as Akono did and either attack or shame their kinswoman's tormentor or demand compensation payment.

2. *If her relatives do not intervene on her behalf, she may leave her husband and return to her own kin.* This option has two shortcomings. First, her relatives may be unwilling to accept her back, either because they are reluctant to return the bridewealth or because they fear retribution by her husband. Second, she will probably lose custody of her children, a cost that many women are unwilling to bear.

3. *A woman may expose her husband to* mali, *"menstrual blood contamination," in order to cause respiratory illness and/or death, or she may collect his hair, cigarette butts, or other "dirty" to use in sorcery.* Although women attributed a number of illnesses and deaths to either menstrual contamination or sorcery, none of them admitted to using either option.

4. *She may take the dispute to the public arena and charge her husband before village or provincial court authorities.* This option requires the support of a woman's male kin for a number of reasons. A principal one is that if the woman's action is successful, her husband will be fined and/or jailed, and she faces his angry retribution. Also, his punishment costs his family scarce cash resources and deprives them of his labor while he is in jail. If she lacks her relatives' support, she and her children may suffer real hardship.

There are problems with the use of the imposed legal system and its norms as a source of sanctuary for beaten women. The Law Reform Commission of Papua New Guinea and the Women and Law Committee have concluded that although wife-beating is against the law, the majority of rural people (women as well as men) seem to be in favor of it and most rural husbands also practice it (Bradley, in press:2). This has implications for the enforcement of laws against wife-beating for, as Chowning has observed, "local government councillors and other village officials almost all strike their own wives and so are reluctant to prosecute other men except when exceptional brutality is involved" (Chowning 1985:88). Recognizing this problem, the LRC made a number of recommendations (Law Reform Commission of Papua New Guinea 1987). Among these were remedial measures designed to improve the way rural village courts handle cases of domestic violence.

Although village courts do have the power to punish assault and to issue Preventive Orders prohibiting further violence, in the past most magistrates did not realize that these powers applied to cases of wife-beating. Consequently village courts usually followed local custom which, in much of Papua New Guinea as in Kaliai, allowed a husband to beat his wife within certain limits (Bradley, in press:6). The LRC suggested measures to educate village magistrates about their responsibilities in cases of wife-bashing, while the Women and Law Committee took steps to make village women aware of their legal rights. The Committee distributed leaflets explaining the law and giving step-by-step instructions on how a person could take a case through the courts. At the same time, the Village Courts Secretariat also sent out leaflets to village magistrates informing them of what had happened in government courts. The leaflets seem to be effective. When village magistrates are made familiar with government law they are more likely to issue judgments consistent with national legal principles rather than local tradition, which may condone wife-bashing (Bradley personal communication, Fitzpatrick personal communication). This encouraging trend suggests that Scaglion and Whittingham are correct when they say that village courts seem to be the most favorable forum for managing domestic disputes presently available to women (1985:132).

5. *She may leave her husband and take a lover or second husband.* This option should be chosen only if all the other alternatives have been unsuccessful for, if she enters into an adulterous relationship without her kin group's consent, they are likely to withdraw support and leave her to her fate.

6. *An abused woman may commit suicide.* Lusi-Kaliai consider this to be an honourable alternative, especially if the woman feels that her husband's act has been unjust. I have argued elsewhere that suicide is one way in which powerless, shamed Kaliai women can get revenge, and that the majority of suicide attempts (two of three) and a high proportion of completed suicides (five of twelve) occurred shortly after the woman had been beaten by her husband (Counts 1980, 1987). A similar relationship between wife abuse and suicide is also reported for North America where recent research by Campbell (1989:23) confirms the conclusion of Stark and Flitcraft that battering may be "the single most important precipitant for female suicide yet identified" (1985:22).

The factors influencing a woman's decision to kill herself are complex. Sometimes the way in which a woman is beaten results in suicide. One consultant observed that a woman who is beaten unjustly will have *ailolo sasi* (literally "bad insides," idiomatically "self pity"), a mixture of anger, shame and despair that may cause her to kill herself. Sometimes the beating is only one aspect of a situation in which the woman kills herself because she is shamed. Occasionally, villagers suspect that a death alleged to have been suicide is in fact due to injuries suffered as a result of marital violence. Sometimes two or more of these elements are present in a suicide case.

The Fate of Assertive Women

Occasionally a Lusi-Kaliai woman feels so strongly about achieving a goal or asserting her rights that she persists in behavior even though she knows she will be beaten as a result. Silimala provides the prototype for this type of behavior, but there are other examples of forceful women in Kaliai myths and folk tales. The fate of these fictitious women — and the delight of audiences when they are killed — demonstrates that aggressive and assertive behavior by women is censured. Still, it does happen. I have seen women determinedly stick with a course of action in spite of warnings — from female and male kinsmen or affines as well as husbands — that they will be beaten. For instance, one woman refused to marry the man her father chose for her, another insisted that her husband must not use family resources on behalf of the children of another wife, while another refused to surrender her rights in a cash crop claimed by her maternal kinsmen. All of these women were threatened with violence if they persisted, and two were beaten for their intransigence. Puri, the woman who defied her maternal kinsmen, threatened to take her case to court and was supported in her claims by her husband. His backing and her willingness to take the dispute into the government arena discouraged her relatives from attacking her physically, although they did advance on her, clenched fists raised, during a public meeting where the dispute was aired (for more details of this case see Counts and Counts 1974:141–149).

The example of Mary is also instructive. In spite of her husband's angry warnings, Mary (who was a first wife) frequently attacked her co-wife. When her husband beat her, she fought back. When he knocked her unconscious and publicly shamed her in an attempt to control her belligerence, she attempted suicide. Bested, her husband no longer interferes when Mary fights with her co-wife. Her cost was high, but Mary won. Are the actions of Mary, Silimala, and other stubborn and determined women aberrant? Or is this a pattern that scholars who attempt to understand domestic violence should note?

This latter possibility is suggested by African sociologist T. M. Mushanga. Using data from Bohannan's edited monograph on homicide and suicide in African societies, Mushanga argues that African wives sometimes 'provoke' their husbands into beating them to death (Mushanga 1977–78:482–483). This is most likely to happen, Mushanga says, among people who are employed in the traditional sector of the economy because they are the ones with orthodox views about the roles of women. They consider a woman's role to be restricted to activities focusing on child care, household and garden chores, and "above all, to remain subservient to their husbands"

(484). These are the men who will not tolerate any "nonsense" about "equality" between women and men. Mushanga continues (484):

> It would appear that the new ideas about women's liberation in communities that are generally traditional may create situations in which the wife may directly or indirectly bring about her own death. This may happen as a result of a woman's attempt to assert her own rights, which may conflict with cultural patterns of behavior and socially accepted responses of a wife towards her husband.

How do we evaluate Mushanga's argument? Is he providing an important indigenous insight into the complexity of marital relationships and family violence? Do women really intend to "provoke" their husbands into killing them? There is a profound difference in a woman's demanding her rights even though she expects to get a beating and a relationship that begins with a husband beating his assertive wife and deteriorates into a situation in which he repeatedly beats and finally kills her in an attempt to force her into submission. Mushanga's analysis, which appears to blame the victim for getting herself killed, does not account for this difference, nor does it attribute to the husband either responsibility for delivering the fatal beating(s) or culpability in his wife's death.

Although Mushanga's analysis is seriously flawed, he does raise an issue that must be addressed. We must recognize and understand the factors that motivate women to persevere in behavior that they know will result in violent retribution. One approach is suggested by Levinson's observation that social change is an ongoing and open-ended process that may effect patterns of domestic violence (1988:451). Mushanga attributes particularly virulent wife-beating to specific kinds of social change. Other scholars also report an increase in domestic violence with modernization. For example, Scaglion associates it with an increase in spousal violence among the Abelam of Papua New Guinea because educated, mobile young Abelam women are less tolerant of abuse, adultery, gambling and neglect on the part of their husbands and more willing to fight back or even to strike the first blow than were women a generation ago (Scaglion 1990). Similarly, in her chapter in this volume, Lateef observes that modern working Indo-Fijian wives assert their rights and refuse to accept total male control unconditionally, even though they may be beaten as a result.

Au Doko, who is a member of the Law Reform Commission of Papua New Guinea and the Women and Law Committee, also points out the relationship between change and wife-beating. She observes that educated, employed women are independent and capable of speaking and thinking for themselves. This conflicts with the traditional notion that the husband is the head of the household and makes the decisions while his wife remains silent.

Consequently, in her opinion wife-beating is an even more serious problem for educated urbanized Papua New Guinean women than it is for traditional women living in rural areas (South Pacific People's Federation 1989:3–5). Some of my female informants insist that wife-beating is increasing, especially among educated Lusi-Kaliai. There are a number of changes in West New Britain that have contributed to a new perception by women of their rights and, therefore at least indirectly, to their being beaten for insubordination. These include increased exposure to Western ideas about courtship and women's rights, and the rejection — especially by educated women — of arranged marriage. One well-educated Kaliai woman who lived with a violent man for eight years insists that two factors relating to modernization — the availability of alcohol and the unwillingness of educated women to submit meekly — contribute to increased violence among educated Lusi-Kaliai. After listing a number of her kinswomen who had endured severe abuse and had left their marriages after their husbands took a second wife, she commented:

> I used to think that there was something wrong with the women in my family. I looked at the marriages of the other village women, and I worried that it was our fault that we were beaten so badly and that our relationships were not stable. But now I realize that it isn't us. It's because we're educated, and we want to have an equal say in things. We want to have our rights. We fight like hell, and this enrages the men. So they look for other women who won't argue with them.

Changes in rights and authority that occur during the developmental cycle of the family also affects the level of violence between spouses. I have noted elsewhere that most wife-beating in Kaliai occurs early in marriage (Counts 1985). This is when each spouse is attempting to assert his/her rights. By the time the couple reach middle age they have probably worked out a mutually acceptable relationship and are more likely to be united by common interests than divided by a struggle over rights and authority. Also, as other scholars have observed, by the time she is middle-aged a woman who is destined to achieve a position of respect and authority has probably done so (for example see Keith 1980; Brown 1982). She may have the responsibility for supervising her daughters-in-law as well as her own children, and she is more likely to recommend (or practice) physical violence toward younger women than she is to be the victim of it (Brown 1982, 1985. Also see Lateef's chapter in this volume for an example of this pattern among Indo-Fijians).

Women may also assert themselves and attempt to achieve a measure of equality with their menfolk in order to become respected, adult members of society. Being beaten may be the cost women must pay to achieve the status of adult person. This approach is suggested by McDowell who attributes the determination of Bun women to assert their autonomy — and the violence of their male kin and husbands who attempt to control them — to the ethos that requires that an individual must maintain a balance between personal autonomy and social relatedness in order to achieve personhood. A shamed, controlled, non-assertive individual is a "rubbish person," not a human being, regardless of gender.

As McDowell reports for the Bun (Chapter 6), Lusi-Kaliai women who defy their husbands and follow a course of action that they know will result in a beating may be following a strategy that permits them to assert their rights, increase their options and expand their boundaries. They accept the beating as part of the cost of achieving a level of autonomy.

As is also true of many battered women in Canada, Lusi-Kaliai women who are beaten by their husbands may perceive themselves, not as powerless victims, but as being stronger than the men who beat them and for whom they, ironically, feel pity (see MacLeod 1987:41 for an excellent discussion of wife-beating in Canada). When viewed in this way, beaten women — in Kaliai as well as in Canada — are not passive victims but are co-actors in an ongoing relationship. They are, at least to some extent, mistresses of their fate.

I must emphasize that the preceding few paragraphs are *not* meant to suggest that a beaten woman deserves what she gets, nor do they necessarily apply to all (nor even to most) occasions of spousal violence. The scenario I describe is limited to those interactive situations in which a woman, in explicit defiance of male authority, asserts herself and is beaten in return. It is surely unnecessary to state that recognition of a pattern of interaction, or an examination of the complex factors contributing to spousal violence, does not imply justification for it or approval of it.

CONCLUSION

While domestic violence and wife-beating are part of family life in Kaliai, there are limits to it. Beyond that, acceptable violence becomes abusive and outsiders will intervene to stop it. A severely beaten woman can sometimes motivate her relatives to intercede on her behalf by remaining passive, while a woman who returns her husband's blows risks losing the sympathy of her kinsmen and takes the chance of being even more severely beaten. Assertive, aggressive Lusi-Kaliai women who defy their husbands or other male relatives are often condemned for their behavior and risk being beaten for it. Nevertheless, women do challenge male authority and demand a voice in choosing a mate or deciding how to distribute family resources. They fight back when they perceive that they are being treated unfairly, and insist upon their rights of inheritance and self-determination. These women remind us that although Papua New Guinea women are often dominated by their menfolk, they are not necessarily passive, pathetic victims. Instead many of them are determined to preserve their autonomy and maintain control over their lives and are willing to risk ill treatment to achieve their goals.

The avenues of relief available to beaten women, whether they are passive victims or persons insisting on their rights, are restricted in Papua New Guinea and may be of limited effectiveness or desirability. The most promising options seem to derive from the programs of public education and legal reform being instituted by the Law Reform Commission and the Women and Law Committee. There is emerging evidence that the efforts of these bodies are bringing about a change in attitudes toward marital violence and creating a new climate in which women may seek protection from physical violence. As a result of their activities, for example, some Papua New Guinea courts now provide women with sanctions against abuse and a forum where domestic disputes can be settled peaceably. Media presentations such as the video *Stap Isi (Take it Easy)* and the cartoon booklet *Let's Talk it Over*, which present alternatives to violence, are widely available in rural area schools, churches, and public meetings. Although the women of Papua New Guinea have far to go before these alternatives are widely preferred to violence, they have made a beginning—one which may be self-sustaining—toward implementing this profound social and cultural change.

NOTES

The research on which this chapter is based was supported in 1966—1967 by the United States National Science Foundation and Southern Illinois University; in 1971 by the University of Waterloo and the Wenner Gren Foundation; in 1975—1976 by the Canada Council and the University of Waterloo; and in 1981 and 1985 by the University of Waterloo and by research grants from the Social Sciences and Humanities Research Council of Canada.

I wish to thank David Counts, Judith Brown, Jacquelyn Campbell, and Ursula Kolkolo for reading and commenting on earlier versions of this chapter.

REFERENCES CITED

Bradley, Christine. In press. Should Human Rights Apply to Wives? — Wife-Beating and the Work of the Papua New Guinea Law Reform Commission. *In* Modern Papua New Guinea Society. Laura Zimmer, ed. Bathurst, Australia: Crawford House Press.

Brown, Judith K. 1982. Cross-Cultural Perspectives on Middle-Aged Women. Current Anthropology 23:143—156.

———. 1985. Introduction *In* In Her Prime: A New View of Middle-Aged Women. Judith K. Brown and Virginia Kerns, eds. Pp. 1—12. South Hadley, Mass: Bergin and Garvey.

Campbell, Jacquelyn C. 1989. A Test of Two Explanatory Models of Women's Responses to Battering. Nursing Research 38:18—24.

Chowning, Ann. 1985. Kove Women and Violence: The Context of Wife-beating in a West New Britain Society. *In* Domestic Violence in Papua New Guinea. Papua New Guinea Law Reform Commission Monograph No. 3. S. Toft, ed. Pp. 72—91. Boroko: Law Reform Commission of Papua New Guinea.

Counts, D., and D. Counts. 1974. The Kaliai Lupunga: Disputing in the Public Forum. *In* Contention and Dispute: Aspects of Law and Social Control in Melanesia. A. L. Epstein, ed. Pp. 113—151. Canberra: Australian National University Press.

Counts, Dorothy A. 1980. Fighting Back is Not the Way: Suicide and the Women of Kaliai. American Ethnologist 7:332—351.

———. 1985. Tamparonga: "The Big Women of Kaliai" (Papua New Guinea). *In* In Her Prime: A New View of Middle-Aged Women. J. K. Brown and V. Kerns, eds. Pp. 49—64. South Hadley, Mass: Bergin and Garvey.

———. 1987. Female Suicide and Wife Abuse in Cross-Cultural Perspective. Suicide and Life-Threatening Behavior 17:194—204.

Keith, Jennie. 1980. The Best Is Yet to Be: Toward an Anthropology of Age. *In* Annual Review of Anthropology, 9. Bernard Siegal, Alan Beals, Stephen Tyler, eds. Pp. 339—366. Palo Alto, Calif.: Annual Reviews Inc.

Law Reform Commission of Papua New Guinea. 1987. Interim Report on Domestic Violence. Boroko: Law Reform Commission of Papua New Guinea.

Levinson, David. 1988. Family Violence in Cross-Cultural Perspective. *In* Handbook of Family Violence. Vincent B. Van Hasselt, Randall L. Morrison, Alan S. Bellack, Michel Hersen eds. Pp. 435—456. New York: Plenum Press.

MacLeod, Linda. 1987. Battered But Not Beaten. . . . Preventing Wife-Battering in Canada. Ottawa: Canadian Advisory Council on the Status of Women.

Mushanga, T. M. 1977—78. Wife Victimization in East and Central Africa. Victimology 2:479—485.

Pacific Islands Monthly. 1987. The Island Press: From the Papua New Guinea Post-Courier, Port Moresby. 58(4):48.

Scaglion, Richard. 1990. Spare the Rod and Spoil the Woman? Family Violence in Abelam Society. Pacific Studies 13(3):189—204. Special Issue: Domestic Violence in Oceania. Dorothy Ayers Counts, ed.

Scaglion, Richard, and Rose Whittingham. 1985. Female Plaintiffs and Sex-Related Disputes in Rural Papua New Guinea. *In* Domestic Violence in Papua New Guinea. Susan Toft, ed. Pp. 120—133. Boroko: Law Reform Commission of Papua New Guinea.

South Pacific People's Federation. 1989. Women's Development in Papua New Guinea. Tok Blong South Pacific People's Federation. (October 1989) 29:3—11.

Stark, Evan, and Ann H. Flitcraft. 1985. Spouse Abuse. Working Paper prepared for Surgeon General's Workshop on Violence and Public Health Source Book. Atlanta, GA: U.S. Public Health Service Center For Disease Control.

Toft, Susan, editor. 1985. Domestic Violence in Papua New Guinea. Papua New Guinea Law Reform Commission Monograph No. 3 edited by Susan Toft. Boroko.

———. 1986. Domestic Violence in Urban Papua New Guinea. Papua New
  Guinea Law Reform Occasional Paper No. 19. Boroko.
Toft, Susan, and Susanne Bonnell. 1985. Marriage and Domestic Violence in
  Rural Papua New Guinea. Papua New Guinea Law Reform Commission Oc-
  casional Paper No. 18. Boroko.

6

Household Violence
in a Yuat River Village

Nancy McDowell

The people of Bun,[1] a small village on the Yuat River in the East Sepik Province of Papua New Guinea, are assertive and volatile, and violence is not infrequent here. In order to understand violence within the household, it is necessary to examine a complex interaction of several factors and not search for any simple cause-effect relationship. It is not that, for example, frustration generates aggression, or that increasing stress is displaced into the nuclear family, or that warriors must be generally aggressive if the society is to survive; although all of these may be contributory, searching for one simple cause for a complex phenomenon is inadequate.

Nor is it possible to seek causes on only one analytical level: ideological, social, and affective factors are all relevant. Specifically, the meaning and incidence of household violence[2] cannot be understood without examining the indigenous conception of person (a cultural structuring), ethos and affect (psychological factors), and social process itself (kinship, power, and politics). The first section of this chapter describes Bun ethos and affect, emotional and psychological tendencies that relate directly to the production of violence. The second section describes Bun views of the world with a particular focus on the structuring of the person, for the process whereby one achieves personhood is seminal in the generation of violence. In the final section, the incidence of household violence is examined.

ON VIOLENCE AND ETHOS

The Bun inhabit a single, small village (Bun), directly upriver from the people Mead (1963) described as the Mundugumor, and in many ways the two are very similar (see Mead 1963; McDowell 1976, 1977, 1978a, 1978b, 1980, 1984a, 1987, and n.d.). Perhaps the most striking similarity between the two is what Bateson (1936) labelled ethos: the emotional tone and tenor

77

of the society. Mead described both Mundugumor women and men as assertive, violent, volatile people. She noted that they also had a great capacity
for joy and generosity as well as other traits Westerners might interpret as
positive, but it was the violence, particularly in the context of childrearing,
that she emphasized.

If one acknowledges the joyful side as well as the more aggressive one,
then Bun ethos is very similar to that of their downriver neighbors. Both
women and men tend to be assertive, volatile and quick to defend themselves.[3] Strength is a major value and virtue, and one of the most obvious ways
to demonstrate strength is through physical violence. There are other ways,
such as sponsoring large and successful feasts, maintaining order in one's
own orbit of influence, provisioning one's family well, demonstrating wisdom
and, traditionally, ritual power. However, physical violence plays an important role in self-assertion. It is a typical reaction to insult and frustration, an
outgrowth of anger; it is a natural response to challenges to one's strength.
Although there do exist some ritual challenges that allow one to demonstrate
strength, to be called weak or inferior provokes anger, which often escalates
from verbal abuse to physical violence.

The expression of anger through physical aggression is a theme in
socialization. Children learn that violence is frequently the proper response
when those in one's environment challenge or frustrate. Children's play
groups are characterized by squabbling that often escalates to violence, and
older siblings with regularity hit younger siblings who are in their care.
Parents often punish children by hitting them, throwing things at them, lash-
ing out in various ways, almost always in anger.

ON PERSON AND VIOLENCE

Autonomy and control are issues faced by people everywhere, but they
seem to be especially significant ones in Melanesia. Elsewhere (McDowell
1978a, 1980, 1984b) I have described how the need to assert one's autonomy
is a central cultural and psychological issue in Bun: one must prove one's
autonomy while simultaneously participating in social relations that always
impair one's desired freedom. The Bun solve this dilemma by basing all internal relations on balanced and symmetrical exchange. One preserves
one's autonomy by not allowing another to control or to be superior; one
remains equal and unindebted. If one escapes being controlled by another,
if one avenges insults and avoids shame and responds to challenges with self-
assertion, then one achieves personhood.[4]

This conception of person is significantly different from the Western one,
which stresses individualism and an acting or core and separate self. Several
ethnographers note that Melanesian persons are defined far more relation-
ally and less individualistically than Western ones (see, for example, Clay

1986; Gewertz 1984; Read 1955; see also Bellah et al. for a description of the Western perspective, and Burridge 1979 for a contrasting view). A Bun person is one who handles the delicate balance between autonomy and sociability by executing transactions that allow for both a relational and autonomous self. There exists a slight gender difference in the attainment of personhood: although both women and men must strike a balance between autonomy and relatedness, men stress autonomy more than women (see McDowell 1984a). Very few people fail completely to achieve personhood, but occasionally someone does. These are people who fall into the familiar category of "rubbish person." It is important to note that much of the process is relative – some people clearly achieve fuller personhood than others or are content to rest with a questionable achievement.

One must, in order to accomplish personhood, transact in three separate modes. First, sharing with close kin is required (while, of course, expecting that they reciprocate). In this domain, affect, closeness, and relational ties are emphasized. But to be a person, it is also necessary to transact in two more formal exchange modes. The first is that of *kamain,* a distant kin tie ritually transformed into an exchange relationship of both material and intangible goods. *Kamain* exchanges must be balanced and equal; if one fails to keep up, shame and a denial of personhood are inevitable. Finally, one must participate in marital exchanges of people, i.e., of siblings. The ideal is that all marriages occur by brother-sister exchange, a transaction in which equality and balance are guaranteed, and the vast majority of marriages are conceived as if they were between brother-sister pairs of classificatory cross-cousins. If a man does not have a sister, he is at a distinct disadvantage, but there are ways in which he can marry anyway (see McDowell 1978b). A deeper problem confronts the man who has a sister but somehow loses her, either to his male kin (to execute their marriages), or to a husband who does not reciprocate with a wife for him. In these cases, the challenge to equity runs deep indeed.

Clearly this process of asserting one's self, achieving personhood by remaining at least equal, maintaining one's autonomy and avoiding control by others (while simultaneously trying to control them), is a political process that is deeply intertwined with the acquisition of power. It played a significant role in the traditional political system in which individual men achieved status by maintaining their strength and controlling others in exchanging and feasting as well as in warfare and ritual. The arena in which one demonstrated one's strength was wider in traditional society, one that included warfare and inter-village raiding; the arena in which it is manifested has shrunk today. One can, indeed one must, demonstrate one's ability to maintain equity in the context of the *kamain* relationship. Because formality and respect characterize the tie, it is not appropriate to win too much – the ideal is equity, and people who violate that ideal by trying to outdo their *kamain* are accused of trying to shame these relations, a serious breach of manners and violation of appropriate kin behavior. The relationship between cross-cousins allows for somewhat more leeway; these relatives frequently provoke one another into a series of competitive feasts in which the goal is to provide so much that the others cannot possibly reciprocate (see, for example, McDowell 1982). Business is providing a new means of asserting one's strength: if one proves one's strength by accumulating money to buy things (such as outboard motors), then one demonstrates strength superior to others. But by far the most significant contemporary arena for proving one's strength, and in which one's strength is most frequently challenged, is that concerning marital exchange.

ON SOCIAL AND POLITICAL PROCESS

Ethos and personhood help to explain the prevalence of violence in Bun, but the pattern of violence must be understood in the sociopolitical context of marriage, for marriage provides the crucible out of which most interpersonal violence between adults emerges. It is within the process of attracting sexual partners and arranging marriages that much of the assertion of self takes place today, and it is within this context that one is frequently frustrated and challenged by others.

Arranging these ideal marriages is enormously complex (see McDowell 1978b) and requires detailed planning and a lot of luck. Rarely do plans work smoothly, for the simple reason that seldom are there classificatory cross-cousins of the appropriate age and sex who are willing to marry the partner indicated for them. Although both men and women speak of these exchanges as if brothers exchanged their passive and yielding sisters, in reality women rarely marry men they do not like. (Women and men both perceive that, like the trouble-makers in Collier 1974, these are idiosyncratic actions of obstreperous women rather than a pattern of resistance to male authority—see McDowell 1984a.) Women assert their autonomy by refusing to marry men to whom their brothers and fathers try to send them and frequently by insisting that they marry men of their own choosing. Men, on the other hand, demonstrate their power by executing what they believe to be appropriate exchanges when they can. The process is made even more complex by the fact that men try to attract unreciprocated women to them. They foil other men's plans by trying to entice women who are not appropriate and by so doing assert their own power to attract and control. Maintaining a marriage and one's power over one's wife, or preserving one's autonomy from one's husband, or choosing one's own husband are all serious aspects of marriage. When an individuals' power and autonomy are threatened, they can generate interpersonal violence.

Marriage exchanges are, then, essentially political processes: they involve ways of manifesting and demonstrating personal power. Disputes about these transactions are not located in either a domestic or public sphere because the spheres, although they do exist (see McDowell 1984a), are not clearly differentiated. In fact, it is precisely the process of arranging marriages that provides the most significant overlap of the public and domestic. Marriages are the foundation of domestic life, but their arrangement involves public and very political process. Violence here, as elsewhere, is not random: it clusters around four related relationships within which power issues and assertions of self are deeply significant: (1) husband-wife; (2) co-wife–co-wife; (3) sister-brother; (4) affines or potential affines. The first two of these are relatively straightforward; understanding the dynamics of the second two is more problematic. Separating these four from the larger context in which they occur allows for more careful attention to each, but marriage is a process that involves all of these people who are embedded together in a single complex.

Physical violence between husbands and wives is commonplace. In just over fourteen months of fieldwork, I recorded thirty incidents of physical violence between spouses, and I am certain that there were many more cases that never came to my attention (the total population of the village during this time was approximately 220). Some couples did not fight physically at all during this period, but at least sixteen did. One couple accounts for six of the incidents, two couples fought four times, one couple fought three times, five couples fought twice, and seven couples fought physically only once during this period. The severity of the physical violence varied; in some instances, a person was only struck once and not physically harmed, but in other cases serious physical damage resulted. One woman's ribs were broken, another woman was badly battered, and in one case a man's collarbone was broken.

Although people say that a quarrel between husband and wife is their own business, bystanders and kin interfere for two reasons. One is that although physical beatings are acceptable, there are limits — excessive damage to another person is not tolerated. Onlookers try to take weapons away to prevent permanent injury or death. The second reason people interfere in a quarrel between wife and husband intensifies and spreads the physical violence rather than curtails it. When a woman is being beaten by her husband, her relatives use the occasion to further quarrels with him. For example, a man might hit his wife because she did not cook, and her brother — angry because of the original marriage exchange or for an entirely different reason — would, under the pretext of helping his sister, attack her husband. In this way, seemingly constrained domestic quarrels ramify and become larger political events. In a case I did not witness, a man hit his wife because no food was ready. Her brother, who had opposed their marriage, decided to help his sister and joined the fray and hit her husband. Later the husband and his brother went into the bush with the wife's brother, and a tree fell on the wife's brother and killed him. No charges were ever brought, but many people speculated that he had been murdered by his brothers-in-law.

Although women usually are the physical victims when they quarrel violently with men, in two cases it was the husband who sustained serious injuries. Women do not always passively accept their husbands' beatings. Sometimes, especially if they are very angry or feel that they have a chance to win, they fight back, and some women initiate the physical aspects of a dispute. In one incident, when people were pulling a canoe out of the forest to the shore the rattan broke and the women who were helping fell down. One husband made fun of his wife. Angry about being ridiculed, she insulted him and would nót cook his dinner. When he tried to calm her down and ease her anger, she stuck a machete through his wrist. Another couple had very dramatic confrontations. In one incident, the husband began to beat his wife, but she grabbed an axe and was prevented from killing him by bystanders (informants believed that she would have killed him if she had not been prevented). On two occasions, this woman initiated the quarrel and hit her husband, even going after him with a spear. The Bun say that men beat their wives with their hands and feet while women tend to use weapons to defend themselves and to harm their husbands. This rule usually seems to hold true, but in the case of this axe- and spear-wielding woman, the husband once became so exasperated that he grabbed a piece of oil palm and bashed her over the head with it.

The reasons wives and husbands quarrel are diverse, but all have to do with power issues — who controls whom in the relationship. This may be a truism for violence between all spouses at some level, but it is in the forefront in Bun. Women often resist new marriages by staying away from their husbands and refusing to behave as wives should, and men frequently respond by beating them. One man's marriage had been arranged to a young girl years before my arrival, and his sister was firmly married to his future wife's brother. He did not wait patiently for his marked bride to mature, and before she was old enough to marry he had an affair with her mother. They had an on-again off-again relationship for about two years; it ended only when the bride gained maturity and the marriage seemed imminent. The bride's mother was disgruntled about the end of the affair and wanted to marry the man herself despite the fact that he was a generation younger and her daughter's marked husband. The bride was young, shy, and easily influenced by her mother, who told her that he would not be a good husband for her and that she should resist the plans that had been made for her marriage. Soon after I arrived, the news broke that the prospective bride had slept with an attractive and unattached young man. In the ensuing argument, she was badly beaten by her brothers, and her lover was slapped around as well. He paid compensation to her intended and the affair ended. It was not clear whether the young man was not seriously interested in marriage with her, or whether she was not strong enough to resist the marriage arranged for her. It was clear that she did not want to marry her marked husband. Helped by her mother's urging, she resisted passively for months. Because she would not behave as a wife — neither as a sexual nor domestic partner — her husband became angry and frustrated. He beat his own mother, who insulted him about the issue, and tried to seduce his wife's sister but was caught and had to pay compensation. People urged him to persist in his bond with the recalcitrant bride and he did so, but at a high cost to her: I recorded four separate occasions on which he beat her for not behaving as she should. She had no support from relatives, other than her trouble-making mother, and eventually gave in. (Note here that although I use this case to examine husband-wife violence, it could also serve as an example of brother-sister violence, adultery, and even mother-adult son violence.)

The reason men frequently give for hitting their wives is that the women did not prepare food or did not work, the implication being that their wives were off doing what they wanted to do rather than what their husbands thought they should be doing. In the case of the husband with the broken collar bone, the ostensible reason his wife hit him with a log was that he wanted to play cards while she wanted him to help her in the garden. On two occasions, husbands complained that their wives were not adequately caring for children and deserved to be beaten for that reason. Sexual and other sorts of jealousy, however, are probably the most important causes of violence between spouses. A husband's belief that his wife may be committing adultery may goad him into violence against her. Women get angry and jealous of co-wives and potential co-wives, and over their husbands' adulteries. When they do so, they insult their husbands and provoke violence even if they do not initiate it. The woman who had broken ribs as the result of a kick from her husband had accused him in obscene and insulting terms of spending all of his money on women while he was away working; she knew that such an insult would provoke him — she only regretted that he acted so fast that she did not have a chance to defend herself. When a man indicates that he may be getting a co-wife (especially if he is having an affair with an eligible woman), his wife will complain, refuse to cooperate, and generally make her displeasure clear. Wives often initiate or provoke violence and make life so miserable for their husbands that the men give up on their polygynous plans.

Another significant way in which women resist the acquisition of additional wives is by taking lovers of their own and causing such disruption that divorce is the only solution. They know that beatings will occur, but some seem to be willing to pay that price. The root of one complex case was a woman's unwillingness to accept a particular co-wife. She made her displeasure known, and her husband avoided the conflict by signing on as a coastal plantation worker for two years. When he returned, his new wife was still waiting for him, but his first wife was having an affair with another man and seemed committed to him. The husband was furious and demanded that she return to him and that he be paid compensation. During the first of several village moots to discuss the case, the wife was severely beaten by her brothers for her behavior; one of these brothers had used her to execute his own marriage and feared that a divorce would undo his own. The adultery-committing couple paid compensation and it appeared that the wife returned to her husband, but she was obviously dissatisfied with the outcome. The lovers continued to meet despite all attempts to keep them apart. The woman was beaten severely by her husband, while her lover was struck by both her husband and his own mother's brother. After her pregnancy was announced, the husband beat the lover in front of the latter's own relatives, who did nothing to protect him. He also tried to beat the wife again, muttering that he would kill her this time, but was prevented from doing so by bystanders. The participants recognized an impasse and took the case to the colonial court in Angoram.[5]

Women do not like to share their husbands and do whatever they can to prevent them from acquiring additional wives. One man was having an affair with an older woman and was considering marrying her. His second wife, favored and beautiful, was deeply resentful and expressed her resentment frequently by insulting her husband, refusing to cook, and being obstinate in various ways (and was beaten by her husband for it; this is the couple who fought at least six times). After one particularly nasty beating, she became enraged and attacked her husband's lover with an axe, nearly fracturing her skull. The husband abandoned thoughts of acquiring a third wife.

Disputes between husband and wife and between co-wives are ethnographically commonplace. The pivotal importance of brother- sister exchange marriage and individuals' attempts to assert themselves within the context of such marriage exchanges generates two additional dyads in which violence is prevalent in Bun, i.e. between brother and sister and between affines (or potential affines).

If executed properly, a brother-sister exchange marriage results in two married couples who are closely connected to one another. Ideally such affines cooperate with each other and support one another in disputes. When the marriages are executed smoothly and with little acrimony, good relations usually are the rule. However, few marriages are arranged and carried out with no trouble; in fact, despite the public ideology that men arrange marriages for themselves, their sons, and their sisters' sons in reality these exchanges are often conflict-ridden. Because of these conflicts, the relations among the major participants are acrimonious and sometimes violent. The brother-sister tie is supposed to be a close one, and in general it is. The tie is especially close with the sibling with whom one participated in a marriage exchange. A woman gives food to this brother regularly and without question; a man provides meat to his marked sister, often over the protests of his wife. But brother-sister pairs often clash violently about arranging marriages. Typically, the brother (with his senior male kin) works out a marriage for himself and his sister without consulting her. When she hears of the plans and learns the identity of her intended husband, she balks and refuses to marry him. She can make her intentions known by announcing her refusal. If her relatives ignore her wishes and go ahead with the marriages, she refuses to behave like a wife. If she already has a lover she prefers to marry she makes this affair publicly known and, by doing so, forces her relatives to deal with her desires in the public arena of a village moot. If she is strong enough, if she accepts the beatings given to her primarily by her brothers, then her will usually prevails.[6] However, some women are not strong enough and acquiesce to the demands of their relatives.

Brothers beat their sisters for other reasons, but most have to do with trouble concerning marriage. It is best to interpret violence associated with adultery in this context because adultery is not just a violation of rights of sexual access; it indicates a desire for divorce and threatens earlier arranged marriages. Thus some women who commit adultery are beaten by their brothers as well as by their husbands. Of the six cases of brother-sister violence that occurred during the period of my fieldwork, four were concerned with arranging initial marriages and two with the threat of adultery to already-existing marriages. Moots are held to settle the dispute, but anger flares and violence erupts. I never saw a woman try to fight back in this context, but informants told me of other cases in which women did defend themselves. Men assert their desires and attempt to control their sisters; women resist control and assert their autonomy in choosing a spouse or terminating a marriage.

Men try to assert themselves in the marriage context in an additional way: they attempt to attract women without laying the necessary groundwork for an exchange. A man engages in sexual affairs in the hope that he can acquire a wife (or additional wives), and sometimes this strategy is successful. But attempted seductions have a price: the woman's brothers resent what they perceive to be theft of their rights to the woman, and their resentment erupts in physical violence. Even if marriages are eventually arranged, conflict and animosity remain because seductions are interpreted as sister-stealing. Sisters are beaten, but so also are their lovers despite the fact that lovers transform into affines with some regularity. It seems appropriate, then, to include certain kinds of violence between affines or potential affines here as well.

Most such violence occurs between men, as in cases of brothers beating their sisters' lovers, but women sometimes get involved in attempts to protect what they perceive to be their siblings' rights. Two brothers from another village married in Bun and brought sisters to exchange for their wives. One of these sisters ended up in an incorrect marriage, and when her husband died she married her deceased husband's father. Her brothers were furious with her and especially with her second husband, but they were unable to do anything about it. They brought another sister to the village to replace the one who had gone astray, and her intended husband waited for her to mature. When it was discovered that she was having an affair with the son of the man who had stolen their other sister, they were furious. They beat the young man, but he was defended by his brothers; the conflict ramified through a larger network as others joined the fray to support a relative. Women participated in this fight as well. Both of the wives of the in-married brothers, who were in fact sisters, feared that their brother was going to be done out of a wife by the same people who had cheated him before. One of them attacked the seducing man's mother for hiding him and his actions from public view; the other attacked the young woman, their brother's potential wife.

CONCLUSION

Violence among kin in Bun must be understood as a part of how the Bun define themselves and achieve personhood. It is when personhood is threatened, when autonomy is in jeopardy, or when accusations of inferiority and therefore inhumanity are made, that one must assert one's self and thereby demonstrate one's humanity. Establishing and situating the self as person is culturally meaningful, but it is also the foundation of political process and the generation of power over others. Physical violence is directed at those who frustrate, who challenge, who evade, who attempt to control, and as such it is an inherent part of the political process as well. Because arranging and maintaining marriages are the central ways in which autonomy is achieved but also threatened, more violence occurs in this context than in any other contemporary arena.

NOTES

1. I conducted fieldwork in Bun for approximately 13 months in 1972—1973 and 6 weeks in 1977 and made two brief visits during 1981. I would like to thank the National Institute of Mental Health, the National Endowment for the Humanities, and Franklin and Marshall College for financial support.

This chapter is a revised and condensed version of an article entitled "Person, Assertion, and Marriage: On the Nature of Household Violence in Bun," *Pacific Studies* 1990. I would like to thank *Pacific Studies* for permission to reprint here.

2. I use the phrase "household violence" here to avoid the more common expression, "domestic violence." In Bun, the domestic and public realms are not clearly delineated, and in fact this kind of violence straddles the line between these two potential domains. See the discussion below about arranging marriages for examples.

3. That there is little or no contrast in gender ethos or, to use Mead's (1935/1963) old terminology, "temperament," does not mean that there are no contrasts in gender ideology, nor does it imply that male and female roles are the same. See McDowell 1984a for a discussion of gender in Bun that relates directly to some of the issues discussed here.

4. I failed to understand the entire process while in the field and cannot answer some significant questions about it. For example, when does a growing child begin the process? Are children non-persons or does another category, perhaps yet-to-be person, exist? Parents begin exchanges in the names of their children. . . . What if they fail to do so? Many such questions remain.

5. Events surprised even close participants, for when asked what he wanted to do, the husband replied that he did not want his first wife back — he only wanted compensation. His first and second wives, recognizing that they had a common goal in facilitating the divorce (the new co-wife did not want to be a co-wife to anyone), formed an alliance and together shamed him in front of a variety of people by asking him, "Why have you made all of this necessary? You're just sexually excited all the time — you only think of female genitals." The ensuing shame, the knowledge that he had little chance in the face of an alliance between the two, and the fear that in reality the colonial court usually favored the woman, made him back down and relinquish his claims on his first wife. The divorce was executed and compensation paid to the husband, and the lovers were free to marry.

6. Fathers are also participants in this; father-daughter violence, however, seems less common and perhaps should be conceived as a subset here. Fathers seem to bluster and shout more than they beat their daughters.

REFERENCES CITED

Bateson, Gregory. 1936. Naven. Cambridge: Cambridge University Press.

Bellah, Robert et al. 1985. Habits of the Heart. Berkeley: University of California Press.

Burridge, Kenelm. 1979. Someone, No One: An Essay on Individuality. Princeton: Princeton University Press.

Clay, Brenda Johnson. 1986. Mandak Realities: Person and Power in Central New Ireland. New Brunswick: Rutgers University Press.

Collier, Jane. 1974. Women in Politics. *In* Women, Culture and Society. Michelle Rosaldo and L. Lamphere eds., Pp. 89—96. Stanford: Stanford University Press.

Gewertz, Deborah. 1984. The Chambri View of Persons: A Critique of Individualism in the Works of Mead and Chodorow. American Anthropologist 86:615—629.

McDowell, Nancy. 1976. Kinship and Exchange: The Kamain Relationship in a Yuat River Village. Oceania 47:36—48.

————. 1977. The Meaning of "Rape" in a Yuat River Village. Ethnology 16:175—183.

————. 1978a. The Struggle To Be Human: Exchange and Politics in Bun. Anthropological Quarterly 51:16—25.

————. 1978b. The Flexibility of Sister Exchange: Case Studies. Oceania 48: 207—231.

————. 1980. It's Not Who You Are But How You Give That Counts: The Role of Exchange in a Melanesian Society. American Ethnologist 82:278—302.

————. 1982. Strength, Autonomy and Alcohol Use in Bun. *In* Through a Glass Darkly: Beer and Modernization in Papua New Guinea. M. Marshall ed. Pp. 257—270. IASER Monograph #18. Boroko: Institute of Applied Social and Economic Research.

————. 1984a. Complementarity: The Relationship Between Male and Female in the East Sepik Village of Bun, Papua New Guinea. *In* Rethinking Women's Roles: Perspectives from the Pacific. D. O'Brien and S. Tiffany eds. Pp. 32—52. Berkeley: University of California Press.

————. 1984b. On Person, Reciprocity, and Change: Explorations of Burridge in Bun. Paper prepared for the Wener-Gren Foundation Symposium no. 95, "Sepik Research Today," Basel, Switzerland, August, 1984.

————. 1987. Exchange and Systems of Competitive Equality in Melanesia. Paper read at the Annual Meeting of the Association for Social Anthropology in Oceania, Monterey.

————. n.d. The Mundugumor: From the Field Notes of Margaret Mead and Reo Fortune. Unpublished manuscript.

Mead, Margaret. 1963 [1935]. Sex and Temperament in Three Primitive Societies. New York: William Morrow.

Read, Kenneth. 1955. Morality and the Concept of Person among the Gahuku-Gama. Oceania 25:233—282.

7

Why Wape Men Don't Beat Their Wives: Constraints Toward Domestic Tranquility in a New Guinea Society

William E. Mitchell

The West, as we know, is fascinated with violence. Western journalists, film makers, and anthropologists working in New Guinea have made the island famous for head-hunting, cannibalism and male-female antagonism. The range of New Guinea societies, however, is great. While the gentler societies lack the riveting appeal of those that are more flamboyantly aggressive, they can be instructive. The Wape of Papua New Guinea's Sandaun (formerly West Sepik) Province are a case in point. Like many other Melanesian peoples, the egalitarian Wape live in a mountainous tropical forest habitat in sedentary villages and are slash-and-burn horticulturalists. Marriage occurs through bridewealth payments, polygyny is allowed but rare, postmarital residence is generally virilocal, and patrilineal clans are ideally exogamous while patrilineages are strictly so.[1] But the Wape differ from a number of the societies with whom they share these customs: Wape men do not beat their wives. This does not mean that conjugal relations are always harmonious, but it is unusual for a man to slap his wife and I know of no instances where a woman suffered an injurious beating from her husband.

Because wife-beating is an accepted custom in many parts of Papua New Guinea and considered by the government to be a serious public health problem (Toft 1985), in this paper I identify some of the factors or constraints that help explain the comparative tranquility of Wape domestic life. These constraints—located on various but intersecting sociocultural, psychological, historical, ecological and physiological levels of analysis—are inextricably bound together in a complex circular relationship. Our present knowledge of this relationship does not warrant the postulating of constraints operating on one level as being more important than those on another, so the general tranquility of Wape domestic life cannot be explained by a simple "cause and effect" model favored by an experimental positivistic science. The explanatory model proposed here is an associational one, more descriptive than causal, whose very circularity is essential to the explanation.[2]

The data for this study, including a review of relevant court records, were collected during an eighteen month field trip in 1970–1972 and brief revisits in 1982 and 1989. Although I have visited many of the villages of the approximately 10,000 Wape during my three trips to Wapeland, my view of Wape society and culture is as seen from Taute village, my principal fieldwork site.

CORRELATES OF WAPE DOMESTIC TRANQUILITY

Ethos and Emotions

The ethos of Wape society is markedly pacific. Although the society is not without its points of stress and the people not without passion concerning their personal relationships, the overall affective thrust of social life is to keep emotions, especially those that might lead to violence, under control. Even before Western contact, when enemy villages engaged in pay-back killings, the attacks might be years apart. Some Wape villages, on learning that the invading whites had banned warfare, abandoned the custom even before government patrols could intervene. During my fieldwork, I never saw a physical fight between men, between women, or even between children. The preferred Wape response to potential violence is conciliatory, not confrontational.[3] When dissension in village life does occur, as it inevitably does, quarrels tend to be defused before culminating in physical violence or, if someone does strike another, he or she does not strike back. As a stranger to Wapeland, I had the first of several personal lessons in their gentle interaction style a few days after I moved into Taute village. When I shouted at a group of children crowding onto the raised and rotting veranda of our temporary house to get off, a man who had befriended me said reprovingly, "Speak softly!" The Wape perceive expatriates, especially men, as unpredictable and potentially bellicose. To gain some control over expatriate emotions, villagers place magical ginger under the house ladder of a visiting patrol officer — and I imagine a visiting anthropologist as well — to soothe him as he climbs down into the village. Another time, when I rebuked a group of men during the building of our house for cutting down the ornamental shrubs that hid the outhouse, they simply turned and silently walked away.

Enculturating a resident anthropologist or Wape children is not always an easy task, but the methods are identical. Aggressive acts are met with disinterest. An enraged toddler is left alone to kick and scream on the ground until her or his reason returns. Children and anthropologists soon learn that public aggression is an embarrassing and non-rewarding activity. Consequently, the Wape restrain the expression of negative emotions toward others and are generally friendly in their everyday village activities. Antipathy toward another person is rarely expressed directly in public though it may be expressed privately to a confidant.

Still, there are times when adults feel so personally transgressed and furious that they must do something more drastic than confiding their anger to a friend. Several alternatives are available. An offended person may gossip openly to others about the offense or, as everyone knows some sorcery, privately execute a punitive ritual. Or, for example, if a man's dog attacks and cripples a woman's piglet and the man makes no attempt to correct the wrong, in desperation she might go to his house and, standing outside, deliver a self-righteous harangue heard by all the neighbors while the transgressor and his family sit silently within. If the problem escalates, a meeting of the entire village is called by one of the concerned parties and anyone remotely involved with the problem should attend; not to go is to compromise one's integrity or innocence. Gathered on the front verandas of the houses surrounding the central plaza, men, women, and even children have their say until finally, perhaps several hours later, a consensus is reached.

I have stressed here the pacific ethos of Wape culture as well as indicated some of the actions resorted to when an individual's emotions must be expressed outwardly, namely, gossiping, sorcery, haranguing, and public meetings. However, none of these actions — regardless of the degree of aggressive intent — usually involve direct physical violence. Later I will discuss two exceptions to this finding that document a darker side of Wape emotions.

The Gaze of the Ancestors

The Wape are not conciliatory solely because they have been socialized to believe that public anger is often unrewarding or humiliating. There is a powerful sanctioning agent that helps to keep their behavior in check: the spirits of their dead ancestors. As Hollan (1988:56) has similarly observed for the Toraja of Indonesia, "Fear of supernatural retribution and social disintegration motivate the control of anger and aggression." The Wape believe that at death, an adult's spirit returns to lineage lands in the forest. The spirit is also believed to be a frequent visitor to the village, where it looks after its descendants by sending illness and bad luck to family enemies. There is a high incidence of illness in Wapeland, testimony enough to ancestral power.

One night while visiting on a neighbor's veranda, I idly inquired about a slight, unidentifiable sound and learned that it was my host's dead father benevolently signaling his presence. Ancestral spirits are believed to see and hear all. This strongly discourages arguments among villagers because a spirit may avenge a descendant by negatively influencing an opponent's hunting, gardening or personal health. For this reason also, individuals occasionally express their anger publicly in Tok Pisin, the region's *lingua franca,* so the older ancestors who never learned it can't understand what is being said.

Frequent disagreements among family members or neighbors can jeopardize the welfare of the entire village. To appease the ancestors, a conciliatory ritual must be held where the opponents speak out to them, announcing that they are now friends and asking the spirits to desist in the punitive interventions.[4] A husband also knows that his wife's agnates as well as her classificatory mother's brothers are concerned about her welfare and, if he mistreats her, may resort to their ancestors or sorcery.

Gender Proximics

Another important factor pertaining to the absence of wife-beating is that Wape society, while acknowledging male-female differences in terms of dress and division of labor, is organized not to polarize gender differences but to de-emphasize them. Husbands and wives use the same paths and sleep together in the same house with their children. Village boys and girls, including teenagers, play at ease with one another. The lightly constructed houses are close together so that aural privacy is at a minimum; even a modestly raised voice is heard by all the neighbors who are also relatives. Menstruating mothers and daughters are not secluded in menstrual huts but remain at home where husbands, if they are not going hunting, continue to eat their wives' food. At puberty, boys begin to sleep separately in a village bachelors' house but they still interact daily with their parents and siblings and usually take their meals with them at home. Nor are boys or youths secluded from their mothers and sisters for initiation into manhood as in some New Guinea societies, where, often brutally, they are cleansed of female contamination in preparation for a warrior's career.

Female Status and Strategies

This is also a society where women and girls do not provide all of the child care. My tape-recorded interviews with male informants are punctuated with a baby-sitting father's asides to his restless toddler or the hungry cries of his infant. Fathers, as well as sons, take an active part in the care of infants and toddlers, especially when the mother is in the forest processing sago or collecting firewood.

This brings us to another important factor to explain why Wape husbands do not beat their wives: Wape women produce most of the food eaten. A typical meal consists of sago jelly with boiled greens – both the result of women's labor – and, with luck, a scrap of meat. While hunting is of great ritual and social importance to men, the introduction of the shotgun has seriously, and in some areas ruinously, depleted wild game.[5] Pigs, of which there are few, are killed primarily for ceremonial exchanges among kin. As monogamy, both in the known past and present, is the Wape norm, a husband is dependent upon a single wife to feed him.

Another point is that a young woman has considerable say in the choice of a husband, signaling a young man in whom she is interested by slipping him a small present of food or tobacco. If possible, women prefer to marry within their natal village and rarely marry into a village that is more than an hour or two walk from their father and brothers. Throughout a wife's marriage — and divorce is unusual — she and her husband are in close contact with her agnatic kin through a continuing series of economic exchanges that necessitates back-and-forth visiting while her brothers hold special ritual sanctions over her children, members of her husband's lineage. By the same token, she is tied to her mother's lineage too, especially to her classificatory mother's brothers who, as already indicated, watch over her well-being and whose homes are available as a place of refuge. A woman who feels that her husband is abusive to her does not hesitate to move in with relatives, where she may stay for a week or more until they return with her to her husband's house. In no case may he seek her return. In the meantime, he becomes dependent on his agnates' wives to feed him or must find his own food. Neither choice is a pleasant one.

The women of a hamlet, or at least the one in which I lived, develop strong solidarity bonds, something I only learned through observation. In the unlikely event that a couple becomes so angry during a quarrel that they begin to shout at each other, women of the hamlet, a few sometimes armed with large sticks, descend upon the house and stand around it until the woman joins them outside.

A factor that relates to the interaction style of women is that they usually do not act in ways to further provoke or escalate a husband's anger towards them but are able to terminate his abuse with a very dangerous and ritualized action. While both Wape men and women are highly sensitive to personal shaming, when a wife is deeply humiliated or shamed by her husband's behavior towards her, she usually does not return the insult but instead attempts suicide. While female suicide attempts are not uncommon in Papua New Guinea, in most communities they appear to be more frequently precipitated by a husband's brutal beatings, as among the Gainj (Johnson 1981) and Kaliai (Counts 1980), than by his shaming words.

Three young wives of our small hamlet unsuccessfully attempted suicide while I lived there by drinking poison made from the root of the deadly derris vine. Interestingly, in each case the woman lived in a household with her husband and one of his parents. In two of the cases a precipitating event was criticism by her husband for not supplying enough food for the family.

There are no reliable suicide statistics for Wape society. But, on the basis of my own data and that of Dr. Lynette Wark Murray (personal communication 1988), the experienced missionary physician who patrolled Wapeland during my initial fieldwork, suicide attempts by unhappy wives, although hushed up by the community, do occur and follow a definite cultural pattern.[6] Because an in-marrying wife's suicide is deeply stigmatizing to the husband's lineage, a woman who survives an attempted suicide finds herself the center of solicitous community attention. It is a desperate way to "get even" with an overly critical or abusive husband but, in the cases I observed, most effective, with the added compensation that it generated a favorable change in his domestic demeanor.

Although Wape men do not often commit suicide (I heard of only one inexplicable case), there is a corresponding dark side to men's behavior. While in the field I observed two instances (Mitchell 1987:197–203) and learned of several others where a man, said to be temporarily possessed by a wandering ghost, attempted to attack fellow villagers with his bow and arrows (cf. Langness 1965). These amok attacks occur only to men and are episodic, often with long periods of lucidity between them. A man so possessed is considered "crazy" by other villagers and is not held completely responsible for his actions. Although the target of a man's attack is socially diffuse with the opportunity to direct part of his aggression toward his wife, he never does.

Diet and Drugs

While the use of drugs, including alcohol, cannot alone make wife-beaters out of husbands, it should be noted that the Wape do not have easy access to alcohol, as is true in some parts of Papua New Guinea where wife-beating is culturally accepted. The addictive substances that are available to the Wape, namely tobacco and betel nut, are not gender differentiated: men and women alike are heavy users of both substances.

Severe protein and caloric deficiency are characteristic of the Wape diet and may, in a highly generalized way, be related to their pacific temperament and domestic tranquility. Sago is notoriously low in nutrients and the mountain-dwelling Wape, unlike most sago eaters who live on the coast or along large rivers, cannot obtain adequate protein from fish. Wape soils are poor and, although sago is supplemented with seasonal garden produce, gardens are small, unfenced and poorly cultivated. Medical growth and development studies indicate the birth weight of the Wape infant is one of the lowest reported in the world and subsequent growth in height and weight is slow with the onset of secondary sex characters correspondingly delayed (Wark and Malcolm 1969). For example, a girl's first menstrual period occurs at a mean age of 18.4 years. There also is a progressive and marked loss of weight with age in both male and female adults. Many villagers suffer from chronic upper respiratory infections and malaria is holoendemic and uncontrolled. Recent studies indicate that the health problems of the Wape are still severe (Pumuye 1985; Division of Health Department of West Sepik 1986). It is hardly surprising that Wape ceremonial life is centered upon curing festivals (Mitchell 1990).

Christian Mores and Government Law

Finally, we must consider the influence of the Catholic and Protestant missionaries and local government officials in respect to the absence of wife-beating in Wapeland. All Wape villages are under the influence of either Christian Brethren or Franciscan missionaries while, more recently, an indigenous fundamentalist church, New Guinea Revival, has also gathered considerable support. All of these churches are strong advocates of a harmonious family life and marital amity. The laws of the country further support these values and government and health officials distribute literature and lecture to villagers about them. But, as we already have seen, "domestic peace" is not a new idea to the Wape people. The importance of the churches' and state's moral rhetoric and sanctions regarding domestic life is not one of innovation, but the reinforcement on another level of the contemporary Wape society's own tradition of domestic tranquility.

CONCLUSIONS

To answer the question of why Wape men don't beat their wives in a country where wife-beating is a major public health problem, I have noted and discussed some of the implicated constraints. These can be summarized as follows:

- A pacific and conciliatory cultural ethos supported by churches and the state
- Non-polarization of gender differences
- Punitive intervention by watchful ancestral spirits
- Women instrumental in selecting their husbands
- Monogamy
- Married couples domiciled among watchful relatives
- Wives as principal food providers
- Near absence of alcohol
- Nutritionally deficient diet
- Solidarity bonds among hamlet women
- Threat of a wife's suicide if her husband shames her

- Women's agnates and classificatory mother's brothers responsive to their welfare

None of these constraints alone can explain the relatively tranquil nature of Wape domestic life. When viewed as an interrelated cluster, though, these constraints help us understand the absence of wife-beating. If a society has very poor nutrition, a pacific conciliatory ethos, low access to alcohol, watchful and succoring neighbors and relatives, vengeful ancestors, husbands dependent on a single wife for sustenance, non-polarization of the sexes, and the threat of a wife's suicide if shamed by her husband, it is difficult to conceive of a marital relationship progressing to a state where a wife is being beaten.

However, this inquiry into the absence of Wape wife-beating has uncovered another form of Wape domestic violence – attempted suicide by females – with a cultural scenario of its own. In desperation, wives humiliated by their husbands "beat up" on themselves and, indirectly, their spouses by attempting to poison themselves. The difference is that attempted suicide, unlike being beaten, is a self-empowering act of rectitude, an aggressive action against one's person that, if one survives, may reshape a damaged husband-wife relationship more equitably. To Wape men, the possibility of a wife's attempted suicide is a sobering symbol for the limits of oppression. To women, it is a desperate act fraught with peril, an act some know is worth the risk.

NOTES

Versions of this paper were presented at the session "Wife-Beating and Wife-Battering: Cross-Cultural Perspectives," at the 1987 American Anthropological Association meeting, Chicago, and in the symposium on "Domestic Violence in Oceania" at the 1989 Association for Social Anthropology in Oceania meeting in San Antonio. This paper originally appeared in *Pacific Studies*, Volume 13, Number 2 (July 1990). I am grateful to Professor Dorothy Counts for suggesting that I prepare a "negative case" on domestic violence from my Wape data and for her subsequent comments. I also wish to thank Dr. Lynette Wark Murray for sharing with me her data on the Wape and Professors Pauline Aucoin and Annette Weiner for their comments on the paper. Fieldwork was supported by a grant (#1 RO1 MH 18039 SSR) from the National Institutes of Health and a faculty research grant from the University of Vermont.

1. For a fuller account of Wape society see Mitchell (1973, 1978a, 1978b, 1987, 1988a, 1988b, and 1990).

2. I wish to emphasize that the explanation offered here is culture specific. For example, the domestic placidity documented for the Dugum Dani in West Irian by Heider (1979:78—84) or, in this volume, for the Nagovisi in the Solomon Islands by Jill Nash, cannot be explained by the same constraints discussed here. For an

exploratory attempt to rank factors in a "multiple correlate" model on the reverse problem of wife-beating and family violence, see Burgess and Draper (1989).

3. On the basis of my 1982 and 1989 observations and information gleaned from villagers as well as government officials and health workers who deal directly with the people, this conciliatory characteristic of Wape domestic life has not changed since my 1970—1972 fieldwork.

4. Because the two shotguns in Taute village were owned collectively by hamlet members, poor hunting was usually explained in terms of ancestral revenge for village dissension. For a detailed discussion of the relationship among hunting, ancestral spirits, and village arguments see Mitchell (1973 and 1987:167—187).

5. During my 1989 visit, however, I was told that wild game is gradually reappearing due to the current prohibition against firearms because of disorder in other parts of the province.

6. See Mitchell (1987:204—208) for ethnographic details regarding the ritualized aspects of Wape wives' suicide attempts.

REFERENCES CITED

Burgess, Robert I., and Patricia Draper. 1989. The Explanation of Family Violence: The Role of Biological, Behavioral, and Cultural Selection. *In* Family Violence, vol. 2 of Crime and Justice: A Review of Research. Michael Tonry and Norval Morris, eds. Pp. 59—116. Chicago: University of Chicago Press.

Counts, Dorothy A. 1980. Fighting Back is Not the Way: Suicide and the Women of Kaliai. American Ethnologist 7:332—351.

Division of Health Department of West Sepik. 1986. Annual Report. Wewak: Wirui Press.

Heider, Karl. 1979. Grand Valley Dani: Peaceful Warriors. New York: Holt, Rinehart and Winston.

Hollan, Douglas. 1988. Staying "Cool" in Toraja: Informal Strategies for the Management of Anger and Hostility in a Nonviolent Society. Ethos 16:52—72.

Johnson, Patricia Lyons. 1981. When Dying is Better than Living: Female Suicide among the Gainj of Papua New Guinea. Ethnology 20:325—334.

Langness, L. L. 1965. Hysterical Psychosis in the New Guinea Highlands: A Bena Bena Example. Psychiatry 28:258—277.

Mitchell, William E. 1973. A New Weapon Stirs Up Old Ghosts. Natural History 82:74—84.

———. 1978a. The Living, Dead, and Dying: Music of the New Guinea Wape. Folkways Record Album No. FE 4269.

———. 1978b. On Keeping Equal: Polity and Reciprocity among the New Guinea Wape. Anthropological Quarterly 51:5—15.

———. 1987. The Bamboo Fire: Fieldwork with the New Guinea Wape (second edition). Prospect Heights, Ill: Waveland Press.

———. 1988a. The Defeat of Hierarchy: Gambling as Exchange in a Sepik Society. American Ethnologist 15:638—657.

———. 1988b. Magical Curing [videocasette film]. Prospect Heights, Ill: Waveland Press.

———. 1990. Therapeutic Systems of the Taute Wape. *In* Sepik Heritage: Tradition and Change in Papua New Guinea. Nancy Lutkehaus et al., eds. Pp. 428—438. Durham, NC: Carolina Academic Press.

Pumuye, Hilary. 1985. The Assessment of Nutritional Status of Children in the Lumi District, West Sepik Province, Papua New Guinea. Community Education for Disadvantaged Children Pilot Project Report, University Printery.

Toft, Susan. 1985. Domestic Violence in Papua New Guinea. Papua New Guinea Law Review Monograph No. 3. Boroko.

Wark, Lynette, and L. A. Malcolm. 1969. Growth and Development of the Lumi Child in the Sepik District of New Guinea. Medical Journal of Australia 2:129—136.

8

Factors Relating to Infrequent Domestic Violence Among the Nagovisi

Jill Nash

INTRODUCTION

This paper discusses the infrequency of physical violence between spouses among the Nagovisi of North Solomons Province (Bougainville), Papua New Guinea. I offer a primarily ethnographic account in discussing this situation. I also will make cross-cultural comparisons when possible.

Sample Size and Estimated Incidence of Violence Between Spouses

There are no figures available for a statistical survey among the Nagovisi, although I can provide estimates of the frequency of various kinds of disputes, especially violent ones. I did not have much interest in domestic violence during my fieldwork, due perhaps in part to its infrequent occurrence; I was much concerned, however, with kinship, family life, and conflict resolution. My sample consisted of several villages whose total population numbered about 200. I heard news about an additional 300 or so people, whom I did not see regularly, but whose genealogies I knew and most of whom I personally recognized. During the two and one half years during which I lived in Pomalate Village,[1] I recorded three episodes in the village, and one from a village just outside the study area, in which a husband assaulted his wife, for a total of four cases.

My impression is that incidents of physical assault between spouses are rare. I never witnessed violence between husband and wife. I did see a physical struggle between brother and sister, between female relatives, and between men. I also heard children crying as a result of being hit by a parent (but did not see the blow struck) or in the course of a tantrum which was part of the provocation for the parent to hit. I also saw a number of arguments which involved shouting or verbal insult. Informants told me news of the day including any violent arguments in other villages. I also heard accounts of violent arguments which had taken place long ago. I no doubt missed hearing of some fights, but Nagovisi take a great interest in conflict, and since most of it leads to court resolution, it is widely discussed. It is unlikely that any occurrence of domestic violence would remain a secret.

FORM AND CAUSES OF ARGUMENTS
BETWEEN HUSBAND AND WIFE

Verbal Insult. As it is a primary way of disputing, a serious insult requires litigation and usually payment of a fine, just as in the case of an injury. Although the amounts asked for insult are less than for injury, in a sense, insults and injuries are considered to be in the same legal category, if not equivalent. Women can compete very well with men in verbal sparring as they cannot in physical conflict; in fact, I have argued that talk (in general) is the source of women's efficacy (Nash 1987). In the past, insults might have led to retaliation with deadly force. Today, this is not the case. Possible reasons for this are discussed below. The following is an example of the sort of insult which may pass between husband and wife: Bernadette[2] asked her husband, Francis, to clean up their toddler daughter's faeces. He said he didn't have a shovel. She then said he should shovel it with his tongue. He got mad and went home to his sister. The sister demanded payment (which she received) for this insult. Bernadette was "dancing with anger" when she said this. Her husband was very lazy and many people felt that his behavior helped to cause the argument. Nevertheless, Bernadette was wrong to say such an insulting thing; consequently, it was appropriate for Francis' sister to ask for a fine.

Property Destruction. Informants claimed that both men and women might destroy property during arguments. My observations seemed to show this to be a particularly female expression of anger. The Nagovisi say that women destroy property because they cannot trounce their husbands, and that husbands destroy property because they do not want to kill their wives.

> Agnes chopped up her husband Simon's bag while we all watched. At the same time, she recited her grievances in a tense and angry voice. Because Simon had declared himself "married" to his newly-widowed sister-in-law, Agnes claimed that Simon had only pretended to show sorrow for his brother and had been lusting after the dead man's wife for a long time. No one intervened.

I have stated elsewhere that the triggering causes of arguments between spouses often seem to be trivial (Nash 1974). These causes include "surprise at the wife's having bought a new saucepan, the alleged withholding of tobacco from the husband, or nagging by the wife that her sick husband seek medical aid" (Nash 1974:65). Although male informants stated that "laziness" might be a reason for a man to hit his wife, in fact, failure to fulfill domestic duties did not appear to be a reason for actual arguments I heard about. Some women who were a bit lazy were never hit nor yelled at, and another, who was not at all lazy, was hit once by her husband, allegedly for not fixing his food as quickly as he wanted it. In some cases, the discovery of a spouse's adultery may cause an argument; in other cases, it is unacknowledged by husband and wife, even when it results in the conception of a child.[3] I do not recall arguments between husband and wife concerning bridewealth amounts or pig prices (such disputes would involve more than a married couple), nor regarding such matters as whether cocoa should be planted.

My field notes show that certain couples seem to go through difficult periods of nearly continual disagreement in which one or the other may resort to violence. Also, some individuals seem more ready to argue, or to hit in argument. These people were fairly young, recently married, and not accustomed to living with each other. One middle-aged man appeared to be having what I hesitantly call a mid-life crisis. Thus, the biographies of individuals and the circumstances of a marriage seem to have more explanatory value regarding disputes, especially violent ones, than do more proximate causes; this observation fits with the lack in Nagovisi of a cultural pattern of the use of violence in arguments.

CULTURAL FACTORS REGARDING THE CONSEQUENCES OF ARGUMENTS AND THEIR RESOLUTION

The consequence of an argument between husband and wife may involve any or all of the following: physical separation or withdrawal from part of domestic life, court hearing, assessment and payment of fine, and reconciliation. Background information on cultural and social practices is provided below to make these alternatives intelligible.

The Nagovisi are matrilineal (i.e, social groups are formed by recognizing kinship links between women and their children) and uxorilocal (i.e., a man moves to his wife's settlement at marriage). Descent groups include moieties, clans, and named and unnamed lineages. Villages are based on a core of matrilineally related women, usually comprising the female members of one or several named or unnamed lineages. Their imported husbands (and fathers) also are residents, as are unmarried males of the matrilineage. Households generally consist of a nuclear family, although it is not inappropriate for unattached relatives (but not the wife's mother) to be included.

Nagovisi have become increasingly uxorilocal since the introduction of cocoa as a cash crop in the 1960s. Before that time, uxorilocality was the ideal, but other forms of residence were tolerated and practiced more frequently than they are today. My survey in 1969/1970 showed 81 percent of all couples residing uxorilocally.

Due to the fact of uxorilocal residence, a man leaves his natal village at marriage to move into the village of his wife. Because most (71 percent) marriages are made between people whose natal villages are less than two miles apart, men find it convenient to visit the homes of their sisters and parents. It is here that a man will return in the event of serious marital discord. In the event of serious disagreements between husband and wife, either may act. Sometimes, a wife will put her husband's belongings outside as a sign that he is to move back to his natal village. More often, a husband will leave of his own accord.[4] When this happens, negotiation begins, the result of which is usually that the wife's kin will pay valuables to the husband's kin. Then the husband returns. By leaving, the husband has raised the ante, so to speak, or registered the seriousness of the event occasioning his departure (e.g., in the example cited above, the directive to use one's tongue as a shovel). He has shown himself to be aggrieved and injured by the treatment of those who are supposed to treat him well.

Husbands can count on unqualified support and sympathy from their matrilineal kin. This is possible because most arguments between husband and wife are not clear-cut cases of wrong-doing on the part of only one spouse, but situations in which the shortcomings of both have figured. Thus, the husband's kin may find it easy to stress the wrongful acts of the wife, ignoring his part in the affair. Another factor in the partisanship of the husband's kin has to do with the balance which should be maintained between affines. Although uxorilocal residence may provide a solidarity group for women which protects them from spousal violence, there is an important advantage for men, too. A man can take an escalating action which is nonviolent by moving to his natal village. This is not seen as a defeat for men, but as shaming wives. It dramatizes the intolerable state that a husband faces during this time of conflict. It is his way of saying that he cannot live with this impossible person.

Men may stay with their wives but cease to eat their wives' food if there is an argument. Usually, he will avoid one food item (e.g., coconut) until a fine has been paid to settle the dispute. The wife continues to cook her husband's food, but is inconvenienced and reminded daily of the unresolved problem.

A favored method of resolving nearly any kind of argument is to go to court. Wrongs can be righted through system of fines, today paid in a combination of cash and shell valuables. Three kinds of wrongs always require such compensation: insult, injury—especially drawing blood—and death (in pre-colonial times). Married couples do not give up their right to sue one another. In fact, the fines paid as a result of arguments are part of the continual adjustments—the evaluation of credits and debits—between husband and wife that go on during the course of a marriage. These adjustments end with the payment (or decision that payment is not required) of death dues after the demise of one of the partners (see Nash 1974 for a longer discussion of these phenomena).

OTHER KINDS OF VIOLENCE

Levinson has recently argued that "wife-beating is part of a broader cultural pattern of violent relationships between persons who reside in the same community" (Levinson 1989:45). I will review below information concerning sexual violence towards women (rape and sexual assault), physical violence towards children, and between women, between men, and between brother and sister. In all of these areas, physical violence is minimal.

Rape. In the course of filling out a questionnaire for the Papua New Guinea Law Reform Commission in 1971, I made inquiries regarding the subject of rape. After much reflection, people recalled a single incident which had taken place 10 miles away in the late 1940s. The rapist had been angry with a male relative of the victim. By and large, people could not quite imagine how rape would work: they said that the woman would cry out and people would come to her aid. Women do not "change their minds" about mutually agreeable fornication to later allege rape. To force a woman to copulate is not considered admirable in any sense, but is disapproved, or more likely considered ridiculous, given the probable consequences. An incident that occurred during my fieldwork may illustrate: a young married woman from my study area was traveling alone to visit relatives in a village about ten miles away. A teenaged male from that village surprised her on the deserted track, indicating his intention to have sex relations with her. The woman slashed the man's shirt with her garden knife, thus repelling him, and proceeded unmolested on her way. This story was retold by men and women in my village with much amusement at the expense of the young man.

Parental Treatment of Children. In Nagovisi, children under the age of five are not usually subject to corporal punishment. With one exception of redirected aggression, in which a mentally unbalanced widow[5] hit her 18-month-old son when her boyfriend told her he would not marry her, any hitting or slapping was directed at older children. This may be for doing something dangerous (e.g., picking through the anthropologist's rubbish pit) as well as for disobedience. I witnessed a struggle between a teenaged girl and her mother in which the daughter was the same size as her mother. In this incident, slaps were exchanged when the girl delayed coming home from church by four hours and did not bring the bread she was supposed to have purchased. The mother's brother came to the assistance of his sister, pulled his niece away, and denounced her.

When older children (aged six to twelve) have tantrums or fight with younger siblings, parents may strike them with their hands or nudge them with their feet. I saw an angry child or heard one screaming only once or twice.

Physical Aggression by Children. Some kinds of physical aggression by little children are ignored. For example, adults react only slightly to a toddler who beats them with a branch. The adult might move out of the way or duck while talking to someone else, but little attention is paid to the behavior. The child is not told to stop.

Children do not usually hit one another in play, nor do I recall chasing and threats to hurt, even though they use knives and sticks as toys. Teasing and insults may cause damage to feelings, however. For example, one five-year-old burst into tears and went home after an older boy mentioned to the general amusement of a group of children that the younger boy had had an erection on a previous occasion. The pattern of going home after an insult starts early.

Discipline by Parents. Parents complain about their children's behavior: frequently heard are the allegations that children are lazy and disobedient. Parents may lecture them on their shortcomings. In Nagovisi, younger children are frightened with warnings about ghosts, snakes or white people, to insure obedience. Informants said that one villager, a former policeman, had punished his son for truancy by the Papua New Guinea police method of "kalabus long san," tying him up in the sun. The child was probably between seven and nine years of age when this happened, since the child quit school after Form II. This is not an indigenous Nagovisi punishment, and all who spoke of this were disapproving.

Child Neglect. Parents in Nagovisi are condemned (by gossip) for being bad parents when their children "do not grow" — are short, thin, or perhaps merely unprepossessing in some way (e.g., subject to insect bites, have especially bad runny noses, or are just shy). A child's growth may be stunted by withholding the appropriate ceremonies in his or her honor (i.e., especially for first-borns), or by not feeding enough. Although this does not fit Western notions of abuse because of the magical concepts involved, it might come closest to a Nagovisi idea of serious and socially disapproved neglect of children. One young widow with four children ranging in age from one- to twelve-years-old appeared to be having trouble feeding her offspring. People would castigate her from time to time and suggest that she ought to remarry. Her very competent mother quite frequently fed and housed the two oldest children.

I should mention that Nagovisi seemed proud of "good" children, even when the children were not their own. People commented favorably upon children who were sturdy, straightforward in their manner, and mature for their age.

Fights Between Women. Women sometimes had arguments with each other which involved name-calling. They could also challenge other women to competitive showing of shell valuables, displays that contained the potential for serious arguments. Also as mentioned above, mother and teen-aged daughter might fight physically. Most conflicts among women seemed to involve those of different lineages, see Nash 1974). I saw the following fight between two women who are classificatory parallel-cousins:

Cecilia stabbed Helena in the head with a comb. The cause was the alleged theft of the comb by Helena's children. Helena had also teased Cecilia, saying she did not have Cecilia's comb, but only had an old broken one. Helena's wound bled briskly for a while and there was much screaming and dramatic gesturing. This resulted in a long court hearing in which Cecilia was denounced. The first fine asked was large, and Cecilia's mother refused to pay, Cecilia herself having no money. Finally they settled on a smaller amount.

Fights Between Men. The fights I saw between men were often intergenerational shouting matches, sometimes aggravated by alcohol. The latter type of argument is discussed separately below. Men were sometimes denounced by other men in angry voices, but did not themselves get angry in return. The causes were varied. Young men at odds with their fathers might tell them to "get out of our village and go back to your own (natal) place." In one instance, a young man spit at his older sister's husband, but physical attacks were more apt to occur if alcohol had been consumed. Young men who had been drinking might attempt to assault their classificatory fathers, but their attempts were fairly ineffectual.

A Struggle Between Brother and Sister. Brothers and sisters are not supposed to fight, but they are responsible for one another's good behavior. Avoidance etiquette and uxorilocal residence makes the expression of strong emotion between brothers and sisters infrequent. Nevertheless, I witnessed one incident, in which a widow and her uterine half-brother struggled publicly. The brother slapped her several times. She had been screaming in support of her lover and chopping holes in her house with a machete. An unrelated man also helped restrain this woman. Afterwards, people said the brother had acted as he had because he was "embarrassed" by his sister's behavior. It was said to have been the right thing to do, and no one suggested that he pay any fine to her or she to him. It is important to stress that the struggle did not stem from a disagreement between the two.

Violence in the Past: Headhunting, Initiation. Like other Solomon Islanders, the Nagovisi took trophy heads in the past during feuding. This practice ended around 1925 with Australian pacification. Old people still had unromantic memories of the days of tribal fighting.

According to informants, the taking of heads might be facilitated by the ingestion of a certain kind of magical powder called *piko,* which was made out of human bone (and other things) at cremations. The effect of *piko* was to turn a man into an angry killer with red eyes and great strength, a *pikonara*. Certain children who showed unusual belligerence were considered to be likely to grow up as *pikonaras*. Although valued in former times, this type of person has disappeared today, according to informants.

An old man in the next village was represented to me as having been a *pikonara* in his youth. People told many stories of his truculence as an adolescent, his numerous stormy marriages, and of his bravery and treachery in World War II. In his old age there was no indication of anything pathological in his personality. On the contrary, he was one of the most intelligent and insightful people in the community. He managed his polygynous household peacefully. The Nagovisi explained that he had become old and was no longer a fighter.

There was no tradition of painful ordeals in adolescent initiation. A small feast might be held for young men after their first killing (or in preparation for it—informants were not clear on this subject), but this was optional. Piercing of the nasal septum was remembered by one informant as very painful: when I asked him whether or not he had cried, he said, "Did I ever!" No ritual significance was attached to this act; it was optional and evidently cosmetic. Girls' initiation, properly done for the first-born daughter on the occasion of her first menstruation, involved no painful acts.

Suicide. Suicide took place in the past and occurs today, sometimes in connection with unhappiness regarding the opposite sex. Protest suicide on the part of young women in the past was directed, not at cruel husbands, but at parents for forcing a marriage (cf. Counts 1980). This kind of suicide was confined to the newlywed bride. This is why parents today, according to informants, do not seek to press unpopular candidates on their daughters. All recent local suicides and attempts I heard of were by men. Men might attempt suicide in reaction to the adultery of their wives. One man killed himself from shame after he was discovered in an adulterous act. Another man killed himself because he believed erroneously that he had killed his child. Sometimes the reasons were obscure; no motive for suicide could be offered, other than hereditary insanity (e.g., "his uncle was crazy, too").

Effect of Alcohol on Violence. It is not possible for me to state now what part alcohol might play today (1991) in arguments. In the late 1960s and early 1970s, only men drank and the bulk of alcohol was consumed at all-night festivities with food and music. At that time, people thought that drinking makes a person lose his strength and, therefore, fights were considered pointless or comic (but see Nero 1990 for a discussion of a situation in which the ability to consume large amounts of alcohol is seen as strength). A sober woman could always evade a drunken man. Women stood together when a drunk was performing. Wives might shout ridicule at drunken husbands for their foolishness, e.g., urinating in public, falling in the mud, dancing wildly, losing clothing, etc. Men did not appear to get angry at this. The only fighting was between men who were drunk; it was fairly ineffectual, except when bottles were used as weapons. Young men got angry at their fathers or other older men when drunk. Men did not seem generally angry at women nor to use drunkenness for an excuse to act on this anger.

One instance of domestic assault took place, however, when the husband was intoxicated. The next morning, when he was sober, he joked about the whole thing—including his own behavior.

COMPARISON AND DISCUSSION

The Nagovisi are different from other societies in that physical violence between married people is neither common nor tacitly condoned. Behavior in the United States presents a marked contrast. According to Straus (1978), in America, a marriage license is a hitting license. Violence between persons who are not related is readily litigable, whereas many barriers still stand in the way of a battered spouse who seeks legal redress, although the situation is slowly changing (Micklow 1988). The contrast here is that Nagovisi have legal recourse in cases of domestic violence, whereas Americans often do not.

Mushanga (1977–78) says in an article on wife-bashing in East African societies that "women ask for it." "Asking for it" consists of ridiculing men and talking back—thus causing the violence to escalate, sometimes to the point of murder. No one believes that women or men wish to be hit in Nagovisi. I do not recall anyone blaming the victim for having provoked violence.

Also, fights in public or in houses with leaf walls draw the attention and intervention of others. People come to the aid of quarrelling couples: they feel that they should interfere. In town, isolation makes it easier to act on violent impulses and to carry them out without interference from concerned relatives or neighbors (cf. Erchak 1984). I knew only one Nagovisi married couple living outside the home area; both were school teachers in Rigo, southeast of Port Moresby, and neither was violent. I heard secondhand of the suicide of a young Nagovisi woman married to a Siwai policeman domiciled in Port Moresby. The woman's uncle had complained to me about her irrational behavior years before this happened.

Two topics to which I have referred above—the influence of matriliny and its concomitants, and the subject of anger—require further discussion. I have described how matriliny-related social features of Nagovisi, including uxorilocality, make it possible for men to separate themselves physically from their wives and thus reduce the possibility of assault. Furthermore, most marriages appear to be congenial. Friedl (1975) has reviewed a whole list of reasons why relationships between husband and wives are not as tense in matrilineal societies as they are in patrilineal ones: ultimately, many of these refer to the fact that the wife is not on trial in a matrilineal society, as she is in a patrilineal one. Nor does the husband in matrilineal societies assume the unenviable position of being a disloyal outsider. In matrilineal societies emotions are not so focused on the marriage tie; rather they are diffused among numerous relatives. Melanesian matriliny, further, has been recently profitably analyzed (Gregory 1982; Strathern 1984; Weiner 1976) as involving a lifelong series of exchanges between affines in which balance is highly valued. In Nagovisi, the idea of reciprocity of actions and material items strongly permeates social behavior (Nash 1987). There is an awareness, from childhood on, that both positive and negative behavior must be repaid.

Although anthropologists are now attempting studies of emotion (Lutz 1988; Rosaldo 1980), the understanding of anger still presents many difficulties. The Nagovisi considered anger to be motivating and energizing; it made possible men's great actions of warfare in pre-European times (Nash 1987). Anger in pre-European times was magically enhanced and the *pikonara* was recognized and valued, if also feared. In domestic relations as I observed them, however, anger was not much in evidence. Crying children were usually labeled "angry" rather than "sad" or "in pain," crying in grief being considered a more adult behavior. Possibly the expression of anger in outbursts is seen as childish and inappropriate for adults. I saw a series of steps in the expression of anger, where insult and property destruction (and for men, withdrawal to the natal village) were enacted first as signs of anger. Social factors do not favor hitting, and therefore it is in a breakdown or loss of control that the occasional instances of domestic violence take place.

Nagovisi seem to take pride in their ability to control the expression of emotion. For example, one informant counseled how important it was in court, for example, to keep one's self-control: "You can't win if you are angry," he said. People dread having their outbursts mocked as a form of gossipy entertainment, as were one woman's cries in labor. Women should be stoic, and the anguished descriptions of perineal pain endured by a young *primipara* were repeated in amusement for weeks by her peers (see also Nash 1987). People often respond angrily, not to an offence itself, but after thinking about it for a while. Thus, angry displays may be rather controlled, as was Agnes' performance, described above.

In summary, domestic violence is rare among the Nagovisi. I would argue that the incidence of domestic violence cannot be zero, however, because some couples will go through difficult times during the course of a marriage and some individuals, by virtue of temperament, are more given to physical violence than are others.

NOTES

Versions of this paper were given at meetings of the American Anthropological Association in Chicago (1987) and at meetings of the Association for Social Anthropology in Oceania in Savannah, Georgia (1988) and San Antonio, Texas (1989). I benefited from the presentations of other members of these sessions and especially from the comments of Dorothy Counts. A slightly different version of this paper appears in Pacific Studies 13(2). I thank the editorial staff of that journal for permission to republish this revision.

1. I was resident in Nagovisi for this time period intermittently between the years 1969 and 1973. Support was provided by National Institutes of Mental Health and the Australian National University.
2. All names are pseudonyms.
3. I should note that people who are aware of some misbehavior on the part of a spouse may "save" their angry reaction until they themselves have caused trouble, and then cite the previous offense as a distraction from or mitigation of their own actions.
4. In the rare event of virilocal residence, the wife leaves.
5. This woman figures in a number of my anecdotes involving physical violence.

REFERENCES CITED

Counts, Dorothy A. 1980. Fighting Back is Not the Way: Suicide and the Women of Kaliai. American Ethnologist 7:332—351.
Erchak, Gerald M. 1984. Cultural Anthropology and Wife Abuse. Current Anthropology 25:331—332.
Friedl, Ernestine. 1975. Women and Men: An Anthropologist's View. New York: Holt, Rinehart and Winston.
Gregory, Chris A. 1982. Gifts and Commodities. New York: Academic Press.
Levinson, David. 1989. Family Violence in Cross-Cultural Perspective. Newbury Park, CA: Sage Publications.
Lutz, Catherine. 1988. Unnatural Emotions. Chicago: University of Chicago Press.
Micklow, Patricia L. 1988. Domestic Abuse: The Pariah of the Legal System. In Handbook of Family Violence, Vincent B. Van Hasselt, Randall L. Morrison, Alan S. Bellack, and Michel Henderson, eds. Pp. 407—434. New York: Plenum.
Mushanga, Timbamanya M. 1977—78. Wife Victimization in East and Central Africa. Victimology 2:479—485.
Nash, Jill. 1974. Matriliny and Modernization: The Nagovisi of South Bougainville. New Guinea Research Bulletin 55, Port Moresby and Canberra: Australian National University Press.

———. 1987. Gender Attributes and Equality: Men's Strength and Women's Talk among the Nagovisi. *In* Dealing with Inequality, Marilyn Strathern, ed. Pp. 150—173. Cambridge: Cambridge University Press.

Nero, Karen. 1990. The Hidden Pain: Drunkenness and Domestic Violence in Palau. Pacific Studies 13(3):63—92. Special Issue: Domestic Violence in Oceania. Dorothy Ayers Counts, ed.

Rosaldo, Michelle Z. 1980. Knowledge and Passion: Ilongot Notions of Self and Society. Cambridge: Cambridge University Press.

Strathern, Marilyn. 1984. Marriage Exchanges: A Melanesian Comment. Annual Review of Anthropology 13:41—73.

Straus, Murray A. 1978. Wife-Beating: How Common and Why? Victimology 2:443—458.

Weiner, Annette B. 1976. Women of Value, Men of Renown: New Perspectives in Trobriand Exchange. Austin, TX: University of Texas Press.

9

Nudging Her Harshly and Killing Him Softly: Displays of Disenfranchisement on Ujelang Atoll

Laurence Marshall Carucci

In parts of the Pacific, the words "domestic violence" conjure up images of men strapping their wives into subservience. The Marshall Islands present a different scenario.[1] Violence does occur there, but it is not necessarily initiated by males. It occurs between siblings and cousins, it is initiated by females as well males, and its very presence so seriously threatens community and family solidarity that it is denied. Nevertheless, intra-family and community violence are integral parts of daily life.

A knowledgeable Marshall Islands man of about sixty patiently explained to me that violence is not found in Ujelang families. It occurs only amongst foreigners. Ujelang people, he insisted, are considerate and loving. I had just witnessed a quarrel between a young couple and knew that physical violence did occur, and that threats of abuse were common. Eventually I understood that he was subtly commenting about foreignness and about the causes of social disruption.

The two who had quarrelled were cross-cousins of the same age. Their marriage was a sanctioned union. Naively, I took them to be very close — "one only" in local terms. Indeed, both were part of a large extended family and members of a small household attached to that larger whole. But these representations of unity did not exhaust their relationship. Because they were members of different clans, the young couple were also opposed, as male and female, as younger and older, as insider and outsider. Each of these opposed components counterbalanced their sameness with foreignness.

The knowledgeable man attempted to tell me how foreignness could be contextually manipulated to lend meaning to the apparent contradictions between what people said and how they acted. Affines, those of different gender and age, as well as people from other lands or other atolls, could be cast as "outsiders" when their actions violated the "codes for conduct" (Schneider 1968) that should be used by group members. As I learned of more instances of violence I began to understand that violence is indeed harmful to the maintenance of solidarity on this small atoll. I also learned how the concept of otherness might expand and contract in order to help maintain a perpetual balance between the necessity for social control and the requirement for close and continuous social alliances.

On Ujelang and Enewetak, the westernmost of the Marshall Islands, wives are seldom severely battered, yet talk about violence and threats of abuse are a communal preoccupation.[2] Indigenous terms of violence permeate daily discourse as mechanisms of social control: *mani* "strike, beat, kill"; *kokurri* "ruin, damage"; *komman joraan* "create harm or damage"; even *maniman nan mij* "beat to death." Though seldom enforced, threats of violence are the means older persons use to control younger siblings and children. Husbands also use threats to control their wives. Significantly, female inflicted magical damage is discussed in similar terms. Violence has a physical form suited to young, warrior-like, men and a magical form suited to old women. Both forms of aggression are dangerous and typify the actions of foreigners. In fact, family members rapidly contain young men's physical violence. Violence inflicted magically is more threatening because it is often lethal, and effective counter magic can be attempted only by a few outsiders who have sources of powerful foreign magic.

While violence on Ujelang and Enewetak is attributed to others, its roots are anchored in patterns of child rearing and socialization. Adults, particularly males, tease children into violence and all boys and girls are taught to throw small paving stones. As boys mature, they replace pebble throwing with wrestling, fighting with fists and clubs, and throwing large rocks. These pursuits, suited to "real men" pose substantial threats that, in the past, were appropriate for young male warriors in training. Circumstances have changed, yet a warrior-like demeanour remains a critical component of masculine Micronesian identity (cf. Marshall 1979; Carucci 1987a). Adolescent males risk ridicule if they continue childish acts like pebble throwing that fail to display real physical prowess. Indeed, Ujelang's first suicide (in 1980) is said to have resulted from a mother's public criticism of her son for actions she considered childlike.

Maturing females are, in contrast, associated with "caring for" and consideration: they epitomize rather than threaten sociality. They create extended families, transmit core elements of identity to their offspring, and maintain the integrity of other social forms. Females are associated with the protected lagoon and with the inhabited village. Women continue to throw pebbles, usually to warn children of impending disapproval or, more aggressively, to respond to the embarrassing quips of suitors. Wrestling is used by older women, but mainly as a form of joking attack, and only the most masculine of Enewetak women fight with their fists. Hurling objects is a woman's mode of physical recourse. An irate wife may throw food, cookware, and a wide array of household items.

Adult women rely on their tongues to fight their battles. While men are said to be physically strong, women become *lej* "acid-tongued." Vociferous vocalization, of course, draws neighbors to the scene. The support of community members bring a physically abusive husband under society's control. As women age they also gain magical skills from their control of internal clan-contained force. Magical skills are often transferred from grandmother to granddaughter within a matriclan and are made efficacious by a mature woman's secret vocal incantations.[3] Evil magic is thought to cause the most violent forms of human suffering, and nearly all severe physical or psychological illnesses are magically induced. Magic is thought to be the most frequent cause of death; death from natural causes is almost an enigma. It is said that no Ujelang or Enewetak people control "bad magic," but magic is said to be a source of danger in all marriages and interactions with outsiders. Many people also modify their dealings with local islanders to avoid (supposedly nonexistent) sorcery.

SOCIAL AND CULTURAL CONTEXTS OF PERSONAL ABUSE

Enewetak and Ujelang are the westernmost of the Marshall Islands. This group of atolls in the central Pacific were granted independence in October 1986 under a compact of Free Association with the United States. The population was reduced to around 140 during World War II (Carucci 1989) but has expanded rapidly in recent years. The group was exiled on Ujelang Atoll from 1948 until 1980 to allow the United States to conduct nuclear tests and related experiments on their atoll. Since 1980, most Enewetak people have returned to their home atoll. Considerable contact is maintained with Majuro and a few other locations in the Marshalls, and recent trust funds to compensate for nuclear-related damages have increased the rate at which outsiders marry into the community. In spite of rapid changes, the group still considers itself to be united by a strong sense of community.

Relations within the community have always been governed by egalitarian ideals and, even though it is ruled by two chiefs, decision making rests with the group. Statuses based on age and gender are not hierarchical, though an elder's position is respected by younger siblings and members of the younger generations. To the degree that overt control over political affairs is taken as a measure, males dominate females. Women have greater access to the magical potency of the clan line than do men, however, and important matters come under greater female control as people move through the life cycle and become ancestors (cf. Carucci 1985).

During childhood, aggressive acts and words are common within the household. Most child rearing is performed by older siblings who seldom use positive reinforcement as a method of socialization. A mother's first warning phrase to deal with undesirable actions, "bad," is followed by "I will beat you." Older siblings use the same phrases, but adults discourage them from physically punishing young children. Indeed, unless a child commits a serious offense, no punishment is forthcoming. Threats of serious violence are followed by inaction. When children chastise younger siblings with slaps or blows, adults reprimand the overseer, even if they do not condone the child's mischief. The same structural logic that unites grandparents and children in opposition to the authority of parents links adults with physically weaker and lower-ranked youngsters against the authority of their older siblings. The standards of how siblings treat one another are social in character rather than abstractly ethical and object oriented. Ujelang strategy teaches youngsters the solidarity of the sibling group (Radcliffe-Brown 1952:66–68) and about external causality. For Americans, events are shaped by individuals who get themselves into and out of situations. Ujelang people act as part of a group to deal with outside occurrences that happen to them. This has critical importance for an understanding of violence.

On Ujelang Atoll the unity of the whole gives people a way to deal with the unpredictability of the outside world (cf. Lutz 1988). In the late 1970s Ujelang residents constantly commented that "RiUjelang, we are all one family." Indeed, the location of the village in the center of the main islet allowed everyone to participate in the affairs of others. From early childhood until death, a person's life is lived in this public arena. Caring for one another – a core requirement for members of a family – is important in the community.

Around puberty boys begin a period of unrestrained free license and exploration not unlike the *taure'are'a* time described by Levy for Tahiti (1973:190 et seq.). During this time the opposition between members of different clans become apparent. Young boys (both cross- and parallel-cousins) refer to one with sibling terms, but young male cross-cousins develop animosities toward each other as a way to preserve close sibling ties with their own sisters who are members of their own clan. Female cross-cousins become similarly disenchanted with one another, though their disputes are less apt to be overt. The newly found antagonisms focus on tales of the sexual exploits of one's siblings. Sexual experimentation among children is coded as play. At puberty a new metaphor of war becomes equally prominent. These sexual battles (cf. Carucci 1980: Ch. II–III) typify the relationships between opposite clans, and youths who formerly interacted as siblings recognize their opposition as cross-cousins.

Disputes involving vocal and physical abuse quite commonly arise among same-sexed youths from different clans. Females, who are culturally restrained from physical violence, vocally defend their brothers. Young men, who are supposed to be bold warriors, force confrontations with male cross-cousins. These confrontations begin with boasting and often escalate into physical violence. They occur in the village—usually in someone's household—but the parties to the disagreement seldom live together. Significantly, disputes between cross-cousins arise between youngsters who were once united by sibling ties as well as by sexual identity. Now faced with their opposition as members of different clans, they feel ambivalence toward their cross-cousins. These ambivalent feelings are expressed in contradictory moments that counterpose fights between cross-cousins with reconciliatory talk couched in terms of siblingship.

The perpetrators of physical violence are young males struggling with the opposing values that separate youth from mature men. Almost certainly seventeen to thirty-five years of age and often inebriated, these fellows are either married and wish they were not, or unmarried and wish they were part of a union. They are, in other words, similar to the members of those categories to which they do not belong and to which they are opposed. The conditions for their symbolic displays of disaffection arise from this contradictory situation.

The ideal Marshallese male is a single warrior who travels around winning physical battles with outside males and sexual battles with females. The same term (*torinae* "war, battle") is commonly applied to both domains. The karate hero Bruce Lee is a modern day analogue of the mythic warrior (Carucci 1980, 1985). *Pojak* "readiness" typifies a warrior's stance and irresistibility (a sort of macho-imbued charisma) characterises his demeanour. During their life cycle, however, males give up these ideal characteristics and are "domesticated"—brought within the female domains of village and household where the responsibilities of providing for a family predominate (cf. Carucci 1985). When performed successfully, these duties help men become village leaders. Leadership positions are valued, but limited in number. Village leaders are "tamer" and less intriguing than are idealized war heroes.

A young married male, who still possesses the attitude and physical form of a warrior, seeks that which he has sacrificed through marriage. His warrior-like actions are often directed toward the person who represents his entrapment, his wife. If he is inebriated, society forgives his behavior because the drink causes him to revert to his naturally aggressive, socially recalcitrant, warrior form (cf. Marshall 1979; Carucci 1987a). This is precisely the sort of performance embodied in the marital disagreement mentioned above. The pair were fighting over the husband's accusations that his attractive wife had slept with her recently pubescent cross-cousin. Indeed, she had joked with the young man, creating reason for jealousy, but there was no evidence of an affair. As the fight escalated, Lahren and Luela each accused the other of infidelity and each denied the accusations. Each insisted the other was crazy and both were correct in that craziness connotes many asocial conditions where interpersonal relationships are out of balance.

Later on the day of the dispute, Luela's grandfather and an elder male from a neighboring land parcel came to visit me. They supported Luela's version of the story (as one would expect of close kin), but condemned her for joking with her cross-cousin. Lahren's actions, they claimed, were wrong because they would damage the marriage. "His thoughts are those of an adolescent male. He thinks he is very strong, a real man, but he does not know how to care for his own family. . . . He goes on and (gets) drunk for a while, walks around for a while, and then returns. And then, in his thoughts, he goes right ahead with his family."

This fight epitomizes the couple's ongoing attempt to define themselves as a legitimately married pair and yet retain the desirable attributes of being single. Luela and Lahren each manipulated one another by claiming the high ground of the adult, and by accusing each other of typical adolescent actions. Luela's joking was appropriate for an unmarried woman but, in her husband's eyes, was evidence of adultery. She contended, however, that she was an ideal married woman while Lahren transformed himself into the irresponsible transient that he accused her of being. Both were trapped between their desire to be treated as adults and the attractions of being single. Alcohol also allowed Lahren to express his temporary rejection of the marriage, since drink transformed his identity into that of an unmarried macho male.

Members of the community with irrevocable ties to both parties were also caught between the different versions of events and sought a new social balance. They warned Luela that adolescent joking is dangerous for married women. They contained Lahren's violence but did not severely sanction it, since severe sanctions might publicly announce that he had abused his marital privileges.[4]

Fights such as theirs are typical of couples in new marriages, but also occur when a pair become disenchanted with one another. By 1989, when Luela and Lahren had four children, their union was stable and disagreements were infrequent.

Why do unmarried males, living instantiations of ideal men, have ambivalent feelings about themselves? One answer lies in the social contradictions that face maturing Marshallese males. Young pubescent males, fourteen to eighteen years of age, often practice their aggressive routines — boasting, competing for the largest catch or most copra, drinking, arguing and, upon occasion, fighting. They are, however, seldom seriously upset with anyone for very long because they are still learning how to portray themselves as young unmarried men. They do not yet face the ambivalence that occurs when they attempt to extend their position. As these young men become older, the disappearance of their cohorts in marriage reminds them of the limited social options that they face. Moreover, irresistibility, which is visible in physical skill and external characteristics (strength, smooth and shiny bronzed skin, jet-black "green-highlighted" hair), is difficult to maintain. As the population of single women in a young man's age bracket diminishes, it is harder for a man to manifest his attractiveness. Mature young women become increasingly interested in other qualities. They may, for example, favor a man with land over one who is physically enticing. Thus, a choice faces the young adult male: marry, and sacrifice his claims to the masculine persona in favor of a future position in the community hierarchy, or remain single and gradually give up the means to maintain his claim to that ideal.

Most young males marry, yet, like Lahren, take on the attributes of single young men when they become disenchanted with marriage. Disillusionment is almost inevitable because it takes years to become a respected elder in the community. In the interim, they have access to power only when they regress to the idealized behavior of the unmarried male warrior.

Single males are always drunk when they enter a household and begin to cause trouble. They may argue with anyone except the youngest and oldest members of the community. If disagreements escalate into fights they never involve female relatives of the same generation. An opponent of the same generation will be another male, usually an older brother or cousin. Or a drunk may attack members of the "plus one" generation. Relatives with whom relationships are strictly governed by respect are apt to be attacked by an inebriated single male since this is the only way for men of low rank to publicly express feelings of disenfranchisement. A man who is in this state of "mindless disinhibition" (MacAndrew and Edgerton 1969; Marshall 1983) or *kadek im bwebwe* "crazy drunk," is not held accountable since he expresses a potential social injustice. Moreover, his drunkenness allows the natural persona of uncontrolled male impulse to emerge in opposition to the unjust constraints of the social order (Carucci 1987a). Close kin help contain the fighting during these moments, and a man's "special mother"(father's younger sister) will plead with him if the fight is serious. Her wails, like those at death, summon the well-socialized spirit of an inebriated young man and stabilize the situation by reuniting his spirit and body.

The condition of in-married young males offers a special opportunity to view how the ambivalence of their situation interacts with definitions of group solidarity. In-marrying men have all of the symbolic weaknesses of newly married indigenous males. In addition, they lack a resident kin network for support and suffer the handicap of not being "really a person of this island." In such cases, the actions of the young male are redefined in terms that distinguish "insider" from "outsider." Outsider actions are always seen as malevolent.

The case of Paisen, a man of about thirty from Saipan, typifies the contradictory situation faced by nearly every in-married young male at some time during his life on the atoll. Paisen had lived on Ujelang for eight years. Originally a sailor, he was adopted by an Enewetak couple, married a local woman, and by 1978 had four children. Ujelang residents often praised Paisen for being a hard worker. Many wished he had married into their families.

In contrast, Paisen's wife, an attractive woman in her late twenties, was renowned on the islet for her sexual activity. On Ujelang (cf. Sahlins 1985), these comments are neither derogatory nor malicious. When Paisen returned to their cookhouse from a drinking circle to find his daughter unattended by the cook fire he accused his wife of attempting to kill the infant through neglect and by sleeping with other men.[5] She could not deny the charges and others agreed.[6]

As the dispute escalated, Paisen, inebriated and upset, threw two large rocks at his wife. At least one of the rocks struck her shoulder, and as she ran away shrieking, her father began yelling at Paisen: "You are really crazy, are you? Leave this place. Just leave, for you are crazy. Are you thinking of killing my daughter? Do you not know the customs of this atoll? Go from this house. Return to your own island and do not think about coming back."

People assessed Paisen's actions differently than they had Lahren's. Paisen was now "very bad." True, his wife had been wrong, but "the people of this atoll do not 'murder' their spouses, they do not throw rocks. In a moment she would have died." When I suggested there were parallels between Paisen and Lahren, others disagreed. Although both had been drinking and both abused their wives, there were differences. Striking and throwing stones were not equivalent, and rock throwing—like the use of knives and guns—was associated with outsiders. In the best circumstances, Paisen was proudly accepted as "one of us." Just as easily, his actions transformed him into a foreigner very different from Ujelang people. He was radically dissociated from "people of this atoll" who "do not murder spouses."

FEMALES AND VIOLENCE

Ujelang associate men with violent acts that are rooted in inherent qualities that tie "maleness" to men's warrior status. They associate females with love and reconciliation, seemingly the antithesis of violence (Carucci 1980). Nonetheless, women use physical force to discipline children, adolescent girls engage in aggressive sexual play, and aging women use supernatural force to control the acts of others.

Mead noted six decades ago (1928) that child socialization in Samoa rests largely with children slightly older than their charges. On Ujelang, children carry babies slung across the hip at an age so young that they weave under the weight. As soon as weaning takes place, youngsters of both sexes take over a good deal of child care. Parents monitor the process, but their role shifts to maintaining harmony among siblings and among the play set which includes relatives and agemates in the neighborhood.

By six or seven years of age girls provide most of the child care, while boys are allowed to range far from home in an unconstrained fashion that continues into marriage. Children admonish younger siblings with phrases like "bad" or "do not (do) your sort of action." When undesired actions continue, scolding is repeated with added emphasis but no enforcement. Physical punishment is so slow in coming that I heard one American comment: "They do not learn how to obey because they go on and on without . . . ever *doing* something about it." Caretakers do move recalcitrant children away from mischief. When infants return to trouble, overseers throw small stones or continue scolding, but do not take decisive action until damage has occurred. Youngsters are hit both by parents and by other children, but battered children are unknown.

Mothers who are principal care givers occasionally swat children, whether they are true offspring, classificatory children, or children through adoption (co-parenthood). The most harsh-tempered mothers beat their children, ring their ears, or drag them by the hair. The latter acts are particularly demeaning since the head is the most highly ranked part of the body. From most women, however, children receive substantial verbal abuse and little physical punishment. This aligns with indigenous stereotypes that categorize outspoken and independent women as "disagreeable or mean-tempered," in possession of "sharp mouths (tongues)." In other words, females who are charged with maintaining the solidarity of the extended family and clan, anchor their punishments in thought and talk instead of action. While these punishments, in their incipient form, are obviously less violent than the physical responses of males, they may be more volatile and dangerous when extended into the realm of magic. Indigenous terms equate malevolent magic and physical violence. Whereas the latter is characteristically associated with males in an ambivalent cultural situation, the former is controlled by females who are denied access to the use of physical force.

"The thoughts of that woman, so great is their damaged character, you could never weigh them." With these words a man warned me of the dangers of an Ujelang woman's magic. People generally say that malevolent magic, like other hostile behavior, is unknown on Ujelang Atoll. Bad magic is attributed to others, particularly to Marshall Islanders, Solomon Islanders,

New Guinea residents, and outsiders to Enewetak and Ujelang. Nonetheless, I have records of many magically influenced local events and, in most instances, mature Ujelang women were involved.

Magic passes through matriclans and is often manipulated by women. A woman with strong magic either inherited the knowledge from clan elders or purchased it from a magical specialist in the Marshall Islands. Males may also purchase magical knowledge or even receive it from clan elders, but their magic also derives its strength from matrilineal sources.

Male magic is often restricted to curing. Young girls likewise use magical knowledge with positive intent, but as a woman ages "sometimes her thoughts are warped" and it is such women who use magic for manipulative purposes.[7] Men who use physical violence and women who practice malevolent magic are both upset with perceived social injustice. Women use love magic and potentially lethal magic to reimpose a morally just order to social relationships that they believe are out of balance.

On Ujelang, evil magic is never practiced openly since this act would contradict the contention that magic does not exist. Women are said, however, to be responsible for magical harm, and the discursive forms used to talk about male physical abuse are also used to describe damage from sorcery. While the blows and death threats of mature single men are dangerous, people fear older women's magic far more. Not only are the effects of magic more lethal than physical aggression but, because magic uses clan force that has a supernatural source, humans have a limited ability to assess the potential damage and to bring the situation back into control.

CONCLUSIONS

A cursory glance at interaction among Marshall Islanders might lead one to draw undue parallels with family violence in the West. Because physical aggression may well be directed against women by young men, one may infer that domestic violence is instigated by men and endured by women. A closer look, however, shows this interpretation to be simplistic and naive.

First of all, violent activities on Ujelang are used to display feelings of disenfranchisement and discontent. Children are never beaten for "wrongs against nature," and adults who use physical beatings or magic do so to communicate feelings of social injustice that must be brought into balance. The people of Ujelang are not empowered with a Western individuality or with the concomitant ability to shape events (cf. Lutz 1988).

Secondly, violent acts occur because they are appropriate for certain role prototypes, not because they are inherent in persons. Young women usually construct their identities using ideal female attributes, but women with the "thoughts of men" may employ physical abuse to communicate their chosen social selves. Likewise, many men use physical force to communicate part of their warrior-like identity, but not all men adopt such aggressive personal styles. Identities, therefore, are actively constructed out of cultural signifiers that take on meaning in relation to prototypes of male and female discourse and practice (cf. Carucci 1980, 1985, 1987b; Shore 1981; Strathern 1981, 1988).

Marshall Islands men and women use violence to point out domestic and village injustice. Restricted abuses may occur in interactions between members of adjacent generations or among siblings, but the most dangerous violence takes place between wives and husbands and between in-laws. Small acts of punishment among kin escalate into volatile forms of abuse among non-kin. Accordingly, men may physically "murder" (beat) their spouses and women "beat their husbands to death" with magic.

Solidarity, rooted in the ideology of bilateral extended families but also applied to the entire community, is the antithesis of violent interaction (cf. Carucci 1980: Chapters II–III). At an ideological level, Ujelang people see both magical and physical violence as typical of outsiders and severe violent acts are consistently attributed to them. For example, residents of New Guinea or the Marshall Islands are said to use the most dangerous forms of magic, while Trukese are particularly "murderous" since they fight with knives and machetes. Even within the community, the most violent actions are envisioned between spouses and in-laws—foreigners who have been brought into the domestic unit (Fortes 1943–44). The violent acts of Paisen are easily recast into those of a foreigner while those of Lahren are attributed to a family that acts "unlike us."

Violent activities are also balanced throughout the life cycle. Ultimately, however, the overt, aggressive acts of young men are less threatening than is the internal, potentially lethal, magical aggression of aging women. Physical acts are contained by the group who surround young men and restrain them while magical acts remain threatening precisely because their parameters cannot be easily delimited and contained. Most importantly, both males and females have ways to express their discontent that line up with the shifting balance of power in the community.[8] The male ideal type, the single roaming warrior, is ultimately replaced by a sedentary male who is partly constrained by matrilines he does not control (cf. Carucci 1985; Kahn 1986). His physical aggression, easily contained by the group, is a metonym of the ambivalent male position. In contrast, females—who initially lack the freedoms young men enjoy—gradually accumulate matrilineal power that expands with the successful transmission of female reproductive force. Their use of magical force—physically passive yet covert, supernaturally inspired, and difficult to control—increases with their own power and age.

To Ujelang residents, both physical and magical violence are inevitable expressions of the inherent capacities of men and women. While mortals may invert these natural forces for ritual purposes, in joking, or as an expression of personal style, they should not believe that, in so doing, they eliminate the distinctions. For earthly beings, there is only the hope of maintaining balance among them.

NOTES

1. A different version of this paper appears in *Pacific Studies* (Volume 13, Number 3, Summer 1990). I would like to thank the editor of *Pacific Studies* for permission to publish in this volume.

2. Research for this contribution was conducted on Ujelang Atoll between August 1976 and September 1978 and on Enewetak Atoll between May 1982 and May 1983. Ujelang research was supported by a grant from the National Science Foundation administered by The University of Chicago while the National Endowment for the Humanities provided funding for work on Enewetak. All interpretations are the responsibility of the author, not of the granting agencies or sponsoring institutions.

3. As indicated below, men also may use magic, but it is primarily manipulated by women and derives its potency from matrilineal sources. As attributes of statuses, things like magical knowledge need not be used solely by females to be associated with them.

4. Lahren here lays claim to mission-inspired rules for adultery, even though he is not a church member. These stiff standards differ significantly from local practice, which permits a wider array of sexual relationships. Luela claims her husband has adhered to indigenous standards in his own conduct.

5. No one was in the cookhouse with Paisen and his wife. I summarize the controversy based on what I overheard from a nearby cookhouse. Only when the encounter became physically threatening did others rush to the scene.

6. Sleeping around could, by indigenous logic, introduce foreign substances into a woman's (white) milk from its connection with the white sperm of her paramours.

7. Thought here includes an emotive component as Lutz notes of *nunuwan* on Ifaluk (1988:93). It is the imbalance of thought/feeling that causes craziness (asocial interaction) for both men and women. The "paths" men and women follow to express their unsettled senses of self stretch along two different vectors.

8. Young women and old powerless men have least access to these modes of expression. Young women threatened by their husbands may take sanctuary with relatives, but old women do not magically kill spouses for them on request. People do fear magical retribution and "straighten" their actions to avoid sorcery. This is fear of the judgments of the magical specialist, however, since evil magic on Ujelang is neither purchased nor performed on behalf of others.

REFERENCES CITED

Carucci, Laurence Marshall. 1980. The Renewal of Life: A Ritual Encounter in the Marshall Islands. Ph.D dissertation. The University of Chicago.

———. 1985. Conceptions of Maturing and Dying in the "Middle of Heaven."
In Aging and its Transformations: Moving Toward Death in Pacific Society.

Dorothy Counts and David Counts, eds. Pp. 107—129. Washington: University Press of America.

―――. 1987a. Jekero: Symbolizing the Transition to Manhood in the Marshall Islands. Micronesica (20): 1—17.

―――. 1987b. Ruwamwaijet im RiAnin: Outsiders Becoming Insiders. A paper delivered at the Annual Meetings of the Association for Social Anthropology in Oceania. Monterey, California.

―――. 1989. The Source of the Force in Marshallese Cosmology. *In* The Pacific Theater: Island Representations of World War II. Lamont Lindstrom and Geoffrey White, eds. Pp. 73—96. Honolulu: University of Hawaii Press.

Fortes, Meyer. 1943—44. The Significance of Descent in Tale Social Structure. Africa 14:362—384.

Kahn, Miriam. 1986. Always Hungry, Never Greedy: Food and the Expression of Gender in a Melanesian Society. Cambridge: Cambridge University Press.

Levy, Robert I. 1973. Tahitians: Mind and Experience in the Society Islands. Chicago: The University of Chicago Press.

Lutz, Catherine A. 1988. Unnatural Emotions: Everyday Sentiments on a Micronesian Atoll and their Challenge to a Western Theory. Chicago: The University of Chicago Press.

MacAndrew, Craig, and Robert Edgerton. 1969. Drunken Comportment: A Social Explanation. Chicago: Aldine Publishing Company.

Marshall, Mac. 1979. Weekend Warriors: Alcohol in a Micronesian Culture. Palo Alto: Mayfield Publishing Company.

―――. 1983. "Four hundred Rabbits": An Anthropological View of Ethanol as a Disinhibitor. *In* Alcohol and Disinhibition: Nature and Meaning of the Link. R. Room and G. Collins, eds. Pp. 186—237. Rockville, Maryland: National Institute on Alcohol Abuse and Alcoholism.

Mead, Margaret. 1928. Coming of Age in Samoa. New York: Morrow.

Radcliffe-Brown, A. R. 1952. Structure and Function in Primitive Society. London: Cohen and West.

Sahlins, Marshall D. 1985. Islands of History. Chicago: The University of Chicago Press.

Schneider, David M. 1968. American Kinship: A Cultural Account. Englewood Cliffs: Prentice-Hall.

Shore, Bradd. 1981. Sexuality and Gender in Samoa: Conceptions and Missed Conceptions. *In* Sexual Meanings: The Cultural Construction of Gender and Sexuality. Sherry Ortner and Harriet Whitehead, eds. Pp. 192—215. Cambridge: Cambridge University Press.

Strathern, Marilyn. 1981. Self Interest and the Social Good: Some Implications of Hagen Gender Imagery. *In* Sexual Meanings: The Cultural Construction of Gender and Sexuality. Sherry Ortner and Harriet Whitehead, eds. Pp. 166—191. Cambridge: Cambridge University Press.

―――. 1988. The Gender of the Gift: Problems with Women and Problems with Society in Melanesia. Berkeley: University of California Press.

10

Preventing Violence Against Women: A Central American Case

Virginia Kerns

It was after dark when Juliana came to get me. "Come quickly," she said. "Thomas is beating my mother." We crossed the yard to Juliana's house, and I could see her grandmother sitting on the steps with her arms folded, a look of subdued anger in her eyes. "No-good man," she murmured. An elderly neighbor, Petrona, stood nearby with another woman, a good friend of Juliana's mother. Petrona called out, "Don't beat your wife, Thomas. Her mother is here." Then both women shook their heads with dismay and Petrona motioned for me to look inside the house. Juliana's mother was leaning against the doorway, her face streaked with tears, while her husband sat on the floor cradling his head in his arms and moaning softly. "Don't cry, *nuguchun* [mother]," I heard him say to her. "Don't cry."

Earlier that day, Juliana's mother had complained to me that her husband spent too much money drinking rum with other men. There was never enough money for food, she protested, adding that she might leave him and go look for work at a citrus plantation in central Belize. "I don't have to beg him for one cent," she said. "I can get some money myself. My mother will take the children. She's old, you know, but Juliana is twelve now and she can help a lot with the other children." She paused, then added, "And if Thomas refuses to leave this house, I'll get some medicine [*arani*] and then he *must go*."[1]

To explain these words and the event fully—to place them in cultural context and also in relation to the personal histories of the principals—would require not just this chapter but a book in itself. The cultural "gestalt" of marital conflict and violence is complex.[2] Even some straightforward questions are difficult to answer briefly at the outset. Why did Juliana say that "Thomas" was beating her mother? What did Thomas mean by calling his wife *nuguchun*, mother? Why did Petrona tell him his wife's mother was there? Who summoned the three women, and why did they stand outside the house watching? What kind of "medicine" did Juliana's mother intend to get? And why did she want Thomas to leave the house if she was planning to leave it herself? I will return to these questions at the end of this chapter, when the answers may be more meaningful, having been given a context.

This case of wife-beating was one of two that I witnessed during a year of fieldwork in a Garífuna (Black Carib) community in Belize, Central America. I was also told of three other episodes that occurred during that year, and about several that had taken place either in the recent past or in different communities. These cases, which both women and men brought to my attention, provide some empirical and ethnographic detail about wife-beating: the incidence, triggering events, types of intervention, levels of violence and severity of abuse or injury, and outcome. By "outcome" I mean whether the abused woman leaves her husband temporarily, permanently, or stays in the relationship.

A central question in many recent studies of domestic violence in the United States concerns outcome: Why *do* some women stay in chronically violent marital relationships? The term "battered wife syndrome" is now used to define "a symptom complex occurring as a result of violence in which a woman has at any time received deliberate, severe, and repeated (more than three times) physical abuse from her husband, with the minimal injury of severe bruising."[3] Research conducted in other countries and a variety of cultural settings suggests that wife-battering is not restricted to the United States or the industrialized West.[4] But neither is it universal. As other chapters in this book illustrate, there are some places where physical violence between husband and wife is very rare and others where wife-battering is all too common. The Garífuna represent an intermediate case, and one that initially seems anomalous: it is a culture in which incidents of spouse abuse are not highly unusual yet wife-battering is practically unknown. Contrary to what might be expected, the overall frequency of conflict does not predict severity of abuse.[5]

I have the agreeable task, in other words, of trying to explain why Garífuna women in Belize *do not* stay in relationships with men who try to harm them, and why instances of serious injury are very rare. To do this, I will focus on the cultural context of marital violence: specifically, on the culturally prescribed means of prevention and intervention ("sanctions and sanctuary"). For the most part it is women who prevent – or at the least, limit – male violence against women. I never learned of a case in which a woman had been severely beaten, to the point of drawing blood or breaking a bone, even when her husband tried to use a weapon. The worst reported case involved a man who hit his wife on several occasions; she left him each time, and finally for good after being badly bruised. People spoke of more violent encounters between *former* spouses or "friends" (lovers who had never lived together). I was told of two different instances in which a young woman stabbed a man, not fatally, for having left her. It was especially unfortunate, people said, that each was a case of mistaken identity.

MEN, WOMEN, AND VIOLENCE

The Garífuna are an Afro-Indian population whose settlements, some fifty towns and villages, lie along the Caribbean coast of Central America, from Belize to Nicaragua. They comprise about ten percent of the population of Belize, and a smaller proportion of the population in the other countries. Several books have been written about various aspects of their culture and complex history.[6] Three of them contain some mention of spouse abuse. One ethnographer notes that a woman who is unfaithful "is severely beaten" by her husband; another remarks that a woman who often quarrels with her spouse and who actually hits him will not easily find another man if she separates; a third states that an abused woman may seek sanctuary in her mother's house.[7]

No one ever told me that a man has the "right" to beat his wife under certain circumstances. Rather, wife-beating is regarded as an unfortunate reality. Men and women agree that a man whose wife is unfaithful is entitled merely to leave her; but, they add, such restraint is unusual. Most view the use of physical force between adults as dangerous, wrong, and all too frequent an occurrence. Only parents, and particularly mothers they say, can legitimately use force, and that is restricted to disciplining young children. A mother has the "right" to "lash" her child for disobedience.[8] She usually does so in public, while other children and adults watch; and the presence of these others compounds the child's fear with deep shame. Years later men and women can recall lashings that were memorably severe. It is surely not coincidental that an ancestor who appears in a dream, complaining of neglect and asking for ritual attention, may threaten to lash the dreamer unless a particular ritual is held.

Violence, as perceived by the Garífuna, often has a supernatural dimension. (By violence, I refer to any act of threatening, attempting, or actually causing bodily pain, injury, or death.) The agents of violence are thought to include a variety of spirits as well as other men and women.[9] Moreover, people can cause injury by using visible, ordinary means (their fists or weapons), or by resorting to supernatural methods (sorcery).[10]

Initially, I wondered if violence were mainly a matter of talk. I noticed that men and women tell, and retell, dramatic stories about disputes that took place many years ago, and that ended in violence: a fight, say, and later a death attributed to sorcery. Recent conflicts, including those between spouses, are also topics of daily talk. And it is not at all uncommon to hear someone air a grievance against another person and then threaten to "beat that bitch" or "that no-good man." (These words may come from either a man or a woman.) In most cases, such threats are warnings, intended to serve notice and protect one's interests. For example, a woman in her thirties who realized that her husband had a female admirer called out to the younger woman as she was passing by (one time too many that day): "I've got a switch here," she said, "and if I see you again I'm going to lash you. Then kick you. Then beat you. Then pay for you" (i.e., pay a court fine for assault). Or again, a young man who thought he'd been cheated by an older one "sent a message" through an intermediary that he was going to get a job so that he could buy a machete and "cut that thief."

Such threats rarely lead to physical assault. Usually the two parties simply avoid each other for some time. If one does confront the other, typically in a very public place, other people gather to listen and watch. As long as the conflict is limited to words, no one intervenes; but physical fighting between men, especially with weapons (a bottle, a stick, or, more seriously, a machete), causes immediate concern. Inevitably, one of the onlookers runs off to summon their kinswomen, preferably older ones, who will try to persuade the men to stop. I heard some stories about women (specifically, sexual rivals) fighting, but without weapons. There was no mention of any serious injury resulting, or of other people intervening; usually, spectators simply gathered to listen and watch.

Cases of male-female conflict often, but not always, involve spouses or lovers (either current or former). Many people voice their reluctance to intervene in marital disputes, citing the adage, "Husband and wife is nobody's business." But if a quarrel escalates, and a man strikes his wife, other women usually do intervene.

Wife-beating: Some Specifics

The proximate causes of wife-beating are similar to those identified in research carried out in the United States. The triggering events include arguments about money (or the man's unemployment or drinking, both of which contribute to the shortage of money), and sexual jealousy or suspected infidelity.[11] In each of the five cases I witnessed or was told about, the man had been drinking before he abused his wife, and three of the men suspected that their wives were having affairs. The incidence of marital violence may also be similar. (This is, of course, mere supposition, since my figures come from a year's observation of one community, while estimates of frequency in the United States are commonly based on random samples and national surveys.) At any rate, the five cases that occurred in one Garífuna community in a year involved eight percent of the co-residential couples. In the United States, from five to seven percent of intact couples admit to kicking or more serious acts of violence in a given year.[12] (A limited survey on marital violence that was carried out in several countries, including Belize and the United States, also suggests that the frequencies may be similar.[13]) As in the United States, marital violence is more common among younger couples than older ones.[14] The average age of the Garífuna men who assaulted their wives was 39 (the range was 32–50 years); the wives' average age was 32 (the range, 23–46 years). Each of the couples was married, had one or more dependent children, and lived in a nuclear family household. (There are about as many extended family households, but younger couples tend to live in the nuclear family type. Slightly over half of the couples in the community are married, although co-residence without marriage is socially acceptable.)

In each of the five cases, other women intervened in some way. Usually they simply stood by as witnesses, shaming the man by their presence and asking him to stop. In the most serious case (discussed below), they helped the abused woman to escape, and did so at some personal risk. She was the only one of the five women who left her husband permanently, returning to her mother's house in another community about forty miles away. Two women whose husbands hit them went away for several weeks, and stayed with sisters who lived in a distant urban area. (Their mothers were no longer living.) Eventually, each of them returned, and there were no further incidents in the following year.

The other two women did not leave. By community consensus, neither was seriously injured (they were pushed and fell down); and each had initiated the physical violence, trying to hurt her husband and not simply to defend herself. One had knocked her husband down when he threatened to hit her. The other, Juliana's mother as it happened, had thrown a bottle at her husband, grazing his cheek.

Significantly, none of the four couples who reconciled had a history of marital violence. A fifth woman, Francisca, left her husband permanently after several days of escalating conflict, in the course of which he had first slapped her, later kicked her, and eventually attacked her with a machete. The events, which I witnessed, are worth recounting in some detail. They provide a "worst case" example of wife-beating, and help to explain why chronic and severe abuse, or wife-battering, is virtually unknown in Garífuna villages in Belize.

WIFE-BEATING: A CASE

Francisca and Matthew had married the year before, shortly after the birth of their son. They lived in her community at first, but moved to Matthew's when he found work at a nearby banana plantation. The fact that Francisca had no close relatives there, and that Matthew was widely known to have a violent temper, particularly when he drank were later cited by many women as the reasons why she should never have agreed to follow her husband.

The first months were uneventful. Francisca often complained of loneliness and made two brief trips to visit her mother. On the second trip, she left her son with her mother, who promised to keep him for just a few weeks and then to bring him back to Francisca. She returned alone to Matthew's community, where in a matter of days rumors began to circulate that Francisca was having an affair with a younger man.[15] Eventually the rumors reached Matthew, who confronted her almost immediately, and, in the course of the argument, slapped her. Her repeated denials finally had some effect, but it was short-lived. Several days later, after he had spent the morning drinking with friends, Matthew brought home a chicken and demanded that she clean and cook it. When she refused, he kicked her, and she ran out of the house and sought refuge at a neighbor's. The woman, who knew Matthew's reputation and was afraid of him, listened nervously to Francisca's complaints, but then reminded her that it is a wife's duty to cook for her husband. She offered some onion, black pepper, and "ricardo" [*achiote*, Spanish] to use for seasoning. Francisca finally returned to the empty house, ingredients in hand, where she prepared the meal and left it on the table.

Later that day, during the afternoon lull, she was sitting in the yard and talking to her neighbor and some other women when someone called her name. Turning, the women saw Matthew approaching, with a glint in his eye and, worse, a machete in his hand. Before Francisca could get to her feet, he had grasped the machete by its blade and begun beating her with the handle. But he was clearly drunk and unsteady on his feet, and finally she managed to pull away. All of the other women had scattered, and now she faced a dilemma: Where could she find sanctuary? She had no close relatives in the community.

Fleeing, she ran past a dozen houses, and finally saw one with the door standing open. She darted inside, bolting the door behind her. The startled owner, a woman in her forties, reluctantly agreed to let Francisca hide for a few hours in another room, and then, after locking the house, went to speak to a neighbor. The two women set off on a pretended errand, but in fact they wanted to learn Matthew's whereabouts. "I don't want her to stay in my house," the one said, fearing for her own safety. "Matthew is a bad, bad man." "We're all women," the other replied, "and it could happen to any of us."

During the next few days, Francisca hid in several different houses. Matthew was said to be looking for her, and so was his mother, but apparently she felt genuine concern. It seems that Matthew's mother had asked him what he had done to his wife, and when he told her, she got angry and said that "Francisca's mother wouldn't like that at all." Everyone agreed that Francisca's mother had the "right" to protect her. Unfortunately, she lived forty miles away, and the journey could take two days.

Finally, the three women who had hidden Francisca made a plan to help her escape and return to her own community. Juliana's mother was one of these women, and she persuaded her younger brother, Raymond, to escort Francisca from the village in the middle of the night. He did so reluctantly, complaining that Matthew would probably suspect him of being Francisca's "friend" (lover) and might try to harm him.

As for Francisca, she swore never to live with Matthew again. Upon returning to her mother's house, she consulted a well-known "obeah man" (a specialist in sorcery) for "medicine" [*arani*] to keep her husband away. She sprinkled the special powder that he gave her along the perimeter of her mother's yard, where it would act as an invisible but powerful barrier to her husband. If Matthew crossed it, the obeah man said, he would sicken and then die. No one else would be affected by the substance.

Within a week, reports of this reached Matthew, who swore that he would "cut" Francisca someday (with a machete). In the meantime, he made no attempt to see her. The three women and the man who had directly helped Francisca — none of them near relatives of hers — continued to worry about their personal safety should Matthew learn of their role in helping her escape. After all, they said, they had no real right to help her, and had done so only because they feared for her life.

WHY WOMEN LEAVE

Wife-battering is virtually unknown in Garífuna communities because women leave abusive men. To explain why they leave, and to do so with brevity, it is useful to begin with a contrasting and more familiar case. Research carried out in the United States suggests that a constellation of factors make it likely that some women will stay in chronically violent relationships. Although these studies often include psychological profiles of battered women, attempting to explain in psychological terms why they stay with abusive men, I want to emphasize that many of the motivating factors are *culturally* based. I have identified at least ten: (1) reluctance to "break up the family" ("the family" meaning a nuclear family household); (2) economic dependence, and a lack of alternative means of support; (3) fear of stigma if the abuse is known; (4) social isolation and domestic privacy, which makes it unlikely that people outside the household see the violence; (5) the absence of intervention, or ineffective intervention (traditionally by male police officers, who are often said to identify with the husband); (6) the lack of accessible and reliable sanctuary; (7) a legal system that defines marital violence as less serious than violence between strangers; (8) a criminal justice system that does not effectively control violent men (for example, by failing to enforce restraining orders); (9) social attitudes of acceptance or tolerance toward marital violence (and a historical tradition in which "laws of chastisement" permitted husbands to use physical force against their wives); and (10) structural inequality between men and women, with women taught to accept a position of social inferiority and subordination.

This summary is by no means exhaustive. It does, however, provide a striking contrast to the conditions in which Garífuna women live in rural Belize. Some of the most important cultural differences have to do with patterns of marriage and postmarital residence, family structure, and conceptions of gender. As I will try to show, these probably help to limit the incidence of wife-beating. They also provide women with the means to protect themselves from chronic abuse, primarily by making it rather easy for them to leave marital relationships and to enter new ones or to remain single. When a couple separates, the man and woman are each free to form a new union, whether or not they were legally married. Divorce is unnecessary and extremely rare.[16]

Although local endogamy (marriage within one's community) is not required, it is both preferred and the common practice. In three villages where I collected detailed census data, slightly over half (57 percent) of the couples who lived together were married; and 85 percent of all the unions, legal or otherwise, were endogamous. Of the remainder, unions involving men and women from different locales, 7 percent of the couples lived in the woman's community of birth, and just 2 percent in the man's. (Francisca was one of only four women who had agreed to live in the husband's community.) Finally, 6 percent of the couples were non-natives.

A consequence of this pattern of marriage and postmarital residence is that the vast majority of women and men in these communities (92 percent and 87 percent respectively, of those with spouses) live near their own relatives. Women say that the chance of financial hardship and physical abuse increases when they live far away from kin, especially their mothers and sisters. A mother has the recognized right to offer her daughter sanctuary, and people often told me that even a very angry man would hesitate to force his way into his mother-in-law's house.

Few women actually seek sanctuary, however, because in most cases intervention is effective. While people prefer to let spouses settle their differences by themselves, if a man begins to hit his wife, someone always alerts older kinswomen and neighbors. These women usually need do nothing more than make known their presence as witnesses to the act. This is said to shame the man, who knows he has no right to beat his wife. In only one case that I was told of, the man "had no shame" and continued to hit his wife until another woman and man, both neighbors, restrained him.

Intervention is inevitable both because the women's kin are usually nearby and have the right (and duty) to intervene, and because marital violence is no secret.[17] Domestic privacy simply does not exist. Houses are not very large or substantial, and daily life is spent outside, usually in public view.

Moreover, these are small communities where people know each other well, watch each other closely, and talk freely about what they see or suspect.

In other words, everyone *does* know what goes on behind closed doors, and people inevitably criticize a man who beats his wife. More to the point, they do not encourage her to stay with him, in order to "keep the family together" or to avoid the stigma of separation or economic hardship. Physical abuse is considered a legitimate reason to leave a relationship, and the expectation is that a woman will separate rather than endure mistreatment. Women do not consider themselves weak, helpless, or inferior to men, nor do men generally speak of them in these terms. There is one notable exception: Many men do say that their *wives* should defer to them. Most women, in contrast, deny that this is a "rule," and say that ideally a marital relationship is one between equals who respect each other.[18] Perhaps this differing expectation of husbands and wives is a source of conflict in itself.[19]

Their allegiance to different extended families also creates some tension between spouses. These families center not on the marital but the mother-child relationship.[20] As a result, while marital separation may cause a "broken household," it does not usually result in a "broken family." Beyond these considerations, even financial need does not compel most women to stay with abusive husbands. A woman can usually count on her mother, siblings, or other close relatives to provide temporary shelter and food until she finds paid work or enters another relationship.

It sometimes happens that such a woman owns the house where she lives with her husband.[21] In that case, she must convince him to leave, and for this purpose she has a strong weapon at her disposal: sorcery. While sorcery is a double-edged sword, which can be used for one's benefit or otherwise, it usually seems to act as an equalizing force in women's dealings with men who try to harm them. Thus, Juliana's mother, who owned the house where she lived with her husband, Thomas, vowed to use sorcery to make him leave. In a sense, this would be her version of an eviction order.

Likewise, Francisca had no need to obtain a restraining order to keep Matthew away from her mother's house; she simply paid an obeah man for protective "medicine" – a supernatural restraining order, as it were.

To return finally to the question raised at the outset, and to give it a summary answer: wife-battering, resulting in serious injury, is practically unknown because women do not stay with men who abuse them. This is not simply a personal decision but clearly a cultural matter. These women have the means to leave and no compelling reason to stay. Most have learned to think of themselves as autonomous adults, and they reject the idea that their husbands "rule" them. The men who disagree, and who expect deference and compliance from their wives, may well be the ones who resort to physical force. The use of violence against women to enforce male dominance is well known from many other cultures, where it is an accepted and pervasive fact of social life. In Garífuna communities, in contrast, it is not sanctioned, nor is it tolerated by women.

The cases of wife-beating that I witnessed help to illuminate some cultural factors that limit the severity (if not the overall frequency) of abuse, and that lead women to leave violent men. Taking an ethnographic approach to marital violence — examining actual cases in some detail, and with knowledge of the cultural context — is also useful in another way. It points up the complex, *cultural* relationship among easily measured variables such as frequency and severity of abuse. A high overall frequency of marital violence may correlate with a high rate of injury in one cultural setting (where intervention is absent or ineffective, for example) but not in another.[22] Understanding the findings of cross-national survey research, and explaining the variation, clearly requires detailed knowledge of the cultural context in which wife-beating and wife-battering occur.

AN EXPLICATION AND EPILOGUE

When Juliana came to get me, she said that "Thomas" was beating her mother. This was the first time I had heard her call him by any name other than terms meaning "father." I had assumed that he was her biological father until, after many months, she casually mentioned that he was in fact her stepfather. When I then asked why she referred to him as *nuguchin* [father], she said simply, "He is my father because he feeds me." Calling him by name that night was not only a sign of disrespect but something of a renunciation.

I have referred to her mother throughout by teknonym, as "Juliana's mother." Like many adults with children, she was as commonly called by her teknonym [*tuguchun* Juliana, mother of Juliana] as by her given name or nickname. Most women bear children, and their primary social identity is as mothers, not as wives. The cultural value placed on motherhood is notably strong, and mother-child ties are central and enduring. When a man calls his daughter, his wife, or another woman by the term *nuguchun* [my mother], he says it with tenderness. So it was when Thomas used this word as he tried to make up with his wife, after they had fought about his drinking.

Petrona had earlier called out to him that his wife's mother was there, watching, and she said this in order to shame him. Of all the witnesses, his mother-in-law's presence had the strongest effect. (Again, many people told me that a man is especially ashamed to treat his wife roughly in front of her mother, and her mere presence is said usually to make him stop.) The other two women later told me that they had come immediately when Juliana summoned them, but with a deep sense of dread: after all, she was calling them to a scene of violence, and they feared for their own safety. It was testimony to their feelings of kinship and friendship that they responded so quickly.

As it turned out, Juliana's mother either settled her differences with her husband or decided to ignore them. The next few years of her relationship with him were reportedly rather tranquil. Her fears about Matthew, however, were realized when her younger brother, Raymond, died suddenly, less than a year after helping Francisca escape. His death came at the age of twenty-eight, without warning or apparent cause in the middle of one night, as he slept. It was widely believed that Matthew had poisoned him.

NOTES

This chapter is based primarily on ethnographic research that was carried out between 1973 and 1981, and which included eighteen months of fieldwork in Belize. I am grateful to the Fulbright-Hays Commission, the Wenner-Gren Foundation, and the University of Illinois for funding my work. A recent experience, serving as a board member of a community shelter for battered women, has given me the opportunity to learn about wife-beating and wife-battering in a second cultural setting, and has helped to provide the basis for comparing "here" and "there." I have learned a great deal from the staff members of the Williamsburg (Virginia) Task Force on Battered Women/Sexual Assault. The views expressed in this chapter are, however, solely my own.

1. All names are pseudonyms, but in every other respect the cases reported in this chapter are factual.

2. In their review of research on wife-beating, Brienes and Gordon (1983:512) write that too often "questions turn upon specific acts, blows, pushes, weapons, rather than the gestalt of the conflict." This may be due to the fact that so much of the research has been carried out using survey techniques, which are better suited to enumerating acts of violence than to understanding the "gestalt."

3. This definition appears in a recent issue of the American College of Obstetrics and Gynecology's Technical Bulletin (1989:1), citing Parker and Schumacher's (1977) study. The title of that issue of the Bulletin is "The Battered Woman." As a member of the ACOG has pointed out, the fact that this problem has been "selected as the subject of a Technical Bulletin is quite significant." It is circulated to the many thousands of members of the ACOG and represents the "standard of care" (John H. Baker, M.D., personal communication).

Brown's (1988) definition of wife-battering differs in that it emphasizes severity of injury without specifying frequency: "The wife is seriously injured, incapacitated, or even killed." It is, of course, very difficult to determine frequency in most ethnographic accounts. (See her discussion, in this volume, of problems with the literature.)

Finally, the term "battered women" is sometimes used very generally to refer to all of those who have experienced any form of "physically injurious behavior" at the hands of a current or former male partner (Margolin, Sibner and Gleberman 1988:93). Such a definition makes no distinction as to frequency or severity of violence.

4. In northern Sri Lanka, for example, a researcher questioned and medically examined 60 battered women referred to him by the police over a three-year period.

The majority suffered from head injuries, and 62 percent had been attacked with a weapon. Each of the women had been assaulted on at least three different occasions (Saravanapavananthan 1982). Also see Levinson (1988:443), who reports that "wife-beating incidents resulting in death or permanent injury" occur in nearly half of the ninety societies in his cross-cultural sample.

5. By "overall frequency of conflict" I refer to all episodes occurring among couples in a community or population during a given period of time. In contrast, perhaps the frequency of abuse *between* a husband and wife does predict severity of injury, as violence may well escalate.

6. See Coelho (1981), Gonzalez (1969, 1988), Gullick (1976), Kerns (1983), Staiano (1986), and Taylor (1951).

7. See Taylor (1951:96), Gonzalez (1969:78), and Kerns (1983:110), respectively. In this chapter, I use the terms "husband," "wife," and "spouse" without any distinction as to the legal status of the relationship (but cf. Kerns 1983:113 on language and terminology).

8. Presumably fathers have this right as well, but I never happened to see a man use physical force to discipline his child. (My informants spoke of mothers as the primary disciplinarians of children.) The right to strike one's child is not reciprocal. For an adult to strike a parent is considered one of the worst moral transgressions, "a sin against God," as many put it (Kerns 1983:106).

9. For detailed descriptions of these spirits, see Staiano (1986:115—126) and Taylor (1951).

10. For detailed discussion of sorcery, see Gonzalez (1970); also see Kerns (1983) and Staiano (1986).

11. According to Okun (1986:50), conflict about financial problems and sexual jealousy are the most common triggering events leading to wife abuse in the United States. Straus, Gelles, and Steinmetz (1980:157) identify the five major issues of conflict as housekeeping, sex, social matters, money, and children.

12. For statistics on wife-beating in the United States, see Okun (1986:39; cf. Straus, Gelles, and Steinmetz 1980:32—33; Gelles and Straus 1988:104).

13. Survey data for Belize were collected for Steinmetz (1981) by a research assistant, who administered a questionnaire to students, presumably in an urban area. The respondents were 231 adolescents, 37 of whom were Garífuna (identified in the article as "Carib," the name by which they were then generally known in Belize). The students answered questions about episodes of violence between their parents. According to the results, marital violence is more frequent among the Garífuna and Creoles than among Spanish-speaking Belizeans. The date of the survey is not given, but comparable data were collected for Steinmetz in several other countries from the mid-to-late 1970s.

14. Straus, Gelles, and Steinmetz (1980:142) conclude that in the United States, "younger couples are more violent" and that violence decreases with age.

15. She was twenty-three, and the suspected lover was eighteen. Such rumors are common in Garífuna communities, and obviously very difficult to verify; young women are the usual subjects, although older women are sometimes suspected of having affairs as well (see Kerns in press).

16. Decisions to establish and to end marital relationships are essentially individual matters, and subject to minimal regulation. Legally married couples who

separate rarely obtain a divorce but commonly form other unions (see Kerns 1983:114—115).

17. See Erchak (1984), Gibbs (1984), and Levinson (1985) on the importance of intervention and the absence of domestic privacy in many cultures; and Beatrice Whiting's comment, quoted in Gelles and Straus (1988:28) on communal residence as a preventive factor in domestic violence (also see Whiting and Whiting 1975:190).

18. The male informants who expressed this view, that women should defer to their husbands, used a highly global statement, "Men rule women." Asked to explain, they spoke of a wife's deference as an ideal (Kerns 1983:92). Coelho (1955:86) notes that, "The position of the woman in the family is in no way to be conceived as subordinate, the principle involved being one of partnership under equal terms, not of one person commanding and the other obeying."

19. According to Finkelhor (1983:19), domestic violence is not only the abuse of power, but is sometimes a response to the perceived lack or loss of power.

20. For a full discussion of gender roles and of family structure, see Kerns (1983:89—104, 120—146).

21. In one community, for example, over 40 percent of the houses are owned by women (Kerns 1983:124). Some of these women are separated or widowed, but many reside with husbands.

22. See Steinmetz (1981), for example, whose preliminary figures from six countries show striking differences in the relationship of three variables: percentage of spouses using violence, frequency of marital violence, and severity of abuse.

REFERENCES CITED

American College of Obstetrics and Gynecology. 1989. The Battered Woman. ACOG Technical Bulletin, Number 124.

Brienes, Wini, and Linda Gordon. 1983. The New Scholarship on Family Violence. Signs 8(3):490—503.

Brown, Judith K. 1988. Sanctions and Sanctuary: Cross-Cultural Perspectives on Violence Toward Women. Manuscript.

Coelho, Ruy Galvao de Andrade. 1955. The Black Carib of Honduras: A Study in Acculturation. Ph.D. dissertation, Northwestern University.

———. 1981. Los Negros Caribes de Honduras. Tegucigalpa, Honduras: Editorial Guaymuras.

Erchak, Gerald M. 1984. Cultural Anthropology and Spouse Abuse. Current Anthropology 25(3):331—332.

Finkelhor, David. 1983. Common Features of Family Abuse. *In* The Dark Side of Families: Current Family Violence Research. David Finkelhor, et al., eds. Pp. 17—28. Beverly Hills: Sage.

Gelles, Richard J., and Murray A. Straus. 1988. Intimate Violence. New York: Simon and Schuster.

Gibbs, James L. 1984. On Cultural Anthropology and Spouse Abuse. Current Anthropology 25(4):533.

Gonzalez, Nancie L. 1969. Black Carib Household Structure. Seattle: University of Washington Press.

————. 1970. Obeah and Other Witchcraft among the Black Caribs. *In* Systems of North American Witchcraft and Sorcery. (Anthropological Monographs no. 1) Deward E. Walker, ed. Pp. 93—109. Moscow, Idaho: University of Idaho.

————. 1988. Soujourners of the Caribbean: Ethnogenesis and Ethnohistory of the Garífuna. Urbana: University of Illinois Press.

Gullick, C.J.M.R. 1976. Exiled from St. Vincent: The Development of Black Carib Culture in Central America Up to 1945. Malta: Progress Press.

Kerns, Virginia. 1983. Women and the Ancestors: Black Carib Kinship and Ritual. Urbana: University of Illinois Press.

————. In press. Female Control of Sexuality: Garífuna Women at Middle Age. *In* In Her Prime: New Views of Middle-Aged Women. Second edition, revised and expanded. Virginia Kerns and Judith K. Brown, eds. Urbana: University of Illinois Press.

Levinson, David. 1985. On Wife-Beating and Intervention. Current Anthropology 26(5):665—66.

————. 1988. Family Violence in Cross-Cultural Perspective. *In* Handbook of Family Violence. Vincent B. Van Hasselt, et al., eds. Pp. 435—55. New York: Plenum Press.

Margolin, Gayla, Linda G. Sibner, and Lisa Gleberman. 1988. Wife-battering. *In* Handbook of Family Violence. Vincent B. Van Hasselt, et al., eds. Pp. 89—117. Beverly Hills: Sage.

Okun, Lewis E. 1986. Woman Abuse: Facts Replacing Myths. Albany: State University of New York Press.

Parker, Barbara, and Dale N. Schumacher. 1977. The Battered Wife Syndrome and Violence in the Nuclear Family of Origin: A Controlled Pilot Study. American Journal of Public Health 67(8):760—61.

Saravanapavananthan, N. 1982. Wife-Battering: A Study of Sixty Cases. Forensic Science International 20(2): 163—66.

Staiano, Kathryn Vance. 1986. Interpreting Signs of Illness: A Case Study in Medical Semiotics. New York: Mouton de Gruyter.

Steinmetz, Suzanne K. 1981. A Cross-Cultural Comparison of Marital Abuse. Journal of Sociology and Social Welfare 8(2):404—14.

Straus, Murray A., Richard J. Gelles, and Suzanne K. Steinmetz 1980. Behind Closed Doors: Violence in the American Family. Garden City: Anchor Press/Doubleday.

Taylor, Douglas M. 1951. The Black Carib of British Honduras. Viking Fund Publications in Anthropology no. 17. New York: Wenner-Gren.

Whiting, John W. M., and Beatrice B. Whiting. 1975. Aloofness and Intimacy of Husbands and Wives: A Cross-Cultural Study. Ethos 3(2):183—207.

11

Men's Rights/Women's Wrongs: Domestic Violence in Ecuador

Lauris McKee

In some traditional Andean communities, wife-beating is a tacitly accepted outlet for male frustration and hostility. In towns and villages of rural Ecuador, younger men generally figure in reports of wife-beating, and one hears of it infrequently among older couples. In the Andean community of Las Flores whose customs are central to this study, mothers commonly warn daughters who would marry that, sooner or later, their husbands will beat them. "That," they say, "is how men are" (*así son*). Maltreatment of one sex by the other not only falls within the range of possible marital comportment, but figures in cultural expectations to the extent that one may view it as part of social structure. Furthermore, in Las Flores, no clear relationship exists between ethnicity and wife-beating: spouse abuse occurs in *blanco, mestizo* and indigenous households.[1]

These social expectations need to be interpreted against another and somewhat divergent reality. The available evidence indicates that wife-beating actually occurs in a minority of marriages in Las Flores and other rural Ecuadorian locales. Its magnitude as a concern must therefore be attributed less to its frequency than to the publicity accorded each occurrence. Gossip gives importance to the *threat* of spouse abuse; it assures its prominence in the minds of the populace as a latent threat to wives and a course of action potentially open to husbands in any marital altercation.

Despite the importance of the subject, this aspect of family relations is, with a few notable exceptions, little documented in Andean ethnographic literature. No systematic study of its frequency in Andean communities has been encountered, although the Boltons' fascinating research documents (through family interviews and recorded lawsuits) reveal a high incidence of conjugal quarrels and wife-beating episodes in Incawatana, Peru (Bolton and Bolton 1975). The lack of information can be partially attributed to the difficulty of collecting systematic evidence. As wife-beating generally takes place behind closed doors, it is most unusual to witness an incident or to be able to substantiate it.

The data for this paper are based on a total of eleven cases that came to my attention (eight of which are drawn from an ethnographically studied randomly selected sample of fifty-two families). One episode took place in the street and I witnessed it together with a crowd of villagers. In four cases I saw the bruises and cuts that evidenced women's abuse on the day following the event. Five other incidents were retrospectively recounted.[2] One case, in which an informant had beaten his first wife to death, occurred several years before my fieldwork, and the informant (now remarried) had served seven years in prison.

GENDER ISSUES RELATED TO WIFE-BEATING

As is almost universally so in the Andes, the world view of Los Flores strongly supports the maintenance of male authority. Although important countervailing tenets also come into play (as we shall see later), we must begin by recognizing the hierarchy of patriarchal control that implicitly justifies the "discipline" of wives and children. Village men have a collective interest in the perpetuation of the sex hierarchy thus established, and individual behavior is monitored by the male community. If a man feels his domestic authority compromised in some manner, the reaction of other men and his reading of his gender role can lead him to beat his wife in the attempt to redeem his status among his peers.

The norm of investing an authority in males that has the potential to be violently pursued is often viewed as derived from a circum-Mediterranean ethos emphasizing honor and shame (Peristiany 1966; Pitt-Rivers 1954, 1977), which was imported to the New World by Hispanic invaders. This ethos predicates male honor on female chastity. "[M]en claim authority over their wives, daughters and sisters, requiring of them moral qualities which they do not expect of themselves — after all, a man cannot afford to have too fine a moral conscience or he would not be able to meet his obligations to his family in the struggle for existence" (Pitt-Rivers 1977:79). Men, though the patterns of justification vary somewhat with class and ethnicity, are responsible for protecting "their" women's chastity, and violation of it by another man is the ultimate insult whose redress may require the death of the violated woman (cf. Taggart 1990).

Among the *mestizos* and *blancos* of Las Flores male superiority is phrased, traditionally, in terms of *machísmo,* a version of the Hispanic-derived model of a dominant masculinity: "The cultural concept involves sexual prowess, action-orientation (including verbal action) . . . but a real *macho* is one who is sure of himself, cognizant of his own inner worth, and willing to bet everything on such self-confidence" (Gillin 1965:509). In writing of the Hispanic ideal, Gilmore (1987:149) states that *machísmo* "spawns a zero-sum contest cosmology in which sexuality becomes a struggle of weakened men against more powerful women. . . . [I]ts motives lie in the emotion of a compensatory assertive sexuality, its expression an eroticized politics—an impulse to dominate, to conquer, and to ward off threats to masculine narcissism. *Machísmo* is nothing if not aggressive—if only in defense of a wounded pride."

In contrast, the indigenous (Indian) ideal of male superiority is differently construed and expressed. It encodes the notion that masculinity carries certain rights and powers, but does not enshrine the particular constellation of qualities attributed to *machísmo*. Although investigators have pointed to the notably aggressive behavior of some Quéchua and Aymara speakers (e.g., Bolton 1973b, Bolton and Bolton 1975; Carter 1977), indigenous social structure is relatively more egalitarian (Belote 1978; Bourque and Warren 1981; Isbell 1978),[3] and traditional cosmology emphasizes duality and sex-complementarity. Yet wife-beating occurs in many indigenous households, and aggression is often seen as a masculine right (see Bolton and Bolton 1975; Carter 1977; Deborah Caro, Linda Belote, personal communications). Indigenous wives are reputed to "give as good as they get." This apprehension may be based upon public observations of women defending themselves against non-kin, but the data on domestic violence fails to document a strong female response against husbands other than abandonment of them. Linda Belote observed a *hempla* ("example"; "morality play") in Saraguro, in which St. Joseph beat the Virgin Mary (literally) into the ground (pounding her into a prepared hole), for the reason, said informants, that "She deserved it."[4]

Olivia Harris, who studied an indigenous group of the Lake Titicaca region, notes that "In Laymi representation, for all the egalitarian sexual ideology, with its complementary division of labor, for all the organization of sexuality around a principle of balanced reciprocity, there are also phallocentric elements. In particular these coalesce around imagery of power and strength. A person who has performed some action out of the ordinary is said to have a big penis" (Harris 1980:80). Carter notes that inebriated Aymara shout "I am a man!" which, depending on the context, can be taken as a general assertion of power, a challenge, or an insult (Carter 1977).

Mestizo Gender Ideals

In Table 11.1, the list of masculine and feminine traits collected from a sample of *mestizo* informants in Las Flores displays the semantic contours of gender ideals. The duality of ideal gender constructs is evidenced in the expressive qualities ascribed to each sex,[5] but it is important to reiterate that these are *ideal* representations: actual behavior—the realm of practice—is

---

TABLE 11.1

GENDER IDEALS

IDEAL MALE TRAITS		IDEAL FEMALE TRAITS	
Men's View	Women's View	Men's View	Women's View
Strong	Strong	Good	Good
Bravo	Good	Tranquil	Tranquil
Honorable	Bravo	Unselfish	Sociable
Exigente	Receloso	Agreeable	Accessible
Rebellious	Exigente	Good-	Unselfish
	Rebellious	Worker	Loving
	Understanding	Serious	Polite
	Responsible	Cheerful	Agreeable
			Docile
			Humble
			Humanitarian

Note a: N = 20 male informants; N = 34 female informants. The data were collected in 1975–1976 (McKee 1980).

Note b: The terms are arranged in an order reflecting frequency of mention. (For example, 'humanitarian' was a trait mentioned by only 10 females, and no males). Rough glosses of the Spanish terms above are: *bravo* ('angry', 'challenging', 'rude'); *exigente* ('insistent', 'demanding'); *receloso* ('mistrustful', 'suspicious').

---

influenced by, but not isomorphic with, the actions and attitudes encoded in the traits listed above.

The trait list stresses the aggressive aspect of male behavior, and the expressive submissive aspect of female behavior, although *men* cite women's role as workers. Women's trait list is longer for *both* sexes. Relative to men, they include more adjectives for their own gender that connote submissiveness (e.g., humble, docile, polite). This is significant given that passivity and cajolery are the culturally expected responses to husbands' violent behavior.

Women share a perception of men that contradicts and softens the *macho* persona. This is reflected in their listing of contrasting qualities: *good-bravo, responsible-rebellious* and *understanding-receloso*. The notion of a dual masculine "nature" may help women view men sympathetically and overlook the contradictions inherent in the role system.

TABLE 11.2

SHARED GENDER IDEALS*

MALE TRAITS	FEMALE TRAITS
Strong Bravo Exigente Rebellious	Good Tranquil Unselfish Agreeable

Table 11.2 is a modification of Table 11.1. It overides frequency-hierarchies and displays only *consensus*-traits — the gender ideals both men and women ascribe to their own sex or to the other. The polar construction of *shared* gender ideals (consensus-traits) is evident here: a physically-active/hostile-defensive masculine dimension is juxtaposed with a passive/accessible-supportive female dimension. The cultural script for inter-sex behavior that can lead to wife-beating seems to be clearly written in this opposition.

The list of male traits (as pointed in emphasis as a cautionary tale) reflects an agonistic symbology: a pattern of initiative and response gauged to protect a man from the predations of others in the social world exogenous to the family (cf. Walter 1981:173). Dealings with individuals not obligated to treat one justly (as are consanguineal, affinal or ritual kinspersons) are portrayed as hazardous undertakings fraught with the possibility of deceit and ruin (an attitude made overt in epigrams and folk tales).[6] Extended into the domestic sphere, however, these responses pattern a man's treatment of his wife if he perceives his dominance as besieged.

Consensus traits for women reflect their ideal family roles as wives and mothers. The adjectives connote a cheerful, accepting passivity that sets standards for women's response to abusive husbands. The lack of role-transitivity in this respect is remarkable. Ordinarily, young women say, they do not fight back or even *remonstrate* with husbands for their maltreatment or for lack of responsibility. Instead, they recruit relatives, *compadres*, or friends to counsel them, or they appeal to a husband's fatherly love, suggesting that witnessing his violence makes his children ill with fright-sickness (*susto, espanto*) (cf. Rubel, O'Nell and Collado-Ardon 1984). Although women deplore their personal experiences of masculine aggression and dominance, they tend to share the world-view that justifies it as necessary to defend family interests against the wider society.

It is important to note that the clustering of traits around polar expressive styles apparently emphasizes certain arenas of action and ignores others. Women's traits relate to their view of domestic behavior, whereas men's relate to their behavior in the extra-domestic world. For example, the gender ideals cited by men and women do not include normative conduct associated with women's business activities in the "world." An agonistic stance is viewed as appropriate to *both* sexes when interacting with non-kin. In defending their own and their family's interests rural highland women are *verbally* aggressive and forceful (and seasoned market women can back up verbal threats with physical ones).[7]

Neither sex makes mention of the sexual component of male "character" although its salience is overtly recognized in customs of socialization thought to ensure its expression (McKee 1980). Equally surprising is men's lack of reference to male qualities advantaging a good worker and their omission of traits that describe the "softer" side of masculine nature. Most men are loving and tender with small children and older men in particular respond altruistically to the needs of others.

The culture poses dilemmas for each sex. Men somehow must find ways of expressing their tender feelings while conveying strength of character; elsewise, their "weakness" targets them for exploitation. Similarly, *women* must display aggression in extra-family dealings in order to defend their interests, but (in the ideal) suppress their instrumentality and power in their marital relations.

The force of gender ideals is seen in an incident involving one of my neighbors, who joined her husband in assaulting two inebriated men who were vandalizing their small bar. She was a strong woman who butchered and roasted whole pigs for sale in the market. During the fracas, she picked up one of the drunks and threw him into the street. Her actions were viewed with universal disapproval by *both sexes* who insisted that she had disgraced herself and her husband by aggressing against a man. These social attitudes, strongly expressed, function to prevent women from retaliating against an abusive husband.

It is clear that consensual gender traits correspond imperfectly and intermittently to reality, and to a degree are even situation-specific. Nevertheless, their "imagery of the extreme" provides the symbols each sex uses in interpreting and evaluating the actions of the other in the process of conjugal exchange.[8]

For this reason, it is important that the world view of Las Flores encodes countervailing tenets that negatively sanction wife-beating. For example there exists the strong conviction that dissension is pathogenic. Conflict can lead to serious illness, not merely for the contenders, but for the witnesses to such altercations. Moreover, the culture has institutionalized a mediation form that specifically deals with marital conflicts. Marriage-godparents (*padrinos*) are specially charged with intervening in conjugal quarrels and helping to resolve them before they escalate to violence. In sum, the assumption of male dominance provides an essential cultural context for wife-beating but is not sufficient in itself to explain its eruption.

ECONOMIC ASYMMETRY IN
THE MARITAL DYAD AND LAND OWNERSHIP

In the cases I have recorded in Las Flores, I will argue that the factors contributing to conjugal abuse were:

1. social expectations derived from gender ideals which make wife-beating a recognized (if deplored) response to male frustration, and
2. the tensions produced when these ideals (featuring male superordination) conflict with an inheritance custom that challenges a man's actual economic status in his marriage.

Whereas certain gender ideals appear to have a broad distribution in rural highland Ecuador, the second factor is related to an inheritance custom specifically practiced in Las Flores. It may, however, point to a potential area of research for other investigators exploring spouse abuse.

To explain those cases wherein wife-beating becomes an *actual* rather than a possible male response, we must consider economic factors, more particularly patterns of land inheritance, as significant variables affecting marital relations. The community of Las Flores is small, agrarian, and strongly familistic. It is located in Tungurahua Province in the central Andean highlands, and is comprised of some 276 households. The majority of the population is *mestizo* (although these people are self-labeled as "whites"), and there is an indigenous minority. The village is located in a valley made productive by a network of irrigation canals. Major crops are citrus fruits, particularly tangerines, and avocados which are sold in the markets of Ambato and Quito. There also are several small factories which produce fruit-flavored liquor (*pisco*). The majority of village families own at least one small plot of land, although some are forced to rent land or to work as day laborers (*peones*). Although education is increasing new career possibilities, the value placed on land remains central in Floreño society. Land ownership is, apart from ethnicity, a major factor differentiating social status.

With this background information in mind, I have looked to exchange theory for explanations that most closely (and economically) approximate the perception of reality reflected in informants' reasoning about wife-beating, and in their own interpretations of episodes of violence. Exchange points to an aspect of marital relationships that deserves more scrutiny; this is the relative status of spouses during the early years of partnership due to asymmetrical control of resources. I will argue that a specific factor contributing to conjugal violence in Las Flores is that young wives often occupy a status economically (and, if one heeds Mauss' theory of exchange, *morally*) superior to their husbands!

Floreñas' status can be construed as (relatively) superordinate because they become landowners at marriage. Throughout the Andes land is a highly valued, scarce good. Families attempt to provide their children with sufficient land for subsistence by the custom of partible inheritance. In other Andean communities, partition can mean that children of both sexes are given property prior to or at the time of marriage, which establishes their economic independence (Beals 1966; Caro 1983, 1985; Flores-Ochoa 1979).[9] The pattern is different in Las Flores, in that the customary *scheduling* of land-transfer from parents to offspring differs by sex. Women are given their portion of their family's lands at the time of marriage, whereas men's inheritance usually is postponed until the demise of both parents. The result is that a wife's inherited land constitutes the sole real property claimed by the newly married pair (although the law supports a husband's right to control property the couple purchases after marriage [Romoleroux de Morales 1975]).

This early settlement can advantage sons in that upon the death of both parents, their real holdings may have increased so that there is more land or better land to be divided among the sons. But however partition is carried out, a completely equal division of real property among offspring is impossible. This is evidenced in the ubiquitous sibling conflicts (often ending in the courts) over the quality or quantity of land each has received.[10]

Also, the danger of partibility, of course, is that as divisions (theoretically) are repeated in each generation, a finite amount of land is passed down to an expanding group of descendants, resulting, after several generations, in plots too small to support a family even at subsistence level. Individual strategies including out-migration function to mitigate this situation. But there are also group-level strategies encoded in customs that facilitate land-reaggregation and temporally restrict land-transmission.

Village endogamy is one way to reaggregate lands[11] and the majority of marriages in Las Flores are endogamous (McKee 1980). At marriage, which occurs between the ages of 16 and 23 for the majority of women, a Floreña generally is given the choice of accepting her filial share of her parents' land immediately, or of waiting until the death of both her parents to inherit. Unless their families are unusually well off, women choose the first option. And though negotiation is possible, in poorer families this means that women relinquish all further claims on the parental estate.

The land a woman inherits remains in her control and does not become the common property of the conjugal society. (By Ecuadorian law, legatees retain sole title to legacies acquired prior to or during marriage [Código Civil 1980: Art. 158]). Nevertheless, the land benefits a woman's husband. Couples generally work together to cultivate the wife's land and its produce *is* viewed as conjugal property (cf. Luzuriaga 1980). In the normal case, when a woman dies, her land is divided among her children; of course, the same is true for any real property a man owns.

In contrast, as noted above, men generally must wait to claim their share of family land until the death of both of their parents at which time the entire family estate is divided among the designated heirs. Postponed inheritance is problematical for several reasons. First, the attrition of family resources may result in little or nothing to inherit. Agricultural catastrophes are frequent occurrences in montane environments (untimely frost, drought, insect plagues and landslides are perennial problems) and debts or disasters can force farmers to sell off land. (Excess rainfall experienced during the El Niño cycle of 1982–1983 rotted crops before they ripened and forced thousands of impoverished farmers to migrate to provincial cities.) Second, lawsuits among siblings can delay actual possession of lands for years (cf. Beals 1966). Third, land quality varies, and partibility, as noted above, disadvantages some of the heirs. Waters (1988) shows a strong correlation between ownership of low-quality land and incidence of out-migration and wage-employment.[12] Fourth, disinheritance of offspring is not uncommon. Preterition is a legal right and occurs when children offend or neglect parents.

Thus, mens' inheritance is contingent on good relations with their parents, and can be used as leverage to induce sons to contribute their energies to parental enterprises. For all the above reasons, men's future inheritances are relatively riskier. A major point here is that the scheduling of inheritance by sex serves a variety of cultural purposes, but disadvantages young men in that the productive yield of a wife's land often is the sole source of equity available to the newly married pair. (A proverb expresses the economic risk marriage holds for men: *"él que se casa pide costal y taza para la plaza"* ("the man who marries asks to be beggared" [to sit with a cup and sack in the plaza]).

Thus, Floreño inheritance customs result in exchange-asymmetry among most spouses early in marriage. If we view the land wives bring into a marriage as a prestation that initiates the relationship (literally, "grounds" it) but that remains unreciprocated in the early years of married life, then husbands, the receivers of the land's benefits, stand in an asymmetrical relationship to wives (Mauss 1954; Lévi-Strauss 1987) or, more colloquially, a wife is "one-up" on her husband. And if, as noted earlier, asymmetry determines the relative status of the pair, then until a husband makes an appropriate return whose benefits accrue to the wife's well-being, he is the temporary debtor (and by the ethics of exchange, the moral subordinate in the relationship), and his wife is the creditor (and moral superordinate; see Mauss 1954; Sahlins 1972; Lévi-Strauss 1987, 1983).

In the usual case, men can and do reciprocate their wives' initial stake, and there are customs that aid them in doing so. First, the debt usually is not large: women's land legacies are small, rarely answering subsistence needs. Second, it is customary for newlyweds to reside with either her parents or his for a few years.[13] Such couples live rent-free and pay only for the food they consume, although they render labor-aid to the household. This permits them to save money for purchase or rental of their own land parcels, and/or to establish themselves in their own house, for neolocal residence is preferred in Las Flores as it is in many Andean locales (cf. Lambert 1977).

In the initial years of marriage, asymmetry can function positively: it promotes continuity in the new relationship, linking the pair by the credit and the debt. The creditor, having invested in the relationship, expects the debtor's eventual return prestation. Once this occurs, the partnership is placed on new terms and (moral) statuses are reversed. Conversely, balance threatens continued interaction.

> The exchange that is symmetrical or unequivocally equal carries some disadvantage from the point of view of alliance: it cancels debts and thus opens the possibility of contracting out. If neither side is "owing" then the bond between them is comparatively fragile. But if accounts are not squared, then the relationship is maintained by virtue of the "shadow of indebtedness". (Sahlins 1972:222).[14]

Initial economic asymmetry usually only lasts a short time. Husbands put aside money during the "grace period" granted by residence with relatives, so that reciprocity is fairly prompt. In some cases, men's inheritances may be forthcoming during this period, or if they remain landless, they find employment for wages that are relatively higher than those allotted to women performing the same work (McKee 1980; cf. Lobo 1986:46). Their contribution, in other words, soon compensates for the bridal "stake," erases their obligation, expands the resource base of the conjugal pair and makes them roughly equal economic partners.

The rarer case is that after a protracted period of time, a husband has not (or cannot) reciprocate. Or else, a wife's business successes augment her initial stake, thus increasing the amount of benefits her spouse is obligated to return. In either event, the pattern and timing of exchange is "off" and the exchange imbalance, and the husband's sense of it, radically increases.

Even so, a safety valve exists: these deficits can be defrayed in non-material ways if other sorts of "capital" are available (cf. Bourdieu 1986). For example, a good deal of "social credit" is awarded a man or woman whose "character," in the opinion of his wife and his neighbors, is good. If a man does his best to meet family and work obligations, and treats *compadres* and neighbors with respect and fairness, his economic failures are largely overlooked as the misfortunes of an otherwise worthy man, and his wife counts herself fortunate to have a "good," "unselfish," and "agreeable" husband.

Conversely, irresponsible husbands (often heavy drinkers) who place their own pleasure above family needs accumulate a "social debit" of ill-will and contempt in both the domestic and public spheres. Even so, such a man may escape public derision *if* he is economically successful; but if his material credits do not defray the emotional costs inflicted by his behavior, the probability of wife-beating will increase.

If an initial economic asymmetry remains unresolved, the passage of time increases social and moral distance between the marital pair. Young couples' capacities as adults are on trial before the village "jury," and an unfavorable assessment soon is communicated via jokes, nicknames and innuendoes. Both sexes are subject to these judgments, but men's economic responsibility is easily monitored, as their labors and recreations tend to be more public and are scrutinized by male peers.

Additionally, the structural asymmetry present in a new marriage often is exacerbated by structural tensions arising from strong continuing ties between the couples and their natal families. Families want to keep their children near them, and, in the early years of a marriage, claim their loyalties to the degree that the conjugal pair can be seen as representatives of two opposing interest groups negotiating an uneasy alliance.

Fortunately, the *padrinos* (godparents of marriage), selected by a betrothed couple, can bridge this gap and mediate marital disputes. Among other duties, *padrinos* should intercede in violent altercations, or better, prevent them by conciliatory counseling. Godparents, who are pledged to be impartial, try to terminate conflicts without involving their godchildren's kindred. The presence of this institution indicates the salience of domestic dissension in the culture.[15]

CONCLUSION

The articulation between institutional structure and social structure is necessarily imperfect in complex Andean communities such as Las Flores. As normative relational patterns cannot satisfactorily address every individual's life-circumstances, dilemmas and conflicts are created that may or may not be positively resolved.

This paper has examined conflicts inherent in the articulation and interaction of two institutions in an Andean community. The sex hierarchy ascribes men a superordinate status, translated as "natural" superiority to women and masculine dominance in the domestic sphere. In contrast, inheritance customs award women control of property upon marriage, and postpone male control of real property for an indeterminate number of years (the lifetime of their parents). Thus, most men begin marriage (paradoxically) as their wives' economic subordinates. By the morality of exchange, as debtors, they also are their moral subordinates.

The question is, why should a society institutionalize a form of property transfer that constitutes a challenge to the gender ideology? A partial answer is that these institutions work positively for *most* families — ensuring offspring's future subsistence, providing each spouse (eventually) with access to new lands donated by affines, and securing for parents the economic cooperation of their young married children. Daughters, who receive land at marriage, remain indebted to parents for the gift; sons await a prestation *predicated* on their continuing filial affection and labor aid.

Furthermore, the tension generated in the conjugal family, when wives are land-lenders, and men are land-receivers, serves other social interests. Bridal bequests generally are small, and postponed male inheritance confronts young men with the necessity to exert their energies and thereby advance the economic status of their newly formed nuclear unit. Shared gender ideals (see Table 11.2), which enjoy a strong and virtually universal consensus, set standards for the attitudes and stances believed necessary to make that advance. In this manner, the economic viability of new families is secured, for most men generally do attain control of property and (in the public's view, at least) their dominance is established.

On the other hand, when male energies and/or ambitions fail, the negative potentials of the system become evident. Despite institutionalized checks and balances (e.g., values on harmony and the family and male reliance on women's property), a man will beat his wife in a demonstration of a "superiority and dominance" otherwise unsubstantiated (in village opinion) through worthy endeavor.

That early marital exchange "should" make men experience feelings of subordination is supported by community response to those who (in pursuit of their own pleasure or their own projects) postpone reciprocation of their wives' contributions. Time is a crucial factor in the public assessment of a man's performance, and once the "grace period" of residence with kin concludes, the social timer (to speak figuratively) is turned on. Social pressure is exerted through opprobrium, but this is expressed as ridicule.

Censure through public ridicule, an institutionalized mode of coercing conformity in Las Flores, can take a variety of forms. Critics may mask themselves on Twelfth Night and read or distribute "wills" (*testamentos*) that are humorous and unmerciful catalogues of individuals' sins and personal deficits. Or on the eve of the New Year, street tableaus of straw-stuffed figures expose officials' corruption or the "secret" activities of local deviants. Nicknames and joking, discussed earlier, are used with cutting effect, and their humor guarantees their diffusion. These criticisms push young men into action: to work harder, to establish domestic dominance, to change their subordinate status. When they are unsuccessful in these goals, they react with violence, to "prove" their manhood by activating the central, agonistic symbols of ideal masculinity.

The argument here suggests that superordination and subordination as moral statuses devolving from dyadic exchange may have different implications if the dyad is a married pair. Marital exchange is formally distinct due to the dimension of relative permanence it brings to the exchange process, and to its special character as a sexual tie that entails both productive and reproductive contributions from exchange partners.

In Las Flores, gender roles predicate and condition the tenor of reciprocal exchange. The wider society, using ridicule as its lever, breeches the secrecy in which families hope to shroud their affairs and forces increased conformity in domestic relationships. The ideal standards of gender are used to measure social value.

But why, one might ask, do women accept this system? Andean women are strong, ingenious, and hard working, essential economic and reproductive partners. Society relies on family cooperation and integrity—for no other social institutions presently exist that could assume the family's functions. It is doubtful that women would tolerate over–expression of the male "right" to domestic dominance: prosecuted too frequently, it would lead to domestic pathology.

The line is narrowly drawn. The potential for abuse and wife-beating is built into the Floreño cultural system, but undue exercise of this "right" would result in family dissolution and social disintegration. The strategies of social actors must operate within these constraints.

NOTES

The material for this paper was collected during fieldwork in 1975—1976, and further substantiated during research in 1982—1984. I am grateful to the National Institute of Mental Health (ADAMHA) who supported the first research period. I also thank the National Science Foundation (Grant #BNS-8210224) and the Fulbright Foundation for their support of my more recent fieldwork and the International Population Program at Cornell University which gave me indispensable administrative and moral support. Insightful and valued comments on drafts of this paper were generously given by Enrique Mayer, Ralph Bolton, Cheryl Pomeroy, Laurence Moore and James Taggart. They, and the agencies who supported me, bear no responsibility for the ideas and conclusions expressed here, which (barring scholarly indebtedness) rest entirely on my shoulders. I wish to express my enduring admiration and affection for my Ecuadorian friends, and to thank them for their patience and unfailing kindness.

1. Native Americans in Ecuador use the term *Runa* in self-reference. Ecuadorians consider "Indian" a pejorative term, and substitute the euphemism *indígenes*. as a term of reference for Native Americans. Most *mestizos* (persons of mixed Hispanic and indigenous descent) use *blanco* self-referentially (cf. Stutzman 1981).

2. The sample of families was originally collected in a study of socialization processes.

3. Egalitarianism may vary among groups, however. See Villavicencio (1973:131) who writes of the Otavaleños of Ecuador and states that "Dentro de la familia la autoridad social y económica reside en el padre, compartida en cierta forma con la madre, quién mas bién se halla sometida a las disposiciones del hombre."

Parallel descent among the Inka (Zuidema 1977), the Andean division of the cosmos into male and female elements and the economic and religious power of noble Inka women all indicate that women's status was relatively higher in the precolombian world. These factors, however, do not necessarily imply a corresponding equality of the sexes extending to all social spheres (Silverblatt 1987). To take another case as an illustration, Confucian ideology divides the cosmos according to masculine/feminine principles (which can mix and interpenetrate in a single being), but it also underwrites a social structure marked by male superiority and dominance, a pattern that persists in Chinese-influenced rural areas of Taiwan (Wolf 1972; Gallin 1987).

4. The prevalence of wife-beating needs much more documentation. At present, we have only bits of information: Levinson (1983), testing (cross-culturally) the hypothesis that the presence of physical punishment in childhood correlates with high levels of wife-beating among adults, found wife-beating common among the Aymara, although child punishment occurred infrequently. An incident of wife-beating is recounted by an indigenous victim in the ethnographic film, "Women of the Andes," and Lobo (1986:15) states that wife-beating and sneak-thievery are the most recurrent crimes in a barriada in Lima whose residents include indigenous migrants from the highlands. Bolton and Bolton (1975) recorded an extremely high incidence of Qolla family violence. Beals (1966) gives us counter-evidence; he heard of only one incident in the indigenous community of Nayón, Ecuador — a report, he says, that was hotly denied by the victim.

5. Gender ideals were first explored in Las Flores during the course of fieldwork in 1975—1976 (and investigated further in other sites in 1982—84) where descriptions of behavioral traits ideal for each sex were collected and compiled.

6. This notion also affects one's contacts with evil, supernatural forces. Demonstrating that one is *bravo* discourages attack by *mal aire*, the illness-producing "evil air" (McKee 1987). Persons who are successful folk-healers (*curanderos*) usually are characterized as *bravo* (McKee 1987).

7. The great majority of market vendors (both *comerciantes* and *feriantes*) and small shop-keepers are women. In commercial dealings, or in social intercourse with non-kin, women actively seek the advantage (a stance necessary to a good bargainer,

and expected by both customer and vendor). But they are most admired if they can drive a hard bargain with cheerfulness and good humour, for joking reduces tension and ill-will generated in competitive commercial exchange (cf. Sahlins 1972).

8. The norms of conjugal exchange are phrased, at their broadest, as the general needs of wives and husbands. In answering these needs, a husband's primary duty is to contribute his earnings to his family (and not to waste them on gambling and drinking). A wife's primary charge is to be frugal, and to augment family income through agricultural work or business enterprises, without failing to give adequate care to children. Mutually held expectations include adequate provision of food whether from the fields or the cooking fire, concern for a partner's health and well-being, and proper performance of the myriad activities essential to an economically viable household. Husbands exact sexual faithfulness from wives; wives hope for the same from husbands, but are aware of peer pressure to involve men in casual affairs.

9. Caro (1983, 1985) notes that the herders of Ulla Ulla, Bolivia, give animals to children at significant stages in the life-cycle, so that at marriage, both husband and wife own herds (also see Flores-Ochoa 1979) and continue to retain ownership of their original animals and all future offspring.

In Nayón, Ecuador, parents who were able to do so gave land to both sons and daughters at marriage. From Beals' sample of families, one can calculate that 54 percent of men (N = 24) married wives who owned land and 47 percent of the women (N = 19) married husbands who owned land (Beals 1966).

10. The *location* of plots is a particular source of contention, for in the vertical environment of the Andes it is desirable to have lands distributed at different altitudinal levels, as each is best suited to cultivation of particular vegetable foods or to pasturage (Bastien 1978; Brush 1977a; Mayer 1974; Murra 1975; Pomeroy 1988; Waters 1988).

11. This is particularly effective if multiple marriages are contracted over time between two families (and brother-sister exchange is a preferred, if now rare, marriage form). Wealthier Floreño families restrict dispersion of family lands by seeking unions between first cousins (though these are proscribed in both sacred and secular law). This custom apparently was common to all social levels in the recent past, for it is found in almost one-third of marriages in the second ascending generation in my genealogical data. Brownrigg (1971) found cousin marriages among an indigenous group in the southern province of Caatnar, but both Beals (1966) and Parsons (1945) report them as rare in the northern Ecuadorian communities where they worked. In Peru, Brush (1977b) finds cousin marriages in Bolivar Province, whereas marriages between kin closer than the fifth degree of relationship are regarded as incestuous in other Peruvian communities (Isbell 1978; Bolton 1973a).

12. Weiss (1985) points to relationships between population growth, farmland shortages and increased urban migration in Ecuador.

13. Patrilocal postmarital residence is supposedly normative, though in my sample of 92 families there were 14 paternal stem families and 8 maternal stem families. Neolocal residence is the ideal, usually achieved after three to five years. There were 47 nuclear families in the sample, and the balance of families were classed as matrifocal, patrifocal or collateral.

14. In fact, *immediate* repayment of an obligation can be construed as an insult (Bourdieu 1986).

15. *Compadres* of marriage may, in fact, be kin of the bride or the groom but their impartiality is believed to be monitored by God. They are duty-bound to refrain from inciting the partisan responses of other kin.

Traditionally, *ajihados* signalled penance and their compliance with their godparents' counseling by kneeling and permitting the latter to whip their backs (Belote 1978; McKee 1980). Bolton and Bolton (1975) state that Qolla godparents threaten to use the whip to coerce obedience.

REFERENCES CITED

Bastien, Joseph. 1978. Mountain of the Condor. Metaphor and Ritual in an Andean Ayllu. Monograph no. 64, American Ethnological Society. New York: West Publishers.

Beals, Ralph. 1966. A Community in Transition: Nayón, Ecuador. Latin American Studies, Vol. 2. Los Angeles: University of California.

Belote, Linda. 1978. Prejudice and Pride: Indian-White Relations in Saraguro, Ecuador. Ph.D. Thesis, University of Illinois, Champaign-Urbana. University Microfilms.

Bolton, Ralph. 1973a. Tawanku: Intercouple Bonds in a Qolla Village (Peru). Anthropos 68 (1—2):145—155.

———. 1973b. Aggression and Hypoglycemia among the Qolla: A Study in Psychobiological Anthropology. Ethnology 12(3):227—257.

Bolton, Ralph and Charlene Bolton. 1975. Conflictos en la Familia Andina. Un Estudio Antropológico entre los Campesinos Qolla. Cuzco, Peru: Centro de Estudios Andinos.

Bourdieu, Pierre. 1986. Outline of a Theory of Practice. Cambridge: Cambridge University Press.

Bourque, Susan and Kay Warren. 1981. Women of the Andes. Patriarchy and Social Change in Two Peruvian Towns. Ann Arbor: University of Michigan Press.

Brownrigg, Leslie. 1971. Cañari Kinship Variations. Paper read at the 70th Annual Meeting of the American Anthropological Association, New York.

Brush, Stephen. 1977a. Mountain, Field and Family: The Economy and Human Ecology of an Andean Valley. Philadelphia: University of Pennsylvania.

———. 1977b. Kinship and Land Use in a Northern Sierra Community. *In* Andean Kinship and Marriage. Ralph Bolton and Enrique Mayer, eds. Pp. 136—152. Washington, D.C.: The American Anthropological Association, special publication #7.

Caro, Deborah. 1983. Land Tenure and Women's Status Among Herders in Ulla Ulla, Bolivia. Paper read at the 82nd Annual Meetings of the American Anthropological Association. Chicago, Illinois, November 16—20.

———. 1985. "Those Who Divide Us": Resistance and Change among Pastoral Ayllus in Ulla Ulla, Bolivia. Doctoral Dissertation, The Johns Hopkins University.

Carter, W. E. 1977. Trial Marriage in the Andes? *In* Andean Kinship and Marriage, Ralph Bolton and Enrique Mayer, eds. Pp. 177—216. Washington, D.C.: The American Anthropological Association, special publication #7.

Código Civil. 1980. Seventh Official Edition. Quito, Ecuador: Corporación de Estudios y Publicaciones.

Flores-Ochoa, Jorge. 1979. Pastoralists of the Andes. The Alpaca Herders of Paratia. Philadelphia: Ishi.

Gallin, Rita. 1987. Wife Abuse in the Context of Developmental Change: A Chinese (Taiwanese) Case. Paper read at the 86th Annual Meeting of the American Anthropological Association, Chicago, Illinois, November 18—22.

Gillin, John. 1965. Ethos Components in Modern Latin American Culture. *In* Contemporary Cultures and Societies of Latin America. Dwight Heath and Richard Adams, eds. Pp. 503—517. New York: Random House.

Gilmore, David. 1987. Aggression and Community. New Haven: Yale University Press.

Harris, Olivia. 1980. The Power of Signs: Gender, Culture and the World in the Bolivian Andes. *In* Nature, Culture and Gender. Carol MacCormack and Marilyn Strathern, eds. Pp. 70—94. New York: Cambridge University.

Isbell, B. J. 1978. To Defend Ourselves. Ecology and Ritual in an Andean Village. Austin: University of Texas Press.

Lambert, Bernd. 1977. Bilaterality in the Andes. *In* Andean Kinship and Marriage, Ralph Bolton and Enrique Mayer, eds. Pp. 1—27. Washington, D.C.: The American Anthropological Association.

Levinson, David. 1983. Physical Punishment of Children and Wife-Beating in Cross-Cultural Perspective. *In* International Perspectives on Family Violence. Richard Gelles and C. Cornell, eds. pp. 73—77. Lexington, MA: D.C. Heath and Co.

Lévi-Strauss, Claude. 1983. Structural Anthropology, Vol. II. Chicago: University of Chicago Press.

———. 1987. Introduction to the Work of Marcel Mauss. London: Routledge and Kegan Paul.

Lobo, Susan. 1986. A House of My Own. Social Organization in the Squatter Settlements of Lima, Peru. Tucson: University of Arizona Press.

Luzuriaga, Carlos. 1980. Situación de la mujer en el Ecuador. Comentarios derivados de una revisión de la literatura. Misión USAID en el Ecuador. Internal Document.

Mauss, Marcel. 1954 [1924]. The Gift. Forms and Functions of Exchange in Archaic Societies. London: Cohen and West.

Mayer, Enrique. 1974. Las Reglas del Juego en la Reciprocidad Andina. *In* Reciprocidad e Intercambio en los Andes Peruanos. Giorgio Alberti and Enrique Mayer, eds. Pp.37—65. Lima: Instituto de Estudios Peruanos.

McKee, Lauris. 1980. Ideals and Actualities: Socialization of Gender in an Ecuadorian Village. Doctoral Dissertation, Cornell University.

———. 1987. Ethnomedical Treatment of Children's Diarrheal Illnesses. Social Science and Medicine 25 (10):1147—1155. Special Issue: Cross-Cultural Perspectives on Women and Health Care, Ruthbeth Finerman and Werner Wilbert, eds.

Murra, John V. 1975. Formaciones económicas y politicas del mundo andino. Lima, Peru: Instituto de Estudios Peruanos. Pp. 59—115.

Parsons, Elsie Clews. 1945. Peguche. A Study of Andean Indians. Chicago: University of Chicago Press.

Peristiany, J.G. 1966. Honor and Shame in a Cypriot Highland Village. *In* Honor and Shame: The Values of Mediterranean Society, J. G. Peristiany, ed. Pp. 173—190. Chicago: University of Chicago Press.

Pitt-Rivers, J. T. 1954. The People of the Sierra. Chicago: University of Chicago Press.

———. 1977. The Fate of Schechem. Cambridge: Cambridge University Press.

Pomeroy, Cheryl. 1988. Fincas familiares multizonales en la vertiente occidental de los Andes Ecuatorianos. *In* Nuevas investigaciones antropológicas Ecuatorianas. Lauris McKee and Silvia Argüello, eds. Quito, Ecuador: Abya Yala Press.

Romoleroux de Morales, Ketty. 1975. Situación jurídica y social de la mujer en el Ecuador. Guayaquíl, Ecuador: Universidad de Guayaquíl.

Rubel, Arthur, Carl O'Nell, and Roland Collado-Ardon. 1984. *Susto*, A Folk Illness. Berkeley: University of California Press.

Sahlins, Marshall. 1972. Stone Age Economics. Chicago: Aldine-Atherton.

Silverblatt, Irene. 1987. Sun, Moon and Witches. Gender Ideologies and Class in Inca and Colonial Peru. Princeton, Princeton University.

Stutzman, Ronald. 1981. El Mestizaje: An All-Inclusive Ideology of Exclusion. *In* Cultural Transformations and Ethnicity in Modern Ecuador. Norman E. Whitten, Jr., ed. Pp. 45—94. Urbana: University of Illinois.

Taggart, James. 1990. Enchanted Maidens. Gender Relations in Spanish Folktales of Courtship and Marriage. Princeton: Princeton University Press.

Villavicencio Rivadenéira, Gladys. 1973. Relaciones Interétnicas en Otavalo. México: Instituto Indigenista Interamericano.

Walter, Lynn. 1981. Social Strategies and the Fiesta Complex in an Otavaleño Community. American Ethnologist 8(1):172—185.

Waters, William. 1988. La Propiedad de la Tierra y la Forma de Producción: Estructura y Transformaciones en Cantón Salcedo, Ecuador *In* Nuevas investigaciones antropológicas Ecuatorianas. Lauris McKee and Silvia Argüello, eds. Quito: Abya Yala.

Weiss, W.A. 1985. The Social Organization of Property and Work—a Study of Migrants from the Rural Ecuadorian Sierra. American Ethnologist 12(3):468—488.

Wolf, Marjorie. 1972. Women and the Family in Rural Taiwan. Stanford: University of California.

Zuidema, Thomas. 1977. The Inca Kinship System: A New Theoretical View. *In* Andean Kinship and Marriage. Ralph Bolton and Enrique Mayer, eds. Pp. 240—261. Washington, D.C.: The American Anthropological Association, special publication #7.

12

Like Teeth Biting Tongue: The Proscription and Practice of Spouse Abuse in Mayotte

Michael Lambek

Lela ndraiky hify fanyekitry. Teeth and tongue live happily side by side most of the time but occasionally the tongue gets bitten. Villagers in Mayotte say people are like this too. In a characteristic spatial idiom for social intimacy they say even people who are in the same place (*mahala raiky*) occasionally fight with each other. Fighting among intimates is wrong and stupid, it is a means of hurting oneself, the proverb seems to say, but it happens. This paper is about why spouse abuse is wrong in Mayotte and how it sometimes happens.

Unlike what is described for most of the societies in this volume, spouse abuse is strongly frowned upon in Mayotte and the incidence appears to be relatively low. Since it is harder to demonstrate an absence than to report a presence, it is critical to begin with the grounds on which my claims are based. My evidence and analysis are not based on surveys or statistics, but rather on a case study approach (cf. Werbner 1984). I have conducted participant-observation fieldwork in a pair of neighboring villages in Mayotte over the course of ten years, 1975–1985. This includes about 18 months residence in these communities. During this time I never witnessed an incident of wife-beating directly. However, without systematically questioning people about the subject, I heard about six distinct cases, and I rely extensively on what people said about them. One of these incidents took place several years before my first visit to Mayotte and another occurred among people whom I did not know, living in a distant village. There were undoubtedly more cases than those I encountered, since a woman who submits to physical abuse may be ashamed of it and may keep quiet for as long as she wishes to maintain the marriage. On the other hand, the number of such additional cases was probably low since the dense settlement pattern makes privacy difficult to maintain, since most abused wives would retaliate loudly, and since I had access to a good deal of local gossip. Moreover, the number of incidents can be contrasted with the much higher rates of violence between people of the same sex; I observed and heard about many more physical fights between pairs of men or pairs of women.

Starting from the cases of spouse abuse themselves, I try to elucidate the local view of why domestic violence is wrong. The paper attempts to understand the meaning of spouse abuse for people in Mayotte and argues in terms of local moral precepts. A shorter section at the end shifts to the level of behavioral and material factors that may affect the incidence of abuse.

First, however, I should say a few words about the general social context. Mayotte is an island, some 275 kilometres square, located in the Comoro Archipelago of the western Indian Ocean, approximately half-way between Madagascar and Tanzania. I worked in a pair of neighboring and closely related villages with populations of about 425 and 150 persons respectively in 1975 and 50 percent more than that a decade later. I cannot say how typical these villages are with regard to the issues at hand. Most of the residents are native speakers of Kibushy, a northern dialect of Malagasy; it is possibly of significance that of the six cases of abuse I know about, three of the violent men were speakers of Shimaore, a Bantu language and the language of the indigenous majority on Mayotte. Although the origins of the first Malagasy speakers on Mayotte are unknown, the ancestors of those among whom I lived arrived for the most part during the nineteenth century either as immigrants from northern and northwestern Madagascar or as indentured laborers from East Africa. (The latter group have lost their original language/s.) Mayotte has been under French control since 1841 but for most of this century prior to 1975 it has suffered, if that is the word, a good deal of neglect from the metropole. Enforced labour on European-owned plantations declined radically at the turn of the century and in 1975 wage labour was a sporadic activity on the part of most men. Most labour was directed to subsistence cultivation on family-owned plots (the use rights to which were often lent freely to other villagers or kin), to fishing in the rich lagoon, and to cash cropping, primarily of ylang ylang. The distilled oil of ylang ylang flowers is a basic element in the French perfume industry and its production during the 1970s provided a relatively good return. By 1985 the situation had changed; male wage labor, often in construction, had become much more important and access to land was significantly restricted. In all periods, however, the production strategy of an ordinary household was marked by its diversification.

Inheritance is bilateral in Mayotte and most women share property rights with their siblings and sometimes with their spouses. As we shall see, Karen Sacks' title, *Sisters and Wives* (1979), is an apposite characterization of the statuses of Mayotte women. The conjugal pair forms the key unit of subsistence production in the village but specific conjugal pairs are far less durable and often less solidary than the deeper ties among siblings. Most important for the present discussion is the fact that virtually all women own their own homes and these homes are usually located in their natal villages, close to their kin. When marriages are village exogamous it is usually, but not always, the husband who moves.

The people of Mayotte are practicing Muslims, but relations between the sexes hardly correspond to the Western stereotypes of Islam. Women are not segregated to any significant extent from men and do not wear veils; nowadays they have a good deal of say in the choice of their first marriage partner and full say thereafter, can terminate a marriage virtually at will, and are frequently public political and ceremonial actors. Motherhood is not the only "career" open to them (Lambek 1988, Lambek in press). However, their privileges and opportunities are not so great as those of men, especially in the spheres of wage labour, cash crop production, and Islamic ritual. Clitoridectomy is not practiced; the one severe obligation placed upon a woman, that she be a virgin upon her first marriage, can be interpreted in a partially positive light as a mark and source of a woman's personal autonomy (Lambek 1983). In effect, defloration is the last moment, not the first, in which other adults have control over her body, and these are her parents, not her husband. If a bride is found not to be a virgin upon her wedding, the only way the groom can retaliate (and he probably won't) is to walk out. If anyone has the right to beat the bride for her lapse, and such an outcome is by no means inevitable, it is her father, and then only for the last time. Finally, a highly relevant aspect of Islam is the prohibition of alcohol. Drinking is minimal, is largely restricted to palm wine among young men and, in the ordinary drinker, it does not produce threatening behaviour.

While I have not actually witnessed a violent incident, knowing local women I cannot imagine that it would be entirely one-sided. The culture in general is characterized by a high degree of verbal assertiveness and oral aggression, often couched in jokes, although the behaviour between husbands and wives is fairly circumspect. If anything, women (of all ages) appear more aggressive than men, although of course there are many exceptions to this generalization from both sexes. Young children in particular are often the objects of verbal aggression. At the same time, physical strength and violence are not idealized, and actual violence makes people uneasy. Assertive behaviour expresses an ethos of equality not domination. In the boxing game (*mrenge*) sometimes practiced by boys, the sparring partners should be evenly matched and they are pulled apart the instant they make contact; it always seemed to me that there was more action in the exclamations of the spectators than in the ring itself.[1] A good deal of "violent" behaviour (as well as sanctions against violence) is also carried out indirectly through both sorcery or sorcery projection, and through harnessing divine justice and retribution, although accusations are rarely made openly.

SPOUSES AND SIBLINGS

The first case of spouse abuse came to my attention when I saw a friend of mine, Ali, a man in his thirties who was the village imam and local intellectual, chasing Zainaba, one of his adult sisters, through the village and shouting at her to leave the community. The story was as follows. On the evening of a Muslim feast day, an ex-husband of Zainaba's had arrived at her home in order to visit his children. Zainaba's current husband Kolo, who was drunk at the time, became enraged and tried to beat Zainaba. Zainaba's brothers and nephews came running to her defense, fending off Kolo, a large, strong man, with sticks. The next day, after consultation with the village elders, Zainaba's relatives announced that they wanted Kolo out of the village. Zainaba and her siblings are members of the village by rights of inheritance and descent from a founder (as well as by residence and participation) whereas Kolo was an outsider, resident only as a result of his recent marriage. The relatives had both the right and the power to force Kolo to leave and public opinion was firmly on their side. They said that they found Kolo's behavior intolerable and were fed up with the domestic quarreling; this was not the first incident and they feared future violence.[2]

They were even ready, they threatened, to take the case to the civil authorities (*sirkal*), an outcome which from everyone's point of view was undesirable and a strategy of last resort. This was a clear-cut and solidary reaction on the part of an abused wife's kin toward her spouse. It illustrates both that domestic violence is unacceptable and that it is not entirely a "private" matter, that the wife's kin will intervene and that they are prepared to render the whole thing "public," whether at the level of the village or the state. What was particularly troublesome to Zainaba's kin was that while their strategy toward Kolo was unambiguous, their obligations vis-á-vis Zainaba herself were not. Zainaba did not wish to separate from her husband and her kin did not have the right to force her to do so. Hence they were presenting her with the unpalatable option of leaving with Kolo, a situation which might presumably put her at an increased risk of violence. The family had never liked Kolo; Zainaba had married him against their express warnings and advice. They were angry with her for helping to maintain a situation of domestic quarrelling and hurt, that after so much mistreatment, Zainaba stood opposed to them rather than to Kolo, claiming that she loved and wanted to stay with him. Ali became infuriated and started chasing Zainaba around the village, screaming at her to leave because she had created and perpetuated a situation of dispute and emotional turmoil with her natal kin (she had "made her mother cry") and because, by rejecting their authority, she was forcing them to make a decision whose likely effect made them feel un-easy. However, as a cooler member of the family expressed it, they would rather lose a daughter (if they had to) than retain this son-in-law.

Kolo left the village three days later, after threatening Ali. (Somewhat to my surprise Ali dismissed the threat, claiming to be much more powerful than Kolo. This confidence came from the sense that the forces of divine justice are much stronger than any attacks, directly physical or by means of sorcery, that Kolo could instigate.) Zainaba stayed behind, out of fear of her mother and brothers (her father was dead). A week later Zainaba's mother received a letter from the leading Islamic cleric on the island, inter-ceding on Kolo's behalf and asking the village to readmit him. Zainaba's mother was furious at this intervention over a matter which she thought was none of the cleric's business. Two days later Kolo appeared with money to give the family in order to effect a reconciliation. Zainaba's kin flatly refused — they said later Kolo had acquired the money by stealing a cow — and so Kolo left a second time. This time, however, Zainaba went with him. Ali said he didn't mind seeing her go since she never listened to her kin any more; when a person doesn't listen to the advice of her (or his) kin things al-ways go badly for them. Moreover, he said, Kolo was Zainaba's eighth hus-band, indicating that she didn't know her own mind and, anyway, eight is always a bad number. Ali added that he could easily do medicine to make Zainaba fall out of love with Kolo and thus choose to stay home, but he wouldn't because he was so angry with her. In his view, Zainaba just liked to cause trouble and deserved whatever treatment she got.

Some weeks after this Zainaba returned home alone, made her peace with her mother, and subsequently married husband number nine. The next time I remember seeing Kolo was ten years later when he started a fight at a spirit possession healing ritual and had to be manually evicted by the patient's hus-band and brothers. He was drunk, capitulated easily, and looked a good deal the worse for wear.

Zainaba's story sets the episode of physical spouse abuse in the wider con-texts of fear, violence, anger, and morality and it counterpoises the legitimate rights and permanent interests of consanguineal kin with the weaker and dif-ferent bonds of affinity. Consanguines are responsible for one another's wel-fare and exert a strong moral influence on behavior. The consanguineal kin are supposed to guarantee the autonomy of the individual, who in turn must show their proper respect. Zainaba's family had expected her to listen to them. It was her consistent rejection of their concern that frustrated and angered them. The emotions that were raised had as much to do with "sib-ling abuse" (in both directions, perhaps) as with Kolo's violence per se. Most of all, the story is about transgressing — again in two directions — the correct limits of autonomy. Kolo had no right to abuse Zainaba and Zainaba had no justification to be so independent from her family as to let herself be victimized by him.

Marital separation (which functions as de facto divorce) is easy and common in Mayotte and not necessarily viewed negatively. A divorced woman often keeps custody of children and in no case need lose contact with them. As adults, Kolo and Zainaba could readily have broken off the marriage and should have done so. As Ali said, when you no longer love a woman you leave, you don't start beating her. Zainaba could also have asked Kolo to go. After the fight she had the freedom to leave with her husband or to stay at home without him, but, out of both common sense and acknowledgement of her kin's legitimate concern, she should have chosen to stay. (Of course, from her point of view, which is not represented here, she may have had good reason to wish to escape the domination of her kin.)

Aside from the violence, the case illustrates more general dilemmas faced by everyone of both sexes in Mayotte: should the "love" and attention one shows one's spouse, and the dependence on them one allows oneself to feel, match that which one shows or feels for one's kin? What should be the correct course of action when these are in competition? In cases without violence the proper course of action, or the one in the best interests of the actor, is not always so easily discernable. Some married couples pride themselves on the length of their union and state that they see themselves as a unity (*ulu araiky*). But, in general, the perspective is different from what we would expect in North America.[3] Thus I have heard women berate their sisters for being loyal to a husband and not changing spouses frequently. From the actor's point of view, emotional investment in the marital relationship may not appear to be particularly secure.

MORAL AUTHORITY AND CORPORAL AUTONOMY

Zainaba's story also demonstrates that violence is not universally frowned upon nor is fear absent from kin relationships. In general, the more solidary the relationship (in descending order, children to their parents, between siblings, between neighbours), the less justifiable the violence. Yet it is precisely in the relationships which are supposed to be the most solidary that transgression of the norms of behavior will give rise to the strongest emotions. Ali's behavior toward his sister was frowned upon (while nonviolent, Ali is viewed as someone too quick to anger; people fear his temper), yet it was understood. Beating a spouse is not understood, or rather it can only be understood in a way that unacceptably devalues the victim.

The issue can be best explored through another case. Sua was discussing with me some reservations about her current marriage to a rather passive man younger than herself. She mentioned that her eldest son had expressed the wish that she return to his father, from whom she had been separated.

He was a vigorous, jovial, and well-respected man and so I was rather taken aback at her categorical refusal to consider the union. She then confided that during their first marriage he used to hit her. They had been residing virilocally in a village about two hours by foot from her natal village. Rumors of the abuse reached her parents who questioned her closely on her visits home, but she always denied it, saying that people were just gossips and that if it were true she would have left him. In a sense, as long as she wished to stay with the man her discretion vis-à-vis her parents was more appropriate than Zainaba's loud quarreling. However, the reason for her silence was a good deal more straightforward than this: she felt humiliated by her situation. Her resentment toward her husband grew and she hit back and eventually left him. Her explanation was simple: "He treated me like a child," she said.[4]

Another story makes the same point from a happier direction. One evening a small group of men were chatting in the centre of the village. One of them recounted how his goat had died that day. It had been taken into the bush to feed but was tethered on such a steep slope that it strangled itself on its own cord. With humorous resignation the man said "if it had been one of my children who had been so careless with the animals I would have beaten him, but what could I do — it was my wife!"

Spouse abuse is illegitimate in Mayotte precisely because spouses ought not to be in a moral relationship to each other of parent to child. A husband should not beat his wife and a wife should not take it if he does. The perpetrator of such violence is in the wrong, but the victim is also partly in the wrong if she puts up with it. If she submits she is acting like a child and if she is going to act like a child she should do so only in relation to her parents and siblings and not in her relation to her husband, since only the former can be assumed to have her best interests at heart. Returning to the first case for a moment, we can now see more clearly how, by allowing herself to be treated like a child by her husband, Zainaba was rejecting her kinship position vis-à-vis her true parents.[5]

The prohibition of spouse abuse cannot be put down simply to the abhorrence of violence per se. One might say, following Margaret Mead on culture and temperament, that a violent individual like Kolo is a misfit in a society like Mayotte. This is true to an extent, but I think one has to look more carefully. The issue is not only the presence or absence or the simple positive or negative evaluation placed on violence, but the means and directions in which it is channelled and more or less appropriately utilized, its meaning in various contexts. Ali chased Zainaba around the village and threatened her in the context of a relationship of siblingship and a situation of legitimate concern and hurt feelings where such behaviour, while incorrect, was not gratuitous. He was, in a sense, berating her "for her own good," something which a husband is viewed as having neither the right nor neces-

sarily the interest to do. Ali would have drawn greater censure and, incidentally, made a good deal more of a fool of himself, had he been chasing his
wife. His behavior had meaningful reference to the channels of deep emotion and moral authority.[6] Likewise, he was confident at being able to har-
ness morally positive mystical violence in order to protect himself from Kolo.

Direct physical violence[7] is acceptable in Mayotte in only two kinds of
relationships and even then it is subject to a series of constraints. The first
is the relationship of adversaries or rivals, people of equivalent status
generally competing for a sexual partner. The second relationship, which is
unidirectional, is that of parents over their children. (The term parents is
broadly defined here and may, in certain circumstances, include siblings.)
In both these kinds of relationships the level of acceptable violence is limited
and bystanders will usually step in to break up the conflict, especially if the
antagonists seem unequally matched, if their statuses are such, e.g. elders,
that the violence embarrasses the audience, if the fight threatens to have
wider repercussions, or if one of the parties seems likely to get badly hurt.
While a fight between young women or men using no weapons might be allowed to run its course and might even be watched with enjoyment by some,
most other violence is stopped quickly. Children receive an occasional cuff
or deliberate single hit with a switch from a parent or Koranic teacher,[8] but
anything of longer duration, especially if the adult seems out of control, will
be stopped by others. For example, I have seen neighbours intervene only
moments after a mother erupted in rage and began hitting her daughter, aged
perhaps eight, for forgetting to fetch firewood. The mother was admonished
that one strike was enough. Parents who resort to excessive violence or for
reasons deemed by others to be illegitimate will be criticized by kin or spoken
about behind their backs by others.

In essence, one of the key differences between childhood and adulthood
in Mayotte is the autonomy that adults have over their own bodies. Children
can be threatened with beatings and sometimes receive them from
caretakers. According to one male informant it is even permissible for a
brother to beat an older sister if he perceives she is doing wrong; significantly, his example came up in a discussion of the control of a girl's premarital
sexuality. Otherwise it is a grave wrong for a person of junior status, younger
in years or in generation, to hit someone of senior status, especially a parent.
An incident in which a youth hit his father was much commented upon in
shocked tones, and the perpetrator of such an act must actively seek his
parent's pardon if he is not to suffer the effects of a curse. Here it is not so
much the physical act per se which is objected to, but the statement it encodes. Hitting a parent reverses the proper direction of authority.

Unlike adults, children can be ordered to do things. Children also suffer
corporal violence in the ritual sphere: boys are circumcised, girls are
deflowered by their husbands, an act often discreetly supervised by their

grandmothers, and children of both sexes must undergo, prior to circumcision or defloration, an inhalation of smoke said to be far more painful than either. The only occasion on which an adult would be smoked is during the course of what local practitioners consider an extreme treatment of last resort to remove a dangerous spirit which has caused a prolonged psychotic break; the aim of the treatment is precisely to enable the patient to regain control over his or her own body. In all other circumstances an adult's body is inviolate. A dying adult is shielded behind a curtain from onlookers and the appearance of corporal autonomy is maintained to the degree that a corpse is never unclothed, even while it is being cleansed and the last traces from the digestive tract removed.

ADULTERY AND THE VIOLENCE BETWEEN RIVALS

The corporeal autonomy of adults is also reflected in sexual mores. Adultery is quite common; yet while injured spouses respond with hurt and anger, they cannot, in the strict sense of the term, punish each other for adultery since neither of them is under the sexual control of the other. If a husband is angry about his wife's sexual exploits (and some men are complaisant), his aggression is more appropriately directed toward his wife's lover. An angry husband may react in any one of three ways: he can leave his wife, he can reduce the amount of material support he provides, or he can fight with the interloper, either physically or by means of sorcery.[9] But the person most likely to retaliate is the wife or girlfriend (or in certain situations even the ex-wife) of the woman's lover.

In other words, where adultery or the suspicion of adultery leads to violence, it is most likely and most appropriately to occur between the parties of the same sex. A woman may attempt to beat up her husband's lover and a man his wife's. When a woman suspects her husband of unfaithfulness before making an accusation she ought to follow him to the other woman's house in order to verify her suspicions and catch the couple in the act. She will then walk in on them, in a cultural scenario known as *mangka vamba*, raise a ruckus, pull her husband away or walk off with his clothes, and perhaps start a brawl with the other woman. Brawls between women may also take place in public, and sometimes escalate to include kinswomen of the major protagonists, although it is felt that senior women should stay out of it. These fights may be rough; I know of cases where the loser has required medical attention. Fights between men are probably less frequent but they may, on occasion, be more violent.[10] One senior man of the village is said in his youth to have lain in wait for his wife's lover with an axe and to have spent some time in prison for wounding him. The level of his violence was directly related to the fact that the interloper was his own classificatory older brother and hence a "parental" figure, precisely the sort of person who should have protected his interests.

This case indicates clearly that the primary injury and hence the retribution is conceived to take place between members of the same sex (though village gossip also said that the wife had treated her husband very badly). Adults have relative autonomy regarding their own sexual behavior; what they do not have the right to do is trespass upon the partners of others. Marriage is a relationship where one has rights *to* the other partner but not *in* her.[11] She can do what she likes (more or less; marriage partners ought to treat each other with respect) but others cannot do with her whatever they like.

In sum, rivals have, in a sense, the right to fight each other. To be beaten by a rival is not to submit to a claim of moral authority because none is intended. Between rivals fighting is a demonstration of equality. But between spouses, quite apart from the physical abuse itself, it is the assertion of the perpetrator, manifest in his act of his illegitimate claim to authority over the victim, which is (or should be) much resented by the latter and by her kin.

FACTORS CONTRIBUTING TO DOMESTIC VIOLENCE

The fact that spouse abuse is conceptually, morally, and emotionally wrong undoubtedly keeps the incidence down but, of course, does not prevent its occurrence. One might expect the incidence of violence to rise where the plausibility of the cultural view is less well supported by social and material factors. For example, in the past when the age discrepancy between spouses was often much greater than today, the husband might more readily have attempted to take on a parental-like role of authority toward his wife. In the present, where women's access to the means of production becomes indirect as the wives of wage earners, they do in fact take on a dependent relationship to husbands (cf. Sacks 1979) and the cultural conceptions might be weakened as a result. Moreover, in the course of such a process of change, structural factors are likely to raise the tensions between marriage partners, e.g. by generating contradictory expectations or by placing an absolute strain on the household budget. Domestic violence might follow. The cultural perspective presented above could only account for why violence might be less than in other societies undergoing similar structural changes. This argument could account for different ratios of violence in different sectors of the population or within the same community over time.

My data will not allow me to do this, but I can say something about the contexts in which violence is more likely to occur in a given rural community where the cultural view presented above remains. Two sets of factors are relevant here, those which weaken the informal social control against violence and those which increase the tensions between spouses. Relevant to both is the residence pattern. Where spouses come from different villages and are residing virilocally it may be somewhat easier for abuse to be carried out than in the more common uxorilocal situation. Also significant is the pattern of seasonal residence in the fields. Many households spend the agricultural season or periods of it in relatively isolated dwellings, quite unlike the densely packed villages. On one occasion when a middle-aged couple returned after a sojourn in the bush the wife issued a complaint of physical abuse against her husband, asking a senior man to mediate between the couple and to propose a form of compensation for the wife. Incidentally, this shows that it is not only a woman's kin who guarantee her safety but that, in the absence of kin, a woman can represent herself.

The reason for this couple's quarrel brings up the most common issue around which marital conflict forms, namely polygyny. Polygyny is an issue both because of the sexual and emotional jealousy and sense of loss it sometimes entails and because of its relevance to debate about the proper ways to spend the household's resources. The wife is in a subordinate situation both because Islam permits polygyny and because she has far less control over household earnings than her husband. Polygyny here is an overt manifestation of an Islamic model of sex roles and conjugal relations which differs from that described earlier and which has been only partially accepted by the community and then more by men than by women. Despite the fact that polygyny is permissible and may, in some situations, be readily accepted, it is often viewed by the first wife as a breach of faith and a disruption, not to say destruction, of common domestic projects.[12] When the threat of polygyny becomes practice, it renders inequality direct, specific, and explicit. Hence I do not think it is unfair to say that in Mayotte, though not necessarily in all societies in which the institution is found, polygyny is itself a form of spouse abuse. Whether that be considered a valid interpretation or not, women faced with polygyny may respond with outright hostility or passive resistance which in turn may sorely try the husband's patience (especially, we might speculate, if he is already feeling guilty or harassed with trying to support two households). The potential for domestic violence rises.[13]

A third kind of factor which increases the level of violence has to do with individual predisposition to violent behaviour. The husband in the first case described in the paper was simply a highly aggressive person. The social factors which might contribute to the etiology of violent dispositions in Mayotte are beyond the scope of this paper, but the existence of "people who like to hit" (*ulu mitia mamanggu*) is recognized in Mayotte. Violent individuals are referred to as *ratsy fangahy,* of bad disposition or personality. Spouses of such people are victims simply because they are within reach and not because of anything intrinsic to the social constitution of marriage.

A final question to ask relates to the factors that discourage an abused woman from leaving her husband and hence perpetuate the conditions that lead to violence. In Mayotte this can be summed up descriptively, to borrow Sacks' (1979) formula, by saying that for some reason sisterhood is outweighed by wifehood, whether this be due to virilocal residence, infatuation, or lack or absence of kin. A potent factor for some women is the fear of poverty. Most women own their houses and household goods and are able to depend on their kin group membership for access to subsistence land, but these things are not sufficient. For the daily necessities—kerosene, soap, salt, clothing—that only money can buy, most women rely on a husband. Some, though by no means all, women find it embarrassing and inconvenient to have to rely on lovers. Husbands are in increasingly short supply and brothers are less reliable since men also have greater expenses and are shifting their investment away both from women and from the wider kin group (cf. Solway 1990). In particular, older women and women with many children may find it hard to find new husbands. This should immediately be qualified by adding that many of them do while other women have built alternate bases of support and may not be interested in remarrying (Lambek, in press).

CONCLUSION

The preceding argument has demonstrated why the people of Mayotte consider spouse abuse to be wrong. I have tried to show that the relationship between spouses is conceptualized at a basic level as one in which violence is inappropriate. In the local view this is not just because violence itself is bad but because the very constitution of the marital relationship precludes it. It is not that women are the weaker sex and must be protected or cherished, but that marriage is a relationship between complementary (but not identical or equivalent) adults who should treat each other with consideration and respect (*ishima*). Perhaps a wife owes her husband respect in a wider range of domains and contexts than the reverse, but this does not change the basic point. Marriage need not be a relationship of great emotional dependency or intensity. The esteem in which one holds one's partner need not be grounded in emotional depth and need not be maintained in the face of evidence that the spouse is not worthy of it. In theory, though people recognize this is frequently not true in practice, letting go of a spouse should be an easy matter. So violence is inappropriate because marital partners are supposed to form a unit of solidarity composed of complements rather than equivalents in which the husband does not have parental-like authority over the wife, and because this unit need not give rise to the sort of violent passions which in other cultures might be idealized. I would suspect that this general view, or something like it, is characteristic of Malagasy speakers throughout Madagascar. A quick and informal oral survey among a number of colleagues with experience in various parts of the island suggests that domestic violence is frowned upon everywhere.

I have demonstrated some of the reasons why spouse abuse is viewed as wrong in Mayotte and have also suggested the conditions under which such moral considerations may be undermined or in which women become vulnerable despite them. These conditions, such as social isolation or economic dependence, may be relevant for the analysis of spouse abuse in any society. But what is more important, I think, is to demonstrate that the presence of a strong disapproval of marital violence can and does work reasonably effectively to control it. Hence recourse to biological arguments is unwarranted. The next step is rather to show how a position such as that taken against marital violence in Mayotte fits into the larger system of gender, marriage, power and prestige. A suggestive beginning for an approach that accounts for the links between marriage systems, gender constructs, and political processes, may be found in the work of Collier and Rosaldo (1981). They attempt to identify the links among such factors as spouse abuse, peer violence, and the cultural emphasis on women's sexuality rather than on motherhood. Although this is not the place to develop a model of social relations in Mayotte along the lines that they suggest, it is clear that the autonomy of women and men, their rights over their respective bodies, the respect in which they should hold each other, and their interests in protecting themselves from rivals are interconnected and are linked to basic social and political processes.

NOTES

Field research was conducted with the financial assistance of the Social Sciences and Humanities Research Council of Canada, the National Science Foundation, the National Geographic Society, and the University of Toronto. I thank Judith Brown for encouraging me to write this paper and all the editors for their patience and helpful suggestions with revisions. Jacqueline Solway has contributed substantially to the argument; her perception of the relationship between the sexes in Mayotte has been invaluable to me. The following individuals have also kindly commented on their experience of spouse abuse elsewhere in Madagascar: Georges Heurtebize, Susan Kus, Victor Raharijaona, and Lesley Sharp. None of them necessarily share my conclusions.

1. I should note that this discussion pertains to the villages in which I lived. An initial residence in town provoked quite a different experience. There, one of my most vivid memories is of children (of mixed sex) playing a game in which the victim buried his head in his arms and had to guess who was rapping him hard on the skull with his knuckles.

2. Even before this incident I had considered Kolo to be potentially violent. He had been one of the very few people to act in a gratuitously unpleasant and even threatening manner toward me, and I was relieved to discover that the community shared my view of him.

3. Nor, here is the perspective similar to the African cases described by Sacks (1979). Not only are wives less subordinate in Mayotte but, as Jacqueline Solway has pointed out to me, the sister/wife contrast in Mayotte is paralleled by a similar duality of status for men. However, in the patrilineal societies analyzed by Sacks, there is no such symmetry; the status of brother is dominant and that of husband is largely absorbed into it.

4. It is a curious fact that the man who beat Sua had also been previously married to Zainaba. For awhile Zainaba and Sua were even co-wives, and it may be that Zainaba has been a victim in more than one of her marriages. Her marriage with this man ended quite differently from Sua's: he discovered she was having an affair and sent her home.

5. Furthermore, in letting her kin become aware of her position and yet not allowing them to help, she was treating them without due consideration and indicating to them that she did not fully know her own mind, hence demonstrating her childlike condition.

6. Had he actually hit his adult sister it might have been a different story.

7. The question of legitimacy of various forms of "mystical" violence, e.g. "sorcery" and retributive prayer, is complex and cannot be treated here, but it should be emphasized that the corpus of violence as it is understood in Mayotte includes much more than direct physical beating.

8. The threat of violence is a major pedagogical tool in the primary Koranic classes.

9. When a man commits adultery his wife can throw him out, hold out for financial recompense from him, or fight the other woman. The fact that a woman can request financial recompense from a husband while a husband can retaliate against a wayward wife by withdrawing financial support indicates the underlying sexual economy. As culturally defined, sex is a woman's resource, cash a man's. One man justified the attack on a wife's lover in the following terms: the man has gone to great expense, he has built his wife a house (this is not all that common in practice but the subsequent disloyalty on the part of the wife is a common story), he buys her new clothes all the time, he supplies her with food . . . and then she takes a lover. Yet this justifies his action against the other man rather than the wife! Adultery shows just how tenuous men's power is; the only thing that makes a woman dependent on a single individual man is her sense of obligation and justice — and of course loyalty is precisely the trait that Mayotte men fear women lack. To a degree the system encourages such disloyalty on the part of women; as long as women are defined as the proper object of men's expenditures a woman can play the field to considerable material advantage (cf. Ottino 1964).

10. The greater occurrence of violence between women may be a reflection of the fact that they have less means of controlling the sexual exploits of their husbands than the reverse or that they feel they have more to lose by a spouse's infidelity. It is also a product of the fact that women consider themselves responsible for minding the taboos (*mitana fady*). When a woman trespasses on another's territory, it is both a violation of expectation and a direct insult. That this is not simp-

ly a product of competition over spouses is indicated by the fact that a woman may feel insulted by a kinswoman's sexual relations with or marriage to a man from whom she has already long since been separated herself, even when there have been several intervening marriages on both sides.

11. This follows Robert Murphy's dictum that "when a man gets married, he thinks that he is marrying a woman, but a bit of reflection on his altered status reveals that he has entered into a state of antimarriage with all women. By defining a tie to one woman, he has defined a status toward all other women" (1980:215). The same holds true in reverse for a woman of course.

12. It is not only the first wife who may experience a breach of faith. Sometimes it is the second wife who discovers only after her marriage that the union she has engaged upon is in fact polygynous.

13. For a means of indirect ("mystical") and sometimes effective retaliation on the part of wives, see Lambek 1980. For such retaliation by the wife's mother see Lambek 1990.

REFERENCES CITED

Collier, Jane F. and Michelle Z. Rosaldo. 1981. Politics and Gender in Simple Societies. *In* Sexual Meanings. Sherry B. Ortner and Harriet Whitehead, eds. Pp. 275—329. New York: Cambridge University Press.

Lambek, Michael. 1980. Spirits and Spouses: Possession as a System of Communication Among the Malagasy Speakers of Mayotte. American Ethnologist 7(2):318—331.

———. 1983. Virgin Marriage and the Autonomy of Women in Mayotte. Signs 9(2): 264—81.

———. 1988. Graceful Exits: Spirit Possession as Personal Performance in Mayotte. Culture 8(1):59—69.

———. 1990. The Practice of Islamic Experts in a Village on Mayotte. Journal of Religion in Africa 20(1):20—40.

———. In press. Motherhood and Other Careers in Mayotte. *In* In Her Prime: New Views of Middle-Aged Women. Viginia Kerns and Judith K. Brown, eds. Second Edition. Urbana: University of Illinois Press.

Murphy, Robert. 1980 [1971]. The Dialectics of Social Life. New York: Columbia University Press.

Ottino, Paul. 1964. La crise du système familial et matrimonial des Sakalava de Nosy Be. Civilisation Malgache 1:225—48.

Sacks, Karen. 1979. Sisters and Wives: The Past and Future of Sexual Equality. Westport, CT: Greenwood.

Solway, Jacqueline S. 1990. Affines and Spouses, Friends and Lovers: The Passing of Polygyny in Botswana. Journal of Anthropological Research 46(1):41—66.

Werbner, Richard P. 1984. The Manchester School in South-Central Africa. Annual Review of Anthropology 13:157—85.

13

Wife-Beating in India: Variations on a Theme

Barbara Diane Miller

A drum, a peasant, a Sudra [laborer], an animal, a woman — all of these are
fit to be beaten.

Tulsidas, The Ramcharitmanas, 16th century

Given all the recent newspaper publicity in the West and in India about
bride-burning murders and the latest case of a young Rajasthani widow im-
molating herself on her husband's funeral pyre in 1987, India looms large as
a society in which wives do not fare well. On a global scale, important
measures of female status such as longevity, literacy, and labor participation
all place India in the lowest ranges. Less recognized is the fact that almost
everything about female status in India varies, sometimes dramatically, by
region, class or caste, and life-cycle stage.[1]

This chapter addresses a particular feature of intrahousehold relationships: the physical abuse — beating or battering — of a spouse — usually the
wife by the husband, in the overwhelming majority of cases cross-culturally.[2] A central issue in intrahousehold violence is dominance: who hits whom
is not a random matter. Throughout the world, children do not generally
beat adults, aged people do not beat the physically fit, and women do not
beat men. These broad statements reflect general truths about power dif-
ferentials in society and in the household. The perspective I adopt here is
that wife-beating in India is caused, both indirectly and directly, by male
dominance.

Male dominance encompasses a complex system of female devaluation
and disenfranchisement in much of India, which puts women at a disadvantage in terms of low intrahousehold status and restricted bargaining
power, a limited range of alternate life courses (outside marriage), and few
escape routes from violent situations. This approach is similar to one
adopted for Western society by Straus (1980), but places more emphasis on

173

patriarchy as the key factor underlying the whole system, with socially contextualized variation throughout the country. Thus, I contend that wife-beating can be added to the list of features of "the male supremacist complex" defined over a decade ago by Divale and Harris (1976).[3]

Within the vast generalization that India is a male dominated society and that spouse abuse there is more likely to mean wife abuse than husband abuse, I seek to discover degrees of variation. Does wife-beating or battering seem more prevalent in regions, classes, and at life-cycle stages where female status is the lowest — for instance, the northern plains area, propertied groups, and young brides?[4] What other social variables are related to the risk of being beaten, to averting risk, or to escaping from a risk-prone context?

A range of factors are involved, all related in one way or another to the nature and degree of a woman's dependence on her marital household. Dependency can be economic — a woman may or may not earn enough money to support herself and her children without her husband and his family. Dependence may also be kinship-regulated — a woman in her marital family may or may not live far from her natal family, divorce may or may not be an acceptable option, and remarriage may or may not be a locally accepted practice. Other factors such as a woman's literacy may be important in her ability to attain some control over her domestic situation. Less amenable to cultural analysis are other factors such as a woman's degree of self-esteem, which may prompt her to leave an intolerable situation and find assistance from the few organizations and shelters that exist to help abused women in India.

Some of these independent variables have been analyzed in the Indian context, and they can provide a framework within which to examine patterns of wife-beating and wife-battering. Unfortunately studies of the dependent variable are rare.[5] At this point in our knowledge, I can do only two things: first, describe the social framework within which wife abuse exists and, second, present some provocative case material gleaned from a variety of secondary sources. The evidence gathered so far does not in any way provide a "data set" by which hypotheses can be tested. We cannot learn if frequency or type of abuse is higher or lower in certain regions or classes or particular life-cycle stages. Rather, the evidence provides a bare beginning for understanding some of the social contexts of wife-beating in India, which may be usefully compared with the other material presented in this book.

THE FRAMEWORK

I attempt to present in a few pages a summary of a model of how to study social variation in women's status in Indian society, which I have been designing and refining over the past decade. This model is necessarily simplified due to space constraints. I collapse several important sub-variables into three super-variables: region, class/caste, and life-cycle stage.

Regional differences in female status are strong in India. In the northern plains region, women appear to have the lowest intrahousehold status in all of India, whereas their status is higher in southern India and in the Himalayan zone in the far north (Berreman 1987; Dyson and Moore 1983; Miller 1981). Indicators of status on which this generalization is based include: juvenile sex ratios, labor participation rates, and literacy. Women in the northern plains tend to have lower labor force participation rates than elsewhere in India. Thus, insofar as income-earning may be an enhancement of intrahousehold power, northern women are more deprived of this possible source of strength.[6] Generally, women in northern areas are less literate than elsewhere in India, and insofar as literacy may be empowering, are relatively deprived of this source of strength. Kinship regulations in northern India are also important limiting factors for women's autonomy: village exogamy is the rule in the northern plains (I use the shorthand term "North" for this region) and marriage distances are long, whereas village endogamy is frequent in the South. Furthermore, hypergamy (marriage of a woman with a man whose family has higher socioeconomic standing than her natal family) in the North means that wife-givers have lower status than wife-takers, while isogamy in the South provides equality between both families. The bride and groom are strangers in the North, but often acquainted with each other in the South as co-villagers or even cross-cousins. This list of socially constructed disadvantages for a bride in the North compared to the South could be expanded, but the ones mentioned provide an adequate, though overgeneralized, background.

Class/caste differences are less amenable to generalization than are regional differences. I have suggested previously that upper class/caste females have lower relative status to males in their class/caste than do women of lower social strata (Miller 1981). Several measures including juvenile sex ratios and labor participation rates indicate that the intrahousehold status of upper strata females in North India is the lowest in all of India. Intrahousehold male dominance in the lower strata appears to be countered by the fact the women tend more to work outside the home for wages and thus gain some economic independence from their husbands. Extended households are more characteristic of propertied, upper-strata groups and may be a context for greater control of females in a patrilineal setting.[7] The absence of a mother-in-law in nuclear households can be seen as a potentially liberating factor for a wife. Poverty, of course, is more prevalent in the lower strata and may provide unknown levels of stress, prompting violence by males. Alcohol abuse by males may be more prevalent in the lower social strata, though I know of no study documenting this possibility.

Life-cycle changes in female status in India are significant (Vatuk 1985). Generally, for adult women in the North especially, the lowest point is the early years of marriage. At this time, the woman has to adapt to a new household situation, has not yet borne children (most especially prized sons), has the hardest chores to do, and the least to eat. The presence of a mother-in-law, who seeks to maintain close ties with her son almost in competition with the new bride, is generally a negative factor for the in-marrying girl. With the bearing of children, especially sons, the domestic power of the wife improves. In later years, as a female head of household with an aging husband or as a widow with sons, she may well assume the pre-eminent position in the household. Wife-battering then logically appears most likely for a young wife, in an extended household, with no children or no sons. This life-cycle pattern iterates to an extent with those of region and class since both patrilineal extended households (Frenzen and Miller 1986; Kolenda 1967) and extreme son preference are more prevalent in the northern plains region than elsewhere in India (Dyson and Moore 1983; Miller 1981).

This broad framework applies more directly to the rural population. The urban elite, and its particular pattern in the North of bride-burning murders, may require a somewhat different approach, beyond the scope of this chapter. As with any model, this one does not provide answers, but is rather meant as a guide in the consideration of the available evidence on wife-beating.

THE EVIDENCE

The examples presented here are gleaned from a variety of sources—primarily ethnographies and articles in journals and magazines with novels as supporting material. This "dataset" constitutes an "opportunistic sample" of sources rather than an exhaustive overview, but it nevertheless offers some useful insights.

Region

A limited collection of secondary evidence cannot reveal much about regional frequencies, but no all-India survey data on wife-beating are obtainable as an alternate source of information. So far, I have cases from all over India, and elsewhere in South Asia, attesting to a very widespread pattern indeed. Authors report that wife-beating is characteristic of several households in the village(s) where they have worked: in the Punjab (Horowitz and Kishwar 1984), Uttar Pradesh (Ahmed-Ghosh 1987), West Bengal (Rohner and Chaki-Sircar 1988), Karnataka (Beals 1980; Dhruvarajan 1989), Andhra Pradesh (Mies 1982), Tamil Nadu (Gough

1981), and Kerala (Gulati 1981). These cases come from states all over India, both northern and southern. Further research of the secondary literature, however, should be done to search for patterns of more frequent reporting for some regions than others; at present this "sample" is just too limited.

Beyond India, a newspaper survey revealed that (presumably for urban, literate respondents) 99 percent of Pakistani women working at home and 77 percent of women working outside the home have been beaten by their husbands (International Women's Tribune Center 1985). In Sri Lanka, an anthropologist reports that wife-beating was "universal" in a village studied in the 1950s (Obeyesekere 1963). In northwestern Bangladesh, a village woman told researchers, "Here in the village the men work all day ploughing with cows. So they think they should treat their women like cows too, shouting at them and beating them" (Hartmann and Boyce 1983:81).

It is doubtful that any region of South Asia is clearly characterized by the absence of wife-beating. Rather the salient question concerns possible regional variation in degree and frequency, and it is for these measures that we lack information now.

Class/Caste

References to wife-beating among both higher and lower social strata are found in the literature, but again we can say nothing about comparative frequency or degree. In eastern India, in a West Bengal village, Rohner and Chaki-Sircar (1988) document wife-beating among both high caste and untouchable groups. From fieldwork done in South India during the 1950s, Gough (1981) notes that in Kumbapettai village, Tamil Nadu, almost all households were known to have had instances of wife-beating. From her study in South India, Mies provides comments from some Kapu (high caste) women in Andhra Pradesh that in the olden days, women were beaten for talking with men other than their husbands and not hiding from their elders (1982:78) and these days for wanting to go to a friend's home for lace-making (1982:134). One of five case studies of poor working women in Kerala, South India, mentions wife-beatings (Gulati 1981:104).

The recent spate of bride-burnings generally involves middle and upper class households in large northern cities (Kishwar and Vanita 1984:224–233; Palriwala 1985), but also in southern cities as well (Krishnakumari and Geetha 1983). In most cases, a young bride is continually harassed by her in-laws, particularly husband and mother-in-law, to bring more gifts from her natal family to her marital household even after the dowry has been paid. When harassment fails, the bride characteristically is murdered by dousing her with kerosene and then lighting her afire. In this way, it can be claimed by her in-laws that she died in a cooking accident. Widowed, the young man is then free to marry again and bring in another bride with her dowry and subsequent gifts. Reports of such cases often mention physical abuse of the bride prior to her murder. For example, here is the story of Kanchan, a 24 year-old stenographer who lived in Delhi:

> On 29 June, she went straight to her parents' house in Malviya Nagar and told them she felt unsafe because her husband and in-laws were persistently demanding money for a scooter, and were ill-treating her. Her husband came at night and forced her to return with him. When she reached home, she was beaten by her husband in the presence of her brother who was also insulted and turned out when he protested. He went to the police station and complained he feared his sister's life was in danger. The police refused to intervene in "family affairs." In the middle of the night, Kanchan's parents were informed that she had been badly burnt and admitted to Lohia hospital. They rushed there but she was already dead (Kishwar and Vanita 1984:224).

We do not know how often such beatings, followed by fatal fire "accidents," occur in India. While most current evidence locates bride-burning deaths in families of the urban, upper and middle classes, the possibility exists that such deaths also occur in other contexts.

Women's Income

Women who work outside the home and earn an income are beaten as well as those who do not. Urban victims of beating and murder for dowry demands are often in the labor-force (Kishwar and Vanita 1984:224–233). Poor working women are also victims (Gulati 1981:104). One particularly revealing case concerns a Tamil woman migrant to Delhi who worked as a domestic servant: "Devaki was beaten frequently by her husband for years when he was sitting idle at home, entirely dependent on her wages for survival. She tolerated this until his death a year ago" (Rani and Kaul 1986:8).

Thus, earning an income is not always a sufficient guarantee that a woman will either be able to use her financial strength to bargain for better treatment in the home or to leave an abusive husband. But the uninvestigated possibility still exists that there may be a greater propensity for income-earning women to cope with an abusive situation by leaving than for non-earning women.

Household Structure

Examples of wife-beating can be found for nuclear as well as extended households. Having in-laws on the scene does not appear to protect a woman from being beaten but rather often seems to exacerbate wife abuse. Beatings linked with in-law instigation are associated with the extreme bride-burning cases mentioned above, as well as village cases. For instance, Rohner and Chaki-Sircar found in a West Bengal village that there are at least eleven high-caste homes where wives have been beaten by their husbands, "often" at the instigation of the mother-in-law (1988). The association of wife-beating in extended households with behavioral control is vividly portrayed in a Punjabi novel mentioned by Kakar (1987): the husband beat his wife because she would not lower her gaze in front of him, and she steadfastly refused to do so even when his parents also insisted that she should.

Yet the presence of a mother-in-law is not a necessary ingredient for wife-beating, as women in nuclear households are also beaten. Cases include the Tamil domestic maid mentioned above (Rani and Kaul 1986) and Devaki, the poor construction worker described by Gulati (1981).

Dowry, Alcohol, and Sex

This congeries of topics includes factors which often appear as proximate causes for wife-beating in the literature. Dowry demands by a woman's in-laws are the most frequently mentioned reason for her ill-treatment. Such references are common for urban bride-burning cases as well as in village settings. Gulati (1981:104) links dowry demands with the frequent quarrels between Devaki, the construction worker and her husband, which generally resulted "in Devaki getting a few blows."

Alcohol consumption by husbands is commonly associated with wife-beating in the literature on India.[8] Horowitz and Kishwar (1984) report that alcohol abuse is routine in the Punjabi village they studied, and that drunk husbands tend to beat their wives. The story of Malarkodi, a Bombay slum-dwelling woman, is particularly stark:

> She had been badly beaten up and killed by her drunken husband. He also kicked her in the vagina. This caused internal bleeding which killed her. We soon came to know the whole story. Some time ago, Malarkodi had run off to Madras with a former boyfriend. Her husband went and brought her back, promising to behave well. But after that, he continued to remind her of her elopement. He used to drink and beat her up. . . . But this Sunday the routine took a fatal turn. She died. . . . When we went to the police inspector of Tilak Nagar to demand Malarkodi's dead body, he said, "Why are you taking up this issue? She was an immoral woman. Otherwise, no sane husband would do this" (Kishwar and Vanita 1984:215).

A husband's demands for sex with his wife are also related to wife-beating. Kakar mentions that interviews with rural women who have migrated to Delhi reveal that the women submit to intercourse for fear of being beaten (1987). A study of sexual behavior in a mountainous area of northern India, Kumaon, found a common pattern of a husband beating his wife as part of sexual activity (Kapur 1987:46–47). This report is confusing because the men assert that it is a sign of love and not, therefore, done in casual extramarital sex, but only with one's wife. When asked about the association between love and beatings, the wives did not seem convinced that the two were related.

WAYS OUT

For the woman who does not wish to endure a domestic situation in which she is vulnerable to beatings, only two options exist: getting her husband to stop beating her or leaving him. Various possibilities exist to empower a woman to do either of these, but as mentioned above, most of these are not options for northern women, particularly northern upper strata women.

Support from a woman's natal kin might be thought to be an important option for all Indian women, but such is not the case. In northern India, a woman's natal family may be many miles away and she is not allowed to travel alone. If she wants to go home, someone from her natal family must come and fetch her. Her natal family's power to influence her treatment is also limited by the fact that its status is generally lower than that of her husband's, due to hypergamy. A much stronger position is afforded a bride in South India due to the proximity of her natal kin and their equality with her marital family.

Divorce is an option limited mainly to lower-class women or to women in elite, Westernized, urban families. In the rural areas, high-caste women would suffer from great stigma if they were to seek divorce, and their options after divorce are narrow. They may either return to their natal families or fend for themselves. Suicide appears as an ultimate way out, resorted to by unknown numbers of women every year because of unhappiness in their marital homes (for comparative information on women's suicide in Papua New Guinea see Counts 1987). The highest rates of suicide among women in several Asian countries occur in the very late teens and early twenties, a point in the life-cycle when the stresses of marriage may be at their worst (Headley 1983; Miller and Kearney 1987).

There are, however, a few cases in the literature of women who threaten to fight back. A low-caste West Bengali woman left her abusive husband and went to her parents' place. Her husband came to fetch her and she yelled at him to go away: "If you come again, I'll throw stones at you and break your head" (Rohner and Chaki-Sircar 1988:51). A woman working as a cashew nut processor in Sri Lanka had a husband who physically assaulted her from the beginning of their marriage (Casinader, Fernando, and Gamage 1987:318). She sent him away, but allowed him to return twice. His behavior improved, she says, because she has threatened to strike back if he assaults her again. A scene in a Punjabi novel mentioned by Kakar (1987) depicts a poor Sikh family in which the husband drinks heavily. His wife quarrels with him about it, and such quarrels often end in violence. But she tries to "give as good as she gets," though his superior strength usually makes him the victor.

One ethnographic report of a wife actually striking a husband is described by Nanda from her research on the *hijras* [male transvestites] (1986:46). The wife in the couple, a *hijra*, was a prostitute, now married to one of her former patrons who wishes that she would discontinue her earlier work. She tells him, "Don't put any restrictions on me," and comments, "If he gives me too much back talk, I give him good whacks." It is telling that this rare case of a wife hitting a husband involves a man in the role of wife.

If a woman is lucky enough to bear several healthy sons and thereby secure her intrahousehold position, and as she ages and gains control of household decision-making, her chances of being beaten are likely to decline. Age, therefore, may bring some freedom from physical abuse (see Brown 1982 on the status of older women cross-culturally).

PSYCHOLOGICAL HINTS

A study of the psychological status of women in India, particularly rural women, is urgently needed. We may expect low self-esteem among girls brought up in cultures where sons are clearly favored.[9] Likewise, low self-esteem might be expected among women socialized to serve others first, knowing that one is the lowest priority in terms of the most basic welfare expenditures on food and health care. Even in homes where daughters are treated as well as sons, they must eventually realign with another household group upon marriage, something most men in India never have to do.

It is not surprising, given the literature indicating women's strong internalization of inferiority, that some women feel they deserve to be beaten. One ethnographer reports that some women say they are beaten because they have done something wrong (Ahmed-Ghosh 1987). A study of four battered urban women, done by the women's group Saheli, found that the women accepted their beatings as part of their subservient role (Research Center on Women's 1986:12). Obviously, however, not all women accept being beaten. Some try to avoid abuse through acceptable options like visits to their natal home, some women threaten to hit back, and others opt out of the situation entirely through suicide.

CONCLUSION

Wife-beating is one part of the wider system of male dominance which pervades much of India and as such cannot be understood fully apart from it. This chapter proposes a framework for looking at variation in wife-beating and reviews some of the evidence available from disparate sources. No systematic study of wife-beating in India has been done, and only a very few case studies undertaken by women's organizations exist. The topic is not an easy one on which to conduct fieldwork, but it is important that such abuse become a topic of research attention. Without careful research, it is difficult to judge the extent of the problem, or which areas and subpopulations are most at risk. Socially focused studies are needed to help determine how one might best devise targeted programs to subvert or circumvent social structures that place women at risk of being beaten as a matter of daily routine, and sometimes to death.

NOTES

This chapter was prepared during a year at the University of California researching gender discrimination in India under the support of the National Science Foundation. Discussions with Deborah Balk of the Graduate Group in Demography and Gerald Berreman of the Department of Anthropology at Berkeley were helpful. Judith Brown's communications about wife-beating and approaches to its study enhanced my thinking on the subject. Joyce Dietrich of the South Asia Program at Cornell University typed the manuscript.

1. Close examination of household-by-household differences within a single village would reveal variation at that level, too. But this chapter considers broader patterns within which individual level data vary.

2. Definitional problems abound; see for instance the discussion in Campbell (1985). Since the data on physical abuse of wives in India are so poor, one cannot even attempt to discriminate much between forms of abuse, such as beating compared to battering.

3. Divale and Harris (1976) consider tribal societies in their analysis, not peasant or industrialized societies in which male supremacist complexes also exist.

4. This model, which states that higher class females have poorer intrahousehold status than lower-class females, depends on within-class male-female comparisons. Anyone comparing the overall welfare of a rich Jat woman with a poor Chamar woman might be able to claim that the Jat woman is better off. But my approach compares, for example, Jat men with Jat women and Chamar men with Chamar women.

5. One could write an entire essay on the methodological problems that would be entailed in a field study of wife-beating.

6. Schlegel and Barry (1986) have analyzed data from 181 nonindustrialized societies and they demonstrate that "women's productive activities have effects on the value accorded to females and the freedom they have to control their own persons" (1986:143). They found a lower incidence of rape where women make a substantial contribution to subsistence.

7. An interesting comparison could be made between the treatment of wives in patrilineal and matrilineal extended households. It may be that in the latter, any abusive behavior toward women would be meted out by brothers on sisters.

8. An association between alcohol abuse and spouse abuse, based on an analysis of African data, is proposed in Erchak (1984).

9. Kakar (1978 inter alia) offers important observations about the treatme.
daughters and their self-esteem in India.

REFERENCES CITED

Ahmed-Ghosh, Huma. 1987. Changes in the Status of North Indian Women: A Case
Study of Palitpur Village. Women in International Development Working Paper
No. 141. East Lansing: Michigan State University, Office of Women in Interna-
tional Development.

Beals, Alan R. 1980. Gopalpur: A South Indian Village. New York: Holt, Rinehart
and Winston.

Berreman, Gerald. 1987. Sanskritization as Female Oppression. Paper presented at
Wenner-Gren International Symposium No. 103, The Anthropology of Gender
Hierarchies. Mijas, Spain.

Brown, Judith K. 1982. Cross-Cultural Perspectives on Middle-Aged Women. Current Anthropology 23(2):143—156.

Campbell, Jacquelyn C. 1985. Beating of Wives: A Cross-Cultural Perspective. Victimology 10(1—4):174—185.

Casinader, Rex A., Sepalika Fernando, and Karuna Gamage. 1987. Women's Issues
and Men's Roles: Sri Lankan Village Experience. *In* Geography of Gender in the
Third World. Janet H. Momsen and Janet Townsend, eds. Pp. 309—322. London: Hutchinson.

Counts, Dorothy. 1987. Female Suicide and Wife Abuse. Suicide 17:194—204.

Dhruvarajan, Vanaja. 1989. Hindu Women and the Power of Ideology. Granby,
MA: Bergin and Garvey Publishers, Inc.

Divale, William Tulio, and Marvin Harris. 1976. Population, Warfare, and the Male
Supremacist Complex. American Anthropologist 78:521—538.

Dyson, Tim, and Mick Moore. 1983. Gender Relations, Female Autonomy and
Demographic Behavior: Regional Contrasts within India. Population and Development Review 9(1):35—60.

Erchak, Gerald M. 1984. Cultural Anthropology and Spouse Abuse. Cultural
Anthropology 25(3):331—332.

Frenzen, Paul D., and Barbara Diane Miller. 1986. Regional Patterns of Household
Complexity in India. Paper presented at the Annual Meeting of the Population Association of America, Chicago.

Gough, Kathleen. 1981. Rural Society in Southeast India. New York: Cambridge
University Press.

Gulati, Leela. 1981. Profiles in Female Poverty: A Study of Poor Working Women
in Kerala. Delhi: Hindustan Publishing Company.

Hartmann, Betsy, and James Boyce. 1983. A Quiet Violence: View from a
Bangladesh Village. London: Zed Press.

Headley, Lee A., ed. 1983. Suicide in Asia and the Near East. Berkeley: University
of California Press.

Horowitz, Berny, and Madhu Kishwar. 1984. Family Life: The Unequal Deal. *In*
Search of Answers: Indian Women's Voices from Manushi. Madhu Kishwar and
Ruth Vanita, eds. Pp. 69—103. London: Zed Press.

International Women's Tribune Center. 1985. Newsletter #32. Quoted in WID Bulletin, January 1987:13. East Lansing: Michigan State University, Office of Women in International Development.

Kakar, Sudhir. 1978. The Inner World: A Psychoanalytic Study of Childhood and Society in India. New York: Oxford University Press.

————. 1987. Eros and Oneiros in Indian Fiction. De Vos Memorial Lecture, Department of Anthropology, University of California-Berkeley.

Kapur, Tribhuwan. 1987. Sexual Life of the Kumaonis: A New Approach to Sexuality. New Delhi: Vikas Publishing House.

Kishwar, Madhu, and Ruth Vanita. 1984. Family Violence. *In* In Search of Answers: Indian Women's Voices from Manushi. Madhu Kishwar and Ruth Vanita, eds. Pp. 203—241. London: Zed Press.

Kolenda, Pauline M. 1967. Regional Differences in Indian Family Structure. *In* Regions and Regionalism in Indian Family Structure: An Exploratory Study. Robert I. Crane, ed. Pp. 147—226. Raleigh: Duke University, Program in Comparative Studies on Southern Asia.

Krishnakumari, N. S., and A. S. Geetha. 1983. A Report on the Problem of Dowry in Bangalore City. New Delhi: The Joint Women's Programme. CISRS.

Mies, Maria. 1982. The Lace Makers of Narsapur: Indian Housewives Produce for the World Market. London: Zed Press.

Miller, Barbara D. 1981. The Endangered Sex: Neglect of Female Children in Rural North India. Ithaca, NY: Cornell University Press.

Miller, Barbara Diane, and Robert N. Kearney. 1987. Women's Suicide in Sri Lanka. *In* Women and Health: Cross-Cultural Perspectives. Patricia Whelehan, ed. Pp. 110—123. South Hadley, MA: Bergin and Garvey Publishers.

Nanda, Serena. 1986. The Hijras of India: Cultural and Individual Dimensions of an Institutionalized Third Gender Role. *In* Anthropology and Homosexual Behavior. Evelyn Blackwood, ed. Pp. 35—54. New York: The Haworth Press.

Obeyesekere, Gananath. 1963. Pregnancy Cravings (Dola Duka) in Relation to Social Structure and Personality in a Sinhalese Village. American Anthropologist 65(2):323—342.

Palriwala, Rajni. 1985. Women Are Not for Burning: The Anti-Dowry Movement in Delhi. Paper presented at Wenner-Gren International Symposium No. 99, Anthropological Perspectives on Women's Collective Action: An Assessment of the Decade, 1975—1985. Mijas, Spain.

Rani, Prabha, and Poonam Kaul. 1986. For Two Meals a Day: A Report on Tamil Domestic Maids. Manushi 35:2—9.

Research Center on Women's Studies. 1986. RCWS Newsletter (Bombay) 7 (3 & 4).

Rohner, Ronald, and Manjusri Chaki-Sircar. 1988. Mothers and Children in a Bengali Village. Hanover, NH: University Press of New England.

Schlegel, Alice, and Herbert Barry III. 1986. The Cultural Consequences of Female Contribution to Subsistence. American Anthropologist 88(1):142—150.

Straus, Murray A. 1980. Sexual Inequality and Wife-Beating. *In* The Social Causes of Husband-Wife Violence. Murray A. Straus and Gerald T. Hotaling, eds. Pp. 86—93. Minneapolis: University of Minnesota Press.

Vatuk, Sylvia. 1985. South Asian Conceptions of Sexuality. *In* In Her Prime: A New View of Middle-Aged Women. Judith K. Brown and Virginia Kerns, eds. Pp. 137—154. South Hadley, MA: Bergin and Garvey.

14

Wife Abuse Among Indo-Fijians[1]

Shireen Lateef

Shanti was a thirty-year-old accounts clerk who was married with four children aged between ten and two. Shanti lived with her husband and his family. Her mother-in-law and sister-in-law disliked her, ill-treated her and made her perform the bulk of the household chores even though she was in full-time paid employment while they were not. Shanti's mother-in-law consistently complained to her husband that she was lazy, disobedient and disrespectful. The complaints led to arguments between Shanti, her mother-in-law, sister-in-law and husband, often resulting in Shanti being beaten by her husband.

Shanti's husband also hit her for reasons besides her mother-in-law's complaint. Sometimes when Shanti expressed her desire to live away from her in-laws or asked her husband when they would get their own house, arguments ensued leading eventually to her being given at least a few slaps. On other occasions she received beatings because her husband was suspicious and jealous, accusing her of fraternizing with other males.

In June 1986, a couple of days after some bad floods when their house was flooded out, Shanti attempted suicide by drinking paraquat (pesticide). While in the hospital she told her friend and work colleague that life had become too unbearable and cleaning up after the floods was the last straw. She said, "You know what they're like at home." Shanti died three days later.[2]

Suicide was Shanti's solution to a life which she perceived to be unbearable and from which there was no other escape. Admittedly, suicide is an extreme and atypical response to the physical abuse to which many Indo-Fijian wives are subjected. A more typical response would be to accept violence as the inevitable fate of being a wife and to bear it in silence.

Physical violence is taken for granted as part of being a wife in the Indo-Fijian society. This is not to imply that all Indo-Fijian wives are subjected to constant physical violence. Rather it suggests that violence is experienced by many Indo-Fijian wives at least occasionally and is accepted by the community as part of a woman's life. Varying degrees of violence are imposed on wives, and their control by the occasional use of the *danda* (stick) is seldom questioned by either males or females.

The threat and use of physical violence against wives is a powerful and effective mechanism for ensuring the maintenance and reproduction of traditional gender relations among Indo-Fijians. However, blatant, overt control of wives through the use of violence is not always necessary since wives control their own behaviour, especially in the face of a powerful and influential familial ideology that stresses the need for female submission to male control. Violence is used as a supplementary mechanism of social control to assert and consolidate male dominance and female subordination within the family.

For Shanti, suicide was the solution for a complex set of problems, not the least of which was physical violence that she encountered in her life as an Indo-Fijian woman. It is within this wider context of an Indo-Fijian woman's life in Suva that I wish to discuss how wife abuse grows out of and supports Indo-Fijian culture.

THE SETTING

The Fiji islands are situated in the southwest Pacific and have a total land area of approximately 7,022 square miles. Fiji acquired independence from the British in 1970. Of a total population of approximately 700,000, Indo-Fijians constitute 50.5 percent and indigenous Fijians 42.4 percent, with the remainder being other Pacific Islanders, Europeans, and Chinese.

The vast majority of Indo-Fijians are the direct descendants of indentured laborers taken to Fiji by the British to work in the sugar-cane plantations between the years 1879 to 1916. After serving periods of indenture ranging from five to ten years, the majority became free settlers, while only a small minority returned to India (Lal 1983).

What passes in Fiji today as Indo-Fijian culture is a syncretic form of Indian culture that was derived from the hegemonic influence of North Indian culture (Jayawardena 1968:438, 1980:431). Little difference exists between Indo-Fijian Hindus and Muslims in family organization, rules and regulations governing women's behaviour, and generally in the social relations of gender.[3] Hence, the term Indo-Fijian is used to refer to both Hindus and Muslims. The women of my study come from different class backgrounds and include both Hindus and Muslims. Few participate in paid employment and those who do tend to be in traditional "pink collar" occupations such as typists, sales assistants, and clerks.

GENDER RELATIONS
AND THE ROLES AND STATUS OF WIVES

Wife abuse among Indo-Fijians must be located and analyzed within the wider context of gender relations within the family in order to explain and understand the nature, reasons, experience and acceptance of this violence.

What follows is an analysis of gender relations among Indo-Fijians with particular emphasis on the ideal roles and status of wives in order to provide the backdrop for a discussion of wife abuse.

The patriarchal, patrilineal and patrivirilocal North Indian family pattern and ideology has generally established hegemonic influence among Indo-Fijians. The essential characteristics of the North Indian family are: male dominance and female subordination, males as the economic providers with females as the economic dependents, spatial and social confinement of women, male inheritance of family property, and females as reproducers of the male lineage and repositories of family honour (*izzat*) (Kishwar 1984; Mies 1980; Gupta 1976; Jeffery 1979).

Any analysis of gender relations and the status of women in the family among Indo-Fijians requires reference to the ideology of *purdah*[4] and to the family and material structure of the household. *Purdah* in the sense of complete veiling and seclusion of women is absent in Fiji, although it is undeniably present in its more subtle manifestations. No clear cut distinctions between Hindu and Muslim forms of *purdah* as identified by Papanek (1973) and Jacobson (1982) are discernible. *Purdah* as it is practiced among Indo-Fijians is a synthesis of the numerous variations shared by both Hindu and Muslim communities in South Asia (Vatuk 1982).

The essential elements of *purdah* are the segregation of the sexes, the sexual protection of women, and the maintenance of family honour. It is this ideology that leads to the creation of separate spheres of existence for males and females; men belong to the public realm of economics and politics, women to the private domestic realm with their spatial movements restricted. Hence, women's role is largely confined to marriage, the performance of household chores, bearing and rearing children and caring for menfolk. These separate spheres of existence result in women being denied access to the labour market; consequently they are rendered economically dependent on males. The ideology of *purdah* also sets the parameters for the deferential relations between males and females and provides the guidelines for female behaviour and demeanour. Since women are perceived as both sexually vulnerable and sexually impulsive, their sexual protection and control is of utmost importance; the honour of the entire family rests in the purity of its women.

Purdah ideology is integrally related to and supports a familial ideology that vests ultimate authority in the father or, in his absence, the eldest male in the household. Both females and younger males are subject to the control of the male head to whom deference is given. This ideology of male supremacy in the family is reflected in the greater importance of male over female children. Male children are viewed as assets since they will become the future economic providers and ensure the continuance of the patriline. Female children are viewed as economic and social liabilities since they are economically dependent and pose a potential threat to the reputation of the family until husbands are found for them (cf. Kishwar 1984; Mies 1980; Gupta 1976). Marriage is both necessary and inevitable for women. Arranged marriages are the preferred and dominant form of marriage because of the limits on spatial mobility and social interactions and strict segregation of the sexes.

The wifely role is pre-eminent in Hinduism and the Hindu law books; the *Dharma Sastras* (Rules of Right Conduct) provide concrete and explicit guidelines for women's roles as wives (Wadley 1977:20). The laws of Manu stress that women must always be controlled by men: daughters by fathers, wives by husbands, and widows by sons. In addition, husbands must be revered as gods despite their failings (Mies 1980:43). "Her only concern in life was to see that all her services needed by her husband were properly performed by her, the satisfaction of her husband being her sole joy in life" (Kapadia 1955:169). Blind worship of husbands is referred to as *pativrata* (one who worships her lord) and is "considered the highest ideal of womanhood in Hinduism" (Mies 1980:44). The lengths to which a wife must go in her duty to serve her husband is a constant theme in both Muslim and Hindu sacred texts, popular literature and films, and folk and oral traditions "often created and propagated by women" (Jacobson and Wadley 1977:125).

A recurring theme at Indo-Fijian weddings is the misfortune of the bride. It focuses on the hardships and difficulties the bride will encounter at the hands of her husband, mother-in-law and sisters-in-law as a newly married woman in her conjugal home. Traditionally, her wedding is a sad occasion for a woman. It is when she leaves the caring and protected environment of her natal family to take up residence in the strange, unknown and sometimes cruel environment of her conjugal family. Many of the wedding rituals, particularly those performed by women, acknowledge and stress the future submissive and subordinate role of wives, the hardships imposed by tyrannical mothers-in-law and the need for women to passively submit to these controls without struggle.

Similarly in Islam, marriage is encouraged and required of women in order to control their sexuality and enable them to realise their most important roles: wife, childrearer and homemaker. Both unmarried males and females pose a threat to the social order of Islam, since humans are believed to inherently possess animalistic sexual urges that need to be regulated and controlled (Minai 1981:12). The institution of marriage is recommended as the legitimate outlet for human sexual instinct and for the propagation of the human race (Madudi 1978:93).

Childbearing and childrearing are women's prime and unique roles in society, and it is through these activities that women make a contribution to society. Furthermore, a woman's natural function in life is to provide for the man "a place of peace and comfort" (Madudi 1978:138). In the *Hadith* (sayings of the

Prophet) "women are assigned the position of fertile fields where men can sow seeds and watch them grow" (Ferdows and Ferdows 1983:57).

Since marriage in Islam is a civil contract, divorce is permissable, while in Hinduism, marriage is a religious sacrament and divorce is, therefore, not permissable. However, Muslim women need the consent of husbands to obtain a divorce, whereas men need no such consent from their wives. Despite legal provisions for separation and divorce, marriage is ideally insoluble and permanent and divorce is considered abhorrent and definitely discouraged among both Hindus and Muslims in Fiji. Familial ideology not only discourages divorce but extols the suffering and sacrifice of women for the benefit of the family. A woman's salvation lies in uncomplaining service to her husband and children irrespective of the husband's bad character, his failure to provide adequate economic support, or his maltreatment of her. Total devotion, respect, obedience and service to husbands is viewed as the true function of wives (Jacobson and Wadley 1977:124).

The privileged position of males within the family is reflected in the specified code of conduct regulating male/female interactions within the family. Respect, deference and distance are the essential features of this code of conduct, supported by the ideology of *purdah*. Interactions between husbands and wives clearly reflect male dominance within the household. Respectful wives do not "answer back" or argue and generally maintain silence when anger and aggression are expressed.

This familial ideology of female obedience, service and subservience to men is further reinforced by the higher status of married women over unmarried women, women with children over childless women, women with sons over those without sons, and older women over younger women. As women get older, bear children, marry off their children, and become grandmothers, the relationship between a husband and wife becomes more egalitarian. Older women have more control over their own spatial movements, social interactions, behaviour, and household decisions and often wield considerable power over younger women (cf. Brown 1982, 1985).

The ideological support for patriarchy and patrilineality is reflected in the veneration of the mother. It is in the service and devotion to her children that a woman is honoured and able to acquire social status and some degree of power (Basham 1974). While ultimate authority rests with males, in many instances older women are the ones who actually exercise this authority on behalf of the family. Senior women have a positive stake in their households and actively work to protect and reproduce the patriarchal, patrilocal family.

THE NATURE OF MARITAL VIOLENCE

The vast majority of my informants have either been subjected to or threatened with violence at some time in their lives. This is not to claim that all women are equally threatened by or subjected to physical violence throughout their lives. Older women—that is women with adult married children—are rarely if ever subjected to physical violence. However, violence pervades the lives of young married women and, occasionally, older women who have yet to consolidate their position in the household.

The form and extent of physical violence imposed on wives extends from a slap, push, kick or shove to solid punches. The most common and consistently used form of violence is slapping the face. Wives are also often pushed against walls, their heads are slammed against walls, and objects are thrown at them. The following case studies illustrate some of the reasons, context and nature of violence imposed on Indo-Fijian wives.

Case Study 1—Sarita

Sarita is 27 years old, married with a 4-year-old son, and working as a high school teacher. Her husband runs a small business and they rent a house in one of Suva's affluent suburbs. They have a live-in domestic worker who performs most of the household chores except cooking.

Sarita met her husband while she was attending university in Suva and hers is a "love marriage." While at university she lived on campus as her parents live in another town. Prior to marriage she lived with her husband for one year and they decided to marry when she became pregnant. Her husband's parents were not happy about the marriage. In their opinion, Sarita did not come from a "good" family and her character was "questionable" since she had lived with their son before marriage. Conflict continues to exist between Sarita and her in-laws.

Sarita and her husband often socialise with other young couples and attend Western-style parties and frequent nightclubs and restaurants. Unlike many other Indo-Fijian women Sarita drinks alcohol and sometimes smokes cigarettes, has an informal relationship with her husband, and interacts with him as an equal.

Even when they were living together Sarita's husband beat her. In recent years these beatings have become more frequent. On two occasions, Sarita left her husband and stayed with a girlfriend until her husband kept harassing her and "begging" her to return. Each time he promised never to hit her again, so for her "son's sake" she returned to live with him.

According to Sarita the main precipitating factor in the violence is "When I ask him too many questions or criticise his parents." However, when he is beating her other reasons also emerge, reasons such as he does not like her smoking and he suspects she is having an affair with his cousin. On other occasions he hits her because he does not like her to go out with her female friends at night, which Sarita occasionally does. On one occasion he beat Sarita because she complained about his mother spreading rumours about her. While beating her, he said, "You talk too much nowadays."

On another occasion, Sarita discovered some love letters from a woman her husband had visited on one of his overseas trips. She confronted him and demanded to know who this woman was and whether she was the reason their phone bill was so high. When he refused to answer, Sarita kept screaming and demanding an answer. At this point, he started hitting her, saying that his mother was right, "I had trapped him into marriage by getting pregnant." He punched her so hard that she fell against the door and hit her head on it. He then picked her up, threw her across the room, came over and started kicking her. Sarita's husband is a big man almost twice her size.

Case Study 2 — Rina

Rina is 30 years of age, married with two small children, and works in a professional occupation. Her husband is a bank clerk, and they live with his parents and his unmarried sister aged 25. Rina is originally from India and her marriage was arranged. Since her family does not reside in Fiji she feels isolated and without support. Her husband beats her, seldom takes her out, and taunts her. When she entered paid employment approximately three years ago, he took all her salary and gave her nothing. Her colleagues at work encouraged her to open her own bank account and not to give her salary to her husband. Rina followed their advice and told her husband she wished to leave him and return to India with the children. Her husband responded by hiding her passport and informing her that he would never give his consent to take the children out of the country.

Her husband beats her for a variety of reasons. Sometimes he beats her when he is drunk and sometimes because his mother complains that Rina does not do any work, is argumentative and disrespectful. According to Rina, her mother-in-law mistreats her, makes her do all the cleaning and cooking for the entire household, and makes up stories about her to her husband. Occasionally he beats her because she confronts him about love letters from other women or because he is generally dissatisfied with her.

The arguments usually commence when be comes home drunk and demands Rina serve him dinner. Invariably he is dissatisfied with the dinner and starts abusing Rina. In response Rina comments on his drunkenness, he slaps her, and both of them engage in verbal abuse. Then he starts beating her for her lack of respect, for opening her own bank account, and for arguing with his mother.

Often while he is beating her he taunts her by saying, "What are you going to do? Where are you going to go? You have no where to go, no one wants you, even your family don't want you. You think you can save your money and go back to India — well, you can't."

Some of Rina's work colleagues verified that Rina is beaten by her husband and that she often comes to work with bruises on her face, arms and legs.

These case studies illustrate the reasons for which wives are beaten by husbands. They can be generally classified as suspected infidelity, insolence, not demonstrating the required deference towards husbands and mothers-in-law, and not adequately performing wifely duties. Violence is used by husbands to demonstrate their anger and frustration, keep women in their place and, most importantly, to assert and display their power and dominant status in the household. The oft quoted threat of *bahuth baath niklii ek jhapar de ga* ["if you talk too much I'll give you a slap"] often becomes a reality.

It is noteworthy that the same words and sentences are used by men as threats to control both wives and children. Often even the husband's tone in speaking to his wife is remarkably similar to that used by both females and males when speaking to children. Alternatively, wives respond to their husbands as they would to their fathers, by speaking in quiet gentle tones that demonstrate their deference.

The precipitating factors for wife abuse are generally varied and confused. Complaints of mothers-in-law, as in Shanti's and Rina's cases, combined with alcohol consumption and general discontent with a wife's behaviour, can result in a man beating his wife. The initial trigger is often something trivial which then escalates, especially if the wife answers back. This is perceived by the husband as provocation. Once the husband is provoked, all his dissatisfactions — including complaints from his mother — with his wife's behaviour emerge. However, neither mothers-in-law nor alcohol alone are sufficient explanation for wife abuse since wives are also beaten when husbands are sober and without encouragement from mothers-in-law. A more adequate explanation rests in the fundamental inequality between husbands and wives, an inequality that gives males the power and privilege to beat wives.

The majority of my informants explained that they complied with and did not resist restrictions placed on them because they feared physical violence by their husbands. For example, many women are critical of their husbands' excessive consumption of liquor yet seldom openly communicate their disapproval because they fear being beaten. Even the threat of violence is a powerful mechanism for keeping wives within the guidelines of proper conduct. Comments such as "my husband would kill me," "my husband will cut my arms and legs off," or "I don't wish to be kicked and beaten" are common from wives even though not necessarily meant to be taken literally.

Despite the threat of violence combined with a powerful ideology demanding compliance, women are not necessarily passive or "pathetic" victims of an insidious system. Women are fully aware of their inferior position, the privileged position of their husbands, and the injustices of the social system. They are quick to articulate their grievances and express discontent to any sympathetic and willing listener. Compliance co-exists with resentment, discontent, and instances of insubordination. Women sometimes engage secretly in rule-breaking behaviour; for example, some wives do have affairs. The instances of misbehaviour and the various strategies women employ to create more space for themselves indicate women do not simply inherit the culture and accept it. Rather, they reconstruct and recreate it through their everyday interactions.

In many cases, women repeatedly engage in the same behaviour that they were beaten for in the past, as in Sarita's and Shanti's cases. Sarita continued to argue with her husband while she was being beaten, and sometimes even deliberately taunted her husband with comments that exacerbated his anger. Wives like these are asserting their right to argue with their husbands and are refusing to accept total male control even at the risk of being beaten.

TENSIONS OF MODERNIZATION

The growth of the Fijian economy, particularly during the 1970s, generated both increased employment opportunities for women and greater prospects for a higher standard of living. Dual income families became more attractive and working women sought after as marriage partners. To reap the benefits of women's paid employment, ideological readjustments were made whereby women are permitted to engage in certain types of paid employment not markedly inconsistent with the requirements of *purdah*. Occupations are acceptable in which interactions with unrelated males are minimal, no night work is entailed and where women can be supervised.[5] Hence some 14 percent of urban Indo-Fijian women are engaged in paid employment (Fiji Bureau of Statistics 1986).

Women's increased participation in paid employment and education, combined with increasing Western modernist influences, has meant that traditional familial ideology is slowly being undermined. Especially among the young middle classes, husband/wife relationships in many ways resembles Western nuclear families. For example, interactions are more informal and relaxed, women are not as constrained spatially and socially, husbands and wives spend their leisure time together, and they espouse a belief in egalitarian partnership-like relationships.

The "modern" Westernised Indo-Fijian woman, often with tertiary education and in paid employment, is increasingly asserting and exercising her rights in this kind of relationship. Economically independent women like Sarita assume they have a right to confront their husbands, demand answers, and argue with them. On the other hand, the "modern" Indo-Fijian male (like Sarita's husband) demonstrates a reluctance to totally surrender ultimate power and control by resorting to violence. Younger Westernised women view this use of physical violence by males as unacceptable and as an important symbol of women's subordinate status and position in the family and community. Women like Sarita question the right of their husbands to subject them to violence and are humiliated and angered by it.

Yet even among these women small doses of violence are tolerated and explained away. They accept the right of males to "slap" them occasionally as a consequence of the enduring traditional ideologies which remain influential although declining in importance. The competing and conflicting ideologies are a source of confusion in gender relations and tension and conflict in these "modern" families.

The problem of co-existing conflicting and competing ideologies is not easily resolved. The old order does not simply disappear to be replaced by a new order. Instead a more complex situation emerges with elements of both orders co-existing. In these instances, physical violence is used as a supplementary mechanism of control, and ideology plays a crucial role in women's acceptance of the use of physical violence by men.

WIFE ABUSE – RECOMMENDED, ACCEPTED, AND SANCTIONED

The vast majority of both men and women accept, seldom question, and even positively sanction men's right to control "their" women by the occasional slap, punch or push. The community views a wife's overstepping the boundaries of proper conduct as sufficient justification for the imposition of physical violence. Abused women who "talk too much," or who aggravate their husbands or his kin, are given little sympathy, since such behaviour is considered to be justified provocation (cf. Chowning 1985; Bradley 1985). Wife-beating is the right and prerogative of husbands and the fate of wives if wives are to be kept in line and properly controlled. On many occasions I heard women recommend a few good slaps to bring certain women back into line. Men often remark that women whose husbands treat them too easily have become spoilt or comment "his wife should be given a few kicks," or "if she were my wife, I'd give her a good beating."

Men who do not beat their wives, especially if their wives are perceived to be "deviant" in some way, are ridiculed by both men and women. In one case a man whose wife ran away with another man was ridiculed for being "weak" and "pathetic." The story goes that "even when he went and brought his wife back, he didn't give her a beating! But her brother gave her a good beating," since she had shamed not only her conjugal family but also her natal family.

Women regard men who do not occasionally slap their wives as being "under the wife's thumb." The English phrase "petticoat government" is used among middle-class men and women and refer to relationships in which the wife is assumed to be dominant because the male never subjects her to any violence. Another common phrase used by both males and females to describe relationships in which wives are not kept under strict control is *uu to apan aurat ke muur pe charhai ke rakhis* ["he has allowed his wife to sit on top of his head"].

Yet extreme cases of physical violence (for example, where the victim requires medical attention) are not condoned. While wife-beating is acceptable, wife-battering is discouraged and frowned upon. On numerous occasions I heard both women and men being critical of husbands who beat their wives weekly, who beat pregnant women, or who cause their wives serious injury. Even mothers who may have initially incited their sons to beat their wives, sometimes intervene to stop their son's crossing the boundaries of acceptable violence, with comments such as, "Don't hit her too much. There's no need to keep hitting her. She's learnt her lesson." At the same time, these phrases imply that a little hitting is all right.

Women's acquiescence and contribution to their own subordination demonstrates the power and persuasiveness of traditional gender ideologies. It could be argued that they have fully internalised these ideologies, since women are part of the system that continually reinforces the status quo. But while ideological subordination of women is an important factor in explaining why women accept and even encourage male violence, it can only provide a partial explanation. Whenever women get the chance they "cheat" the system by harbouring resentment, expressing discontent, and engaging in acts of insubordination, even when it results in violence. Their willingness to break the rules is evidence that their ideological subordination is neither thorough nor complete (cf. Jeffery 1979).

Explanations based on the ideological subordination of women also fail to take account of the fact that women are not just pathetic victims of an overwhelming system and may have a positive stake in maintaining the status quo. Senior women of the household, for example, enjoy the respect of younger members (both male and female) and wield considerable power and authority over younger women, especially daughters-in-law. Sons have a particularly close relationship with their mothers and show immense respect and affection for them. In fact, as sons get older they are likely to intervene and protect their mothers from any violence imposed by their fathers. Usually a husband stops hitting his wife when their sons are old enough to protect her. At this later period of the life-cycle a woman reaps the benefits of having endured the hardships of being a young wife and daughter-in-law in a strange and sometimes hostile environment and, in turn, is likely to impose similar hardships on other women (Brown 1982, 1985). Her suffering, patience and conformity as a young woman is rewarded when her sons bring wives for her to supervise and control. As a senior woman her loyalties and interests are invested in the household of her sons. As such, she actively works to protect the reputation and honour of her family and to reproduce the status quo.

Such a system creates divisions between women in the household rather than generating solidarity against men. The divergent interests of women partially explains why they encourage or recommend physical violence for other women, especially for their female affines. Stereotypical images of tyrannical mothers-in-law, wicked sisters-in-law and oppressed daughters-in-law in the popular culture of Hindi films reflect the competition and conflict between women of the same household — between mothers-in-law and daughters-in-law, between the wives of brothers, and between sisters-in-law. Mothers compete with wives for their sons' affections. Wives of brothers compete for their mothers-in-law's support and patronage, and for a greater share of the household resources for themselves and their children. Sisters compete with their brother's wife for his affection. These conflicts are structural barriers that prevent women from realising their common interests and from taking joint action against either males or the system.

At another level the system that oppresses women also cares for them and protects them from the harsh realities of the outside world. Increasing unemployment, lack of job opportunities and the absence of an adequate state welfare system means that women, especially those not in paid employment, are dependent on the family-based household for their livelihood. It is no wonder that both young and old women have a positive stake in ensuring the survival of the traditional household. The economic support provided by the males of the family is a powerful mechanism that ensures women conform and actively work to perpetuate the system. Without this financial support women could easily be rendered destitute.

Against this background, the non-conformity and insubordination of the younger, economically independent modern wives makes sense. Unlike older and more traditional wives, they do not have a positive stake in maintaining the status quo since they are not economically dependent on males for their livelihood. Because they are members of modern, Westernised, nuclear families, their sons will set up their own separate households and are, therefore, unlikely to bring wives for them to control and supervise in the future. Furthermore, modern younger women living in nuclear households can afford to espouse a general aversion to male violence against women since they are not subjected to the same degree of tension, conflict and competition that is suffered by women living in traditional family-based households. The costs of insubordination for young modern wives are not as great as for the more traditional wives since they do not have a similar investment in sustaining the system. No rewards for patience and conformity await them in the future.

Abused Wives — What Options?

The powerlessness of wives becomes glaringly obvious when we search for options available to victims of violence. In short, the vast majority of wives have few options but to endure the violence, wait for seniority, and hope to be reborn as males in their next life.[6]

The taunts of husbands like Rina's, such as "Where can you go?" "No one wants you." "Who will feed and keep you?" "Your family does not want you back," are generally true. The majority of women have nowhere to go since they are economically dependent on their husbands and their families prefer they remain married. Such women are locked into violent relationships because of an ideology that stresses the permanency of marriage and a lack of alternatives. This explains why economically dependent wives are hesitant to confront their husbands and to fight back.

Returning to her family of origin is seldom a viable option for an abused woman. Her parents may have died or become economically dependent on their sons. Although brothers traditionally have the responsibility for maintaining sisters and their children if their husbands divorce them, in reality economic pressures and family tensions make this unlikely. Occasionally, however, women do return to their natal home if their marriages are exceptionally violent and no children are involved. In one instance, for example, a woman without children who needed hospital treatment on numerous occasions and became very ill was finally taken back by her financially independent parents. More often than not, however, parents will attempt to talk violent sons-in-law (sometimes through his parents) out of such behaviour and coax their daughters into persevering with the marriage. Marriage is meant to be permanent and women's suffering within marriage is taken for granted.

Even modern Westernised working wives who are not totally dependent on their husbands are hesitant to leave violent marriages. As with Sarita, they leave their husbands for short periods but almost inevitably return, only to be again subjected to violence. On her income alone, Sarita's son was likely to be denied the opportunities he could otherwise have. Although fathers are generally required to continue providing support for their children after divorce, support orders are difficult to enforce in Fiji, as they are in many other countries. Divorce for women like Sarita could also mean the risk of losing custody of their children.

Because divorce in Fiji, except after five years separation, can only be obtained through claiming fault by one party, the potential exists for women to be seriously disadvantaged. If women are proven to be at fault as in failing to fulfill marital obligations, they could be denied maintenance or custody of their children. Hence, fear of losing their children and concern about their future welfare are among the main reasons for women's reluctance to leave violent husbands.

There are also other reasons. Young modern women claim they cannot contemplate divorce because it would bring shame on their natal family, they would be the targets of gossip and rumour, and they would receive little support from their families. This lack of support is evident in the greater proportion of Indo-Fijian females, as compared with ethnic Fijian women, who receive welfare support, statistics confirmed by welfare officers of both groups. The majority of women receiving welfare whom I interviewed claimed they were deserted, thrown out, or maltreated by their husbands and in-laws and that their own families either did not want them, or could not afford to take them back. The fate of many divorced Indo-Fijian women who end up as destitutes requiring welfare and food handouts from charities acts as a powerful deterrent to divorce. At the same time it keeps women submissive and tolerant even of violent marriages.

For some women, like Shanti, the absence of viable alternatives when their patience and tolerance is finally exhausted leaves them only one option: suicide. By committing suicide they communicate to their families, friends and acquaintances the suffering they have endured and the lack of alternatives. They also may attract some sympathy. Suicide by Indo-Fijian women appears primarily to be an escape from an intolerable life.

A disturbing 203 reported cases of suicide by Indo-Fijian women were recorded by the Fiji Bureau of Statistics between the years 1977 and 1982 compared with 25 among indigenous Fijian females. Indo-Fijian women who commit suicide are mainly under the age of 30, an age which coincides with the period in their life when they are likely to have the least power and control (Haynes 1984). Haynes found that the major precipitating factors for female suicides (where families chose to provide reasons) were marital and family (in-laws) conflict (1984:435). The choice of suicide as a solution by so many Indo-Fijian women is an indictment of the insidious system under which they are forced to live rather precarious lives.

CONCLUSION

The threat and use of physical violence is a powerful mechanism by which husbands exercise and assert power and control over wives. While the enduring influence and persuasiveness of familial ideology ensures female submission with little male intervention, the occasional use and persistent threat of violence consolidates male dominance and female subordination within the family. The presence of violence as part of the taken-for-granted world of being female is indicative of the status of women in Indo-Fijian society.

NOTES

Much gratitude is owed to Dorothy Counts for her encouragement, insightful comments, and suggestions on an earlier draft of this paper. Thanks are also due to Ruth Walker for her typing. An earlier version of this paper dealing with domestic violence in general was published in *Pacific Studies* 13(3) July, 1990. I wish to thank *Pacific Studies* for permission to reprint here.

1. The research for this paper was undertaken as part of a wider study on gender relations among Indo-Fijians in Suva. The data were gathered between 1983 and 1987. No reference is made to the May 1987 military coup in Fiji as the data were gathered prior to the coup.
2. This paper is dedicated to the memory of Shanti, who was a gentle and unassuming woman. She was not just another one of my informants but a friend of the family's and someone I had known for nearly ten years.
3. This is not to imply that no divisions exist or that Indo-Fijians constitute a homogenous group. On the contrary, divisions between Hindus/Muslims, North Indian/South Indian, urban/rural, rich/poor all exist. Hinduism and Islam is practised with great fervour and marriage is endogamous by religion.
4. *Purdah* literally means "curtain" (although in common usage it refers to the various modes of secluding women either by confining them to an enclosed space or by veiling them), the strict segregation of the sexes, the "symbolic sheltering" (Papanek 1973) of women and a moral code of conduct (cf. Jeffery 1979; Vatuk 1982). *Purdah* is practised throughout North India among both Hindu and Muslim communities (see Jacobson and Wadley 1977; Jeffery 1979; Papanek 1973; Sharma 1980), although distinctions between Hindu and Muslim patterns are known to exist. The ideology and numerous manifestations of *purdah* are deeply ingrained in the South Asian socio-cultural system, and it has been retained (albeit in a modified form) among Indo-Fijians. It can be viewed as the major organising principle for the controls on women's sexuality, spatial movements, social interactions, behaviour, demeanour and the sexual division of labour. For a more detailed discussion of *purdah* ideology see Lateef (1990).
5. For more details on appropriate and inappropriate occupations see Lateef (1986).
6. When I asked women the question "What do you hope to return as in your next life?" virtually all replied "Male."

REFERENCES CITED

Basham, Arthur L. 1974. The Wonder that was India. London: Fontana.

Bradley, Christine. 1985. Attitudes and Practices Relating to Marital Violence Among the Tolai of East New Britain. *In* Domestic Violence in Papua New Guinea. Susan Toft ed., Pp. 32—71. Port Moresby: Law Reform Commission of Papua New Guinea, Monograph No. 3.

Brown, Judith, K. 1982. Cross-Cultural Perspectives on Middle-Aged Women. Current Anthropology 23:143—156.

————. 1985 Introduction. *In* In Her Prime: A New View of Middle-aged Women. Judith K. Brown and Virginia Kerns, eds., Pp. 1—11. South Hadley, Mass: Bergin and Garvey.

Chowning, Ann. 1985. Kove Women and Violence: The Context of Wife-Beating in a West New Britain Society. *In* Domestic Violence in Papua New Guinea. Susan Toft ed., pp. 72—91. Port Moresby: Law Reform Commission of Papua New Guinea, Monograph No. 3.

Ferdows, Adele K., and Amir H. Ferdows. 1983. Women in Shi' i Fiqh: Images Through the Hadith. *In* Women and Revolution in Iran. G. Nashat ed., Pp. 55—68. Boulder, CO: Westview Press.

Fiji Bureau of Statistics. 1986. Report of the Census of the Population. Suva: Government Printer.

Gupta, A. R. 1976. Women in Hindu Society. New Delhi: Jyotsna Prakashan.

Haynes, Ruth. 1984. Suicide in Fiji: A Preliminary Study. British Journal of Psychiatry 145:433—438.

Jacobson, Doranne. 1982. Purdah and the Hindu Family in Central India. *In* Separate Worlds: Studies of Purdah in South Asia. Gail Minault, ed. Pp. 81—109. Delhi: Chanakya Publications.

Jacobson, Doranne, and Susan Wadley, eds. 1977. Women in India: Two Perspectives. Columbia, MO: South Asia Books.

Jayawardena, Chandra. 1968. Migration and Social Change: A Survey of Indian Communities Overseas. Geographical Review 58:426—442.

————. 1980. Culture and Ethnicity in Guyana and Fiji. Man 15(3):430—450.

Jeffery, Patricia. 1979. Frogs in a Well: Indian Women in Purdah. London: Zed Press.

Kapadia, Kanailal M. 1955. Marriage and Family in India. London: Oxford University Press.

Kishwar, Madhu. 1984. Some Aspects of Bondage. *In* In Search of Answers: Indian Women's Voices from Manushi. Madhu Kishwar and Ruth Vanita, eds. Pp. 230—241. London: Zed Press.

Lal, Brij. 1983. The Girmitiyas: The Origins of the Fiji Indians. Canberra, Australia: Australian National University Press. (Also Journal of Pacific History)

Lateef, Shireen. 1986. Because They Have Nice Uniforms: The Career Aspirations of Schoolgirls in Suva, Fiji. *In* Development in the Pacific — What Women Say. Pp. 45—47. Canberra: Australian Council for Overseas Aid Publication.

————. 1990. Rule by the Danda: Domestic Violence Among Indo-Fijians. Pacific Studies 13(3):43—62. Special Issue: Domestic Violence in Oceania. Dorothy Ayers Counts, ed.

Madudi, Sajed A. 1978. Purdah and the Status of Women in Islam, Fourth Edition. Lahore, Pakistan: Islamic Publications.

Mies, Maria. 1980. Indian Women and Patriarchy. Conflicts and Dilemmas of Students and Working Women. Sarah K. Sarkar, trans. New Delhi: Concept Publishing Co.

Minai, Naila. 1981. Women in Islam: Traditions and Transition in the Middle East. N.Y.: Seaview Books.

Papanek, Hanna. 1973. Purdah: Separate Worlds and Symbolic Shelter. Comparative Studies in Society and History 15(3): 289—325.

Sharma, Ursula. 1980. Women, Work and Property in North-West India. London: Tavistock Publications.

Vatuk, Sylvia. 1982. Purdah Revisited: A Comparison of Hindu and Muslim Interpretations of the Current Meaning of Purdah in South Asia. *In* Separate Worlds: Studies of Purdah in South Asia. H. Papanek and G. Minault eds., Pp. 54—78. Delhi: Chanakya Pub.

Wadley, Susan. 1977. Women and the Hindu Tradition. *In* Women in India: Two Perspectives. Jacobson, Doranne, and Susan Wadley, eds., Pp. 113—139. Columbia: South Asia Books.

15

Wife Abuse and the Political System: A Middle Eastern Case Study

Mary Elaine Hegland

If a wife goes bad (said the mullah in explaining the Arabic of Surah 4, verse 34 of the Qor'an), or if there is a difference between husband and wife, first he should scold her and speak with her. If that does not work, he should become *ghar* with her — stop interacting with her. If that does not work, he should administer corporal punishment — but there should be no resulting marks on her body — it should not turn black and blue.

INTRODUCTION

Although wife abuse is common in Iran, it is a subject which has received almost no attention from scholars and little has been written on it. The purpose of this article is to examine the problem, to show the connection between wife-beating and the Iranian political system, and to raise questions for further research. The data on which this analysis is based come from my own research as well as from published sources. The two case histories of wife abuse presented exemplify social process in a political system characterized by arbitrariness and the need to dominate. The degree to which a woman could be abused depended upon the power relationships and resources that people were able to muster in their continuous effort to control others and to avoid being manipulated themselves.

THE RESEARCH

My data are from my 1978–1979 field research in the village of Aliabad in southwestern Iran as well as other periods spent in Iran between 1966 and 1978 and from interviews in the United States between 1987 and 1990 with mainly middle-aged Iranian women (who had received some of their education in America) as well as their mothers and aunts visiting from Iran. During my research in Iran between June 1978 and December 1979 I did not interview my informants specifically about wife-beating, but my interviews in the United States did focus on the topic.[1] Most of the events I describe here occurred between June 1978 and December 1979, although I also recount incidents that happened within the memory of informants. As it is not possible to ascertain current conditions in Iran I use the past tense.

THE VILLAGE POLITICAL SYSTEM AND WIFE ABUSE

In 1978 and 1979 Aliabad was a large village of some 3,000 people located half an hour by bus away from the outskirts of the city of Shiraz, capital of the province of Fars in southwestern Iran. Local political factions battled for control over agricultural land and the powerful position of headman for the absentee landlord. Because there was only a weak centralized government before the oil boom of the 1960s and 1970s, local factions had to rely on the strength of their fighting men for political power. During the relative anarchy of the revolutionary period between 1978 and 1980, local police control declined and competition between local factions in Aliabad resumed. (For more discussion on the political system of Aliabad, see Hooglund [Hegland] 1982.)

In the local political system, young men were valued as fighters while women were valued as reproducers and as the means of creating or solidifying relations with other groups through marriage. Women's work and hospitality were invaluable and their role was central in producing support for their kinsmen in the local system, where repetitive and intense social interaction was required to maintain political alliances. (For more discussion of the roles of women in the Aliabad political system see Hegland 1986b.)

Although devalued as persons, women were valued as resources (see Vieille 1979). If men could control women, they could utilize their labor, so important in the political process. Women were also valuable as a means of demonstrating control and authority. The protection of dependents of both sexes, and their submission and obedience, effectively signaled to other political actors the dominance and political strength of a leader and his faction.[2]

In this fluctuating, authoritarian village political system, men demonstrated their superiority by intimidating others. To make others — enemies, followers, and dependents — afraid of them, they engaged in acts of violence. It was incumbent upon those in authority to instill "respect," or more accurately fear, in those for whom they were responsible in order to extract the required compliance and correct behavior. Children and women were chastised in order to force them to live up to the expectations of the system. According to Erika Friedl, who has been conducting research on women's issues and child rearing in Iran,

> The beating of children is an educational device. In my village research site, children have to be beaten to keep them on the right path and if a woman misbehaves, she has to be beaten for the same reason. Beating is a teaching device, but it's also a means of dealing with insubordination and dissent. (Personal communication, October 4, 1989)

In order to carry on their political and economic struggles, the older generation had to control the younger generation. Young men were needed for their labor and their fighting abilities. In addition to the political work a young man might carry out for his father, sons were often a main source of money, work, and other resources for their parents. Young women were needed for their labor power and for their reproductive capacities.

Parents obtained a wife for their son, but they often sought to minimize the contact and affection between the couple, fearing that the wife would compete for the resources produced by him. By physically abusing his wife the son served the purposes of the older generation and the kin group as a whole.

In Aliabad, people were the most important resource. Control over property was not secure; rather one needed people and their connections to get and keep control over land and other resources. Women were a means of gathering people and connections and were, therefore, valuable and carefully controlled. Often women learned the political importance of controlling people and sought to build their own power by influencing others.[3]

The treatment of a young bride was sufficient to quell any thoughts of independence. Generally, she improved her situation and gained power by fulfilling her duties and producing children. Whereas a younger woman was kept in line through force and intimidation, an older woman developed a stake in her husband's family and kinship group. Because of her children, she was willing to do whatever she could to support the interests of her husband's family. She gained power in proportion to her effectiveness in working for the family and keeping family members under control. Young women and young men learned that the best way to gain power and a more comfortable life was to manipulate the system, to build up a power base, to become the people who controlled and intimidated others. From being a weak and subservient bride herself, a woman often turned into a mother-in-law who tightly controlled and even aided in the abuse of new daughters-in-law (see also Brown 1982, in press; Mernissi 1987; and Rassam 1980). Older women exchanged their services as controllers of young women for acceptance and status in their husbands' family. A woman wanted the approval of her husband and the community that resulted from her good management of her daughter-in-law. She also wanted to retain the devotion of her son rather than lose it to the younger woman.

MARRIAGE, KINSHIP, AND THE EXPECTATIONS OF WOMEN

When I was born, the minute they told my mother it was a girl she began to
cry bitterly. She refused to feed me for three days. She was ashamed in front
of her in-laws. But my aunts were happy and showing the baby to everyone.
Then my aunts tried to tell her—you should be ashamed, she's a lovely baby,
you should be happy—so she gave up and fed me. She thought it was shameful for an important man to have a daughter.

These words of an urban friend illustrate the lesson learned by girls at an
early age: they are valued less than boys. Girls were not expected to promote
their own interests but to be available to others for service. They were raised
to be homebound, obedient, and extremely concerned about their reputa-
tions.

A number of factors made a wife subservient to and dependent on her husband. Young women were carefully guarded, married off young—ten to
twelve was not unusual in the recent past (see also Guppy 1988:44 and Haeri
1983:242, 243)—and then subdued as new wives. An age difference of ten
or more years between bride and groom was typical, and the bride usually
had a lower level of education than the groom. Most girls were removed
from school at puberty and were, therefore, unable to obtain an education
that might allow them to support themselves.[4]

The requirement that a bride be a virgin caused girls to be sheltered, isolated, and inexperienced in dealing with others outside of a small group of
family, kin, and neighbors. Traditionally, Iranian women were not allowed
to make decisions concerning their own lives (see also Farmanfarmaian
1976).[5] Every effort was made to keep women economically dependent and
therefore unable to leave the control of their fathers, husbands, or brothers.

In my village research site, if a woman were to work, the male in charge
of her would be considered unable to support her, a shameful state of affairs. Although girls from less economically comfortable families worked in
the local carpet shop, they were taken out before marriage.[6] Only some
twelve adult women out of a village of about 3,000 did some work for money
outside of the home. All except one of these women were single, widowed,
or the wives of men who could not support them.

Young village women were supposed to stay at home as much as possible
and were to turn to close neighbors and relatives for companionship (see
Friedl 1983:222). This isolation in a watchful group of female guardians
restricted the access of young women to potentially helpful connections and
the examples set by more independent women. They had little or no perception of alternatives. Young women could only leave the village in the company of relatives. After extracting a promise of secrecy, one village woman

told me of her friendship with a city woman whom she visited periodically and who helped her out with little gifts. This type of friendship was unusual.

Men were raised to be aggressive, to devalue women and their activities, to use violence to get what they wanted, and to demonstrate the power and strength required for political survival. Men were expected to keep control over their womenfolk; failure to do so meant a loss of standing for the entire family. Many men were willing to use corporal punishment to extract obedience and maintain control, and they received social support for doing so.[7]

Most women were not able to escape from abuse. Beatings emphasized their position of subservience and dependence and kept wives cowed and acquiescent. People were not eager to intervene, and some women counselled patience; this is what women must tolerate and live with. Forcible defloration on the wedding night, compelled sexual intercourse, and beatings were acts of male dominance and female submission that were a repeated reminder to the woman of her position of relative powerlessness and the necessity of obedience to her husband and others in authority over her.

A woman generally had to come to terms with a violent relationship without external help. Separation and divorce were shameful and, because women rarely could support themselves, were possible only if their fathers or brothers were willing to take on the economic burden and the embarrassment of sheltering them. As she was no longer a virgin, a divorcee would enter a second marriage with even less leverage than she had enjoyed in her first.

The requirement that women must protect the reputation, the *qaybat*, of the family generally made them reluctant to talk to others about how their husbands treated them and kept them quiet about abuse. Ziba, in the case study below, even denied the abuse when her mother asked her about it.[8] The repeated invasion of their persons, the attacks against their bodies which they felt they must tolerate, and the stories of the beatings and forced sexual relations endured by other women formed for wives a bleak image of their lives and the relative hopelessness of changing their situation.

The Iranian kinship system is bilateral and couples generally maintain ties with both sides of the family. Village endogamy was the rule. The association between a young woman and her own family was usually close. Shortly after marriage a bride was expected to visit her parents for a few days, and during her marriage a woman maintained her connection with her natal family and usually visited often at their home.

A wife was not to complain of mistreatment from her husband. Her husband was expected to maintain complete authority over her and her father had no right to interfere. However, since her relationship with her father and brother continued, they were assumed to still care for her and be concerned about her welfare. It did not speak well of a man's position and power if his daughter or sister were consistently mistreated and others in the community were aware of it. Should it come to the attention of a woman's father that her husband was beating her excessively, her father might provide a refuge for her. He would take no action against the husband, however, for a man had full authority to treat his wife as he wished and no father wished to become involved in controversy over a daughter's treatment.

The result of these contradictions was ambivalence about the responsibility for married women that lent itself to manipulation and negotiation between a woman's husband and her male relatives. The outcome of the negotiations depended on the relative power of the husband versus the woman's father or brother.

Iranian men beat their wives and sisters when the women challenged the hierarchical, authoritarian system. If wives disobeyed husbands or talked back to them, if they did not immediately and cheerfully perform the labor required of them, if they were not sufficiently submissive and sympathetic to in-laws, they were punished. Correct behavior was not enough; correct *affect* also was owed to superiors. Brothers were in charge of sisters; they were responsible for correct behavior by a sister toward other males and their obedience to superiors—including themselves. Beatings reminded women of their duties and of their relatively defenseless position in the social system.

Wife abuse, then, was a result of the hierarchical and violent nature of the political system and became one more arena where men vied for political power, thus perpetuating the system. Abuse also effectively taught young women that the best way to beat the system was to join it and become manipulators and abusers themselves—often as older women through their sons.

WIFE-BEATING IN IRAN

Wife-beating was common in Iran. Almost every Iranian whom I questioned in the United States related stories of abuse. According to a city woman who had visited a number of villages and who was on close terms with several village women who came to work for her as maids,

> Among villagers, wife-beating is very, very common; they do it all the time. In my country it is common among poor people. Naneh Kayvan (her maid and close friend from a village) said all villagers beat up their wives (Personal communication, October 21, 1989).

Ethnographic short stories (actual occurrences written in short story form) by Friedl (1989) support these observations. In Friedl's book we read of a brother who beats his sister for greeting her cousin in public, and of another brother who beats his sister for talking back (Friedl 1989:48, 132). Husbands beat their wives because they are disobedient, insubordinate, or bad tempered; because they talk back or complain about the husband's mother and sister; as a result of complaints from his sister; to reprimand for adultery; or because the husband felt upset and frustrated (Friedl 1989:50, 55, 64, 69, 84, 94, 95, 226). Some people argue that wife-beating does not occur in urban areas or among well-educated peoples (see Bauer 1985:173 for example). There is, however, evidence that it occurs in towns and cities as well as villages and is common among all classes.[9]

Wife-beating in Aliabad

Wife-beating was not discussed openly in Aliabad. On one occasion I was present when a young woman wept softly as she told her older neighbor about abuse from her husband. Another young woman told about episodes of physical abuse from her husband and said that in frustration she had wept and repeatedly hit her head against the wall. In thinking about his upcoming wedding, a friend revealed the fear that he might come to beat his wife; his father beat his mother.

Two cases which came to my attention resulted in separation. First is the case of "Ziba," the daughter of a village headman, who cleverly obtains what she wants by living up to the ideal of a "passive" and obedient daughter. In the second case, the relatives of "Goltaj" told me about her situation with her husband. In both cases the relative political power of the protagonists was related to the outcome of their conflict over the wife abuse.

Ziba told me her story when I visited her father's home during her stay there.

> I was married two years ago. . . . When I went, I had earrings, bracelets, and other jewelry. My husband's sister took them from me. She said, "The price of gold is going up—let me sell them for you and give you the money"—and then she never gave me the money. My mother-in-law took the money that was given to me at the time of my wedding. When the baby was born she took the money that was given to me at this time too.
>
> My husband is twenty-two; he works at the gravel factory. When they get extra money from their shares and he buys me a lamb so I get meat, my mother-in-law is jealous. She's jealous of anything I get. I haven't had a new *chador* (veil) or anything else since I was married—my mother-in-law won't allow it. She won't allow her son to visit my parents. She says, "What do you want to do there?"
>
> When I wash the baby's clothes, she asks me, "Why are you constantly washing the baby's clothes?" If I'm washing clothes and the baby is lying in the sun, she won't pick her up—even though the baby is her son's child. She

complains to her son, "Look, she comes and washes clothes in the *hoze* (small courtyard pool)." Where *should* I wash them?

At first he believed his mother, but then he came to realize it was his mother's fault. He gets 3,500 tomans a month.[10] Someone who gets this salary should have his own rooms by now, should have a home. But his father buys and sells animals. His father says to him, "Lend me some money; I want to buy an animal" — and then doesn't give the money back.

He used to come home from the factory and would laugh and joke with me a couple of hours, I swear! But then they said bad things about me. They said, "Your wife is no good." Then he would come home and go over to their room. I would wait without eating dinner — I felt it was better to eat together — and then when he came back at midnight, he said his mother had pressured him into eating dinner there. They said bad things about me so that he would come home from the factory and stay over there until bedtime, and even then when he came home he wouldn't talk to me, as they had told him not to. What sort of a life is this? A person is alone all the time and then even in the evening alone, going to sleep alone to wake up in the morning and be alone.

I never told my mother how it was for me. When the neighbors told her, and she asked me about it, I'd say they were lying.

Then on that day, the father came home shouting and swearing and said the shepherd had taken the animals to drink and two of his lambs had fallen in the water and drowned. They told me and I didn't say anything. He kept on shouting and going on.

When he came home, they told him that two of the lambs had died and I wasn't sorry about it, I didn't take it hard. He beat me from eight at night and continued to beat me until twelve midnight. At twelve o'clock I fell asleep without being aware of anything, not even the thought of my father and mother.

When I woke up I was ill, and I kept vomiting — I hadn't eaten dinner or lunch the day before. They took me to my father's and my parents took me to the hospital. My husband stayed with me the first two days in the hospital. All of the doctors and nurses came to ask me how I got bruises all over my face and body. I said I fell down a stairs — they doubted it. His mother and father scolded him because he stayed with me. They kept telling him to get a divorce. He said to them, "I haven't got tired of this wife, I want my wife, I want this wife."

When I got out of the hospital, I came to stay with my parents. His parents kept encouraging him to get a divorce. At first, at night he ate supper here at my parents' house and then went there to sleep. But his parents scolded him. He wanted to move to another home, but they wouldn't let him, so he stopped going home after work. He wanted to move in with his mother's brother on the other side of the highway. His uncle had told me, "I know what my sister's like — come and live with us." So he took a pickup truck to his parents' house to get his stuff. They wouldn't let him take it. Then they fought with the uncle who then fought with my husband, saying, "Why are your parents like this?" Finally, the aunt came over to my parent's house to get me to come back. They want me back now so that their son will come back. But I wouldn't go, and then the aunt fought with them.

I won't go until my husband comes back. I will only go if my father tells me to go. They won't let me have any of my clothes and things. Finally my parents told him, "She doesn't have any clothes; she has to wear her sister's clothes," so he got me a blouse and a couple of loose house pants, but no shoes. Now I'm waiting to see what my husband and my father will say. Now I'm in my father's house. I'll do whatever he says.

It's because of his parents. Whenever he beat me, it was the parents who ordered him to do it. He always swore his parents ordered him to do it. He was always sorry afterwards. He would realize his parents were wrong. I used to work so hard. I swept my mother-in-law's house and did so much.

Although Ziba blamed her husband's parents for her troubles, her mother felt Ziba's husband was also at fault. "Ziba and the baby have been here for forty days," she said, "and he has never asked about his daughter. Some people just don't care about their children."

Sometime later as I was hurrying through a village alleyway, I heard a call; Ziba had seen me and urged me to come up and see her new home. She was pleased with her modest, second story room. Now that she and her husband were away from the influence of his parents, she indicated, things were much better.

In spite of abuse, not all women were entirely cowed. Ziba managed to get a home for herself and her husband away from his parents and against their will. The same political system in which women were used as a means of forming alliances between families also allowed them to use their intermediate position to achieve their own aims.

Ziba behaved passively, as a proper young woman, saying "I'm in my father's house. I'll do whatever he says." Ziba's success in the competition over her husband was due to her father's eminence in the village. Publicity over her battering enabled Ziba to obtain her father's support for the couple's move to their own home. His father-in-law's respected position in the village community also helped the young man (who did not wish to lose his wife) to stand up to his parents.

Goltaj's husband, Mehdi, often physically abused her and had several times sent her back to her father's home. When he wanted his wife back, he would send his mother to fetch her. Finally Goltaj's brother Cyrus did not hand her over to the mother when, at Mehdi's direction, she came to fetch her. Cyrus insisted that Mehdi himself, along with several of his male kin, must come after her and they must talk the matter over. Mehdi refused. On the evening of December 8, 1978, Mehdi attacked and stabbed his brother-in-law Cyrus in the side, seriously wounding him. The attack occurred during the religious self-flagellation procession of mourning for the martyrdom of Imam Hosein. Mehdi said his attack was prompted by loyalty to the shah as he was a monarchist and Cyrus was a village leader supporting the revolutionary forces, but the whole village knew Mehdi was furious over Cyrus's refusal to return Goltaj to him.

Crowds of visitors, anxious to show their support for Cyrus against Mehdi, came to see Cyrus in the hospital. The incident brought about a shift in village opinion from pro-shah or at least accommodating to the shah's regime, to pro-Khomeini and pro-revolution. If this is how shah supporters behaved, villagers felt, he and his followers should be ousted.

Cyrus gradually recovered. On February 11, 1979, during the hubbub of the day the government fell, several people beat Mehdi up. He was taken into the nearby city and when he returned, he went to Cyrus's courtyard. He called for Cyrus's uncle (this man was also Cyrus's step-father and Goltaj's father)[11] and when he came to the door, Mehdi and the others so severely beat the older man's head with large sticks that he was taken to the hospital. In a vengeful mood, a crowd attacked the shop belonging to Mehdi's mother's brother, pulling down the roof, taking goods and candy, and tearing up the *chadors* from Mecca.

Although some members of the clan thought they should kill Mehdi to demonstrate that they were not weak, no further violence occurred; rather, Cyrus's clan pursued the matter through the court system. Later in the summer, Cyrus's new bride commented on the case:

> Goltaj is sixteen. She was fourteen when she got married. Cyrus was against her marrying Mehdi — boys are together in the alleyways, so they know each other better. But his step-father said to him, "So, are *you* going to support her then?" She has been living with her father for about a year now. They get 600 tomans every month from the husband for her and the child's expenses. It would be better if she got the divorce; then they could get the money from the brideprice and so on. Sometimes her husband says he'll give her a divorce, sometimes not. His family tell him, "Divorce her. She's no good; you can't get along with her."
>
> Now they're waiting for a hearing in court to see what will happen. If she didn't have the little girl it would be all right; she could get married again. But it's rare for a divorced woman with children to remarry — her new husband wouldn't accept the children. (Goltaj's sister-in-law, bride of Cyrus, July 17, 1979)

In October of 1979 I learned from Mehdi's sister that Mehdi had gone to get his daughter. The little girl was now with Mehdi's mother who lived with him and cared for the child. According to Mehdi's sister, the couple were going to get a divorce.[12]

Both of these cases reveal the determination of parents to retain control over their sons and to avoid losing them to the daughters-in-law. Ziba was in competition with her husband's parents over her husband and the resources he provided. A widow, such as Mehdi's mother, often felt especially dependent upon her son and thus vulnerable to loss of influence over him.[13]

The case of Goltaj illustrates one important reason why women will not complain of ill treatment or leave their abusing husbands. If they do, their children are generally lost to them. When Mehdi came to get his baby daughter no one stopped him because everyone recognized his right to his child.

A husband also had the right to mistreat his wife. Goltaj's relatives did not mobilize to protect her or to get revenge on Mehdi for beating her.[14] It was only when Cyrus was injured that his kinsmen took action. Injury to a male could not be tolerated.

Cyrus was a popular young man in the village and he had a larger kinship group than did Mehdi. Although Cyrus had stronger backing in the village, Mehdi had counted on the intervention of forces outside of the village. Mehdi believed he had the power of Iranian government forces behind him. If necessary, local gendarmes and other government bodies such as the court system would back him in his violence against Cyrus, he believed.

Up until that point, the rural police had protected pro-shah individuals in the village. Mehdi's stabbing of Cyrus took place, however, in the midst of the revolution when the balance of power was in flux. Villagers sensed the decline in the power of the pro-shah forces. Their analysis of political conditions, together with their outrage at the stabbing of Cyrus, led the majority of villagers to swing their support to Cyrus and the pro-Khomeini revolutionary forces. The Pahlavi government fell about two months later on February 11, 1979. Mehdi lacked support either within or outside the village, whereas Cyrus was connected to the new government. Goltaj did not go back to her husband's home for more abuse but stayed with her brother and father. Mehdi was furious at Cyrus for providing a refuge for Goltaj but could do nothing.

CONCLUSION

The men in Aliabad were pressured by the authoritarian political system into obeying their elders in exchange for receiving valuable resources — such as wives. The men, in turn, abused their wives, cowing them and usually leaving them with the feeling that they had few alternatives but to submit to their husbands. Their labor was, then, often put to use in the political system. As they grew older, women, through bitter experience, learned how to survive and use their resources and manipulate others to gain power. Among their more precious resources were their sons. Older women who had suffered under the senior generation in their husbands' families in turn tyrannized their daughters-in-law.

Although wives were valued for their labor and reproductive capacity, their in-laws often felt they must be controlled and distanced from their husbands. Parents who relied upon the income and labor of their son, considered it to be in their best interest for their daughter-in-law to be abused, cowed, helpless, and submissive rather than a part of a decision-making husband-wife team. In turn, a young wife often felt it was in her own interests to leave her in-law's home and tried to persuade her husband to move.

In the authoritarian, hierarchical village political system, wife abuse was just one way in which inferiors were connect to superiors. Sons who were dominated by their elders in turn subjugated their wives and older women — who had been suppressed in their youth — encouraged the repression of their daughters-in-law.

In Aliabad, however, such relationships were not necessarily static, but rested on power differences that might change. For example, sons working in the new jobs available as a result of the oil boom were less dependent upon their fathers and less subject to the wishes of the older generation. Or women might have more access to resources such as education and jobs and be less susceptible to abuse from their husbands. A young bride might develop resources and a power base in her husband's home or a women accrue power over her lifetime. Eventually an older woman might be surrounded by loving children and caring for a helpless and socially isolated old husband who had previously abused her.

Men with greater political power could both abuse their wives with greater impunity and could more readily protect sisters and daughters from abuse. A man, because of his attachment to his abused daughter or sister and out of concern for his own reputation, might provide refuge for her, especially if he were in a more powerful political position than the abusive husband. If, however, the husband were politically powerful, the abuse would be less likely to come to public attention. In Aliabad abused wives were subject to the vicissitudes of the political system. Political change might alter the relative power of in-laws, and such changes would affect sanctions against abuse and the sanctuary available to an abused wife.

The case of Ziba shows how an apparently helpless abused wife was able to use abuse by her husband, her obedience to social expectations, and the higher status of her father over her husband to gain a home for herself and her husband separate from her in-laws. In the hierarchical, fluctuating political system of an Iranian village, wife abuse could become an issue in political competition among male in-laws. As seen in the case of Goltaj, the ability to abuse a woman or to protect a woman from abuse changed with the fluctuating political power of the protagonists.

NOTES

The name of the village and all names of persons have been changed in order to protect privacy. For research and writing funding, I am grateful to the Social Science Research Council and the American Council of Learned Societies; the Anthropology Department and The Southwest Asian and North Africa program of SUNY, Binghamton; the Educational Foundation of the American Association of University Women; the Center for Near Eastern and North African Studies of the University of Michigan, Ann Arbor; the National Endowment for the Humanities; Franklin and Marshall College; and Santa Clara University. My deep gratitude goes to those women who shared with me their often distressing stories of mistreatment, and especially to some of my close friends who revealed painful memories in hopes of helping to bring about positive change. Generous assistance and constructive criticism has been provided by Akbar Aghajanian, Erika Friedl, Patricia Higgins, Anne Marie Ominski, Nancy Tapper, the editors of this volume, and others whose names are best not mentioned.

1. One of the reasons for the dearth of social science material on wife-beating and battering is likely the reluctance of researchers to tackle these sensitive topics.

2. See also Papanek (1973, 1979, and 1984); Sharma (1983); Sanday (1981); and Vieille (1979).

3. For discussion of women's labor and its political importance as well a women's activities in politics see Hegland (1986b and in press). For discussion of political system and process see Hooglund (Hegland) (1982) and Hegland (1986a).

4. Although the fiance of one young woman, the daughter of an enlightened school teacher, gave his approval for her to attend university, the future father-in-law rejected her plans to have a career. "My son is perfectly capable of supporting her," was his outraged comment.

5. In a dramatic illustration of this point, Erika Friedl relates the words of a woman who resisted her marriage: "I was about ten or eleven then, before I even had my first period, but I had grown quite a bit and no longer was so weak and skinny. I cried and screamed and kicked and scratched and bit like a cornered cat, but they just beat me up, my mother and my father did. My sister cried with me. My father's brother, when he came to sign the marriage contract, even clobbered me with his rifle butt until I said yes "(Friedl 1989:185, 186; see also Guppy 1988:32, 40, 43, 56, 156).

6. Many men elsewhere in Iran also did not wish their wives to work. Farmanfarmaian states, "In Iran we have discovered that many divorces and family disputes result from the wife's desire to work and the husband's refusal to give consent" (1976:28— 29). See also Guppy (1988:30) and Friedl (1981).

7. A researcher reports on a father who supported his son-in-law's beating his daughter and, in fact, urged him to use a chain for flogging her (Fathi 1985:155).

Not all Iranians share these attitudes or feel that wife-beating is acceptable. One urban Iranian woman told me, "My father thinks anyone who beats his wife is out of his mind."

8. Friedl related an aunt's comments about her niece: "I myself have seen her with a black eye, her veil drawn half across her face. 'The cow hit me,' she said. The cow indeed" (1989:94).

9. Although one urban informant felt wife-beating is not common among the educated, stating, "The educated don't beat up their wives unless they get very mean and aggressive," other indications are to the contrary. During the course of conducting research in Iran in summer of 1989, Erika Friedl asked an Iranian social scientist and his wife about wife-beating: "At first they said it was a class thing. The lower classes do it more. Then they looked at each other and one would say, 'So and so beats his wife,' and the other said, 'And so and so in such and such a department does it,' until between the two of them they came up with a whole list of wife-beating cases in the academic community" (Erika Friedl, personal communication, October 14, 1989).

Educated Iranian friends living in the United States told me of the physical abuse of their relatively well-educated female relatives in Iran, and of their own physical abuse and that of their friends here in the United States. According to Erika Friedl (personal communication, October 4 and 14, 1989), wife abuse appears to be increasing in Iran. In recent years the responsibility for controlling and punishing women has become shared by larger circles of men. After the revolution, groups of men calling themselves "Whippers of Naked Women" roamed the city to chastise improperly covered women. Revolutionary guards, of course, feel themselves responsible for the correct behavior and appearance of all women. For an example, see Friedl (1989:85—86). Also see Hegland (1982:500 and 1983:188). With government-required *hejab* (modesty), the State has also taken upon itself the functions of monitoring and controlling women.

Wife abuse appears to be common, at least in some areas, elsewhere in the Middle East as well. See Sawsan el-Messiri (1979:538); Nayra Atiya (1982); Nawal El Saadawi (1983); and Wedad Zenie-Ziegler (1988) for example.

10. In the late 1970s, there were about 7.5 tomans to the dollar.

11. It was not uncommon for a man to marry his brother's widow.

12. Both cases have characteristics similar to those found by researchers in wife abuse in the U.S. and elsewhere. See Campbell (1985); Levinson (1988); Masumura (1979); Walker (1979 and 1984); and Yllo and Bograd (1988).

13. Other stories told of great control by mothers-in-law, such as the mother-in-law sleeping between the couple! See also Ghalem (1984) and Friedl (1989:94).

Upper- and middle-class women, as well as village women, have marital problems because of interference by their in-laws. In his analysis of 285 cases, an Iranian psychiatrist found marital problems causing difficulty for 40 percent of the women. The leading marital issue among these women was the "woman's struggle to free herself from in-law interference." (Bagheri 1981:47)

14. In cross-cultural research on wife abuse, Masumura found that "in most societies, wife abuse, whether homicidal or not, does not call forth revenge by the wife's kin" (1979:55). Vieille has likewise found Iranian village women to be devalued (1979:197—456).

REFERENCES CITED

Atiya, Nayra. 1982. Khul-Khaal: Five Egyptian Women Tell Their Stories. Syracuse: Syracuse University Press.

Bagheri, Abbas S. 1981. Precipitating Factors of Neurotic Reactions in Middle and Upper-Middle Class Persian Women (Iran). The International Journal of Social Psychiatry 27:47—51.

Bauer, Janet. 1985. Demographic Change, Women and the Family in a Migrant Neighborhood of Teheran. *In* Women and the Family in Iran. Asghar Fathi, ed. Pp. 158—186. Leiden: E. H. Brill.

Brown, Judith K. 1982. Cross-Cultural Perspectives on Middle-Aged Women. Current Anthropology 23:143—156.

———. In press. Introduction to the First Edition and Addendum. *In* In Her Prime: New Views of Middle-Aged Women. Second Edition. Virginia Kerns and Judith K. Brown, eds. Urbana: University of Illinois Press.

Campbell, Jacquelyn C. 1985. Beating of Wives: A Cross-Cultural Perspective. Victimology 10:174—185.

Farmanfarmaian, Khodadad. 1976. Women and Decision Making: With Special Reference to Iran and Other Developing Countries. Labour and Society 1:25—32.

Fathi, Asghar. 1985. Social Integration in the Traditional Urban Family. *In* Women and the Family in Iran. Asghar Fathi, ed. Pp. 151—157. Leiden: E. J. Brill.

Friedl, Erika. 1981. Women and the Division of Labor in an Iranian Village. Middle East Research and Information Project Reports, 95:12—18.

———. 1983. State Ideology and Village Women. *In* Women and Revolution in Iran. Guity Nashat, ed. Pp. 217—230. Boulder: Westview Press, Inc.

———. 1989. Women of Deh Koh: Lives in an Iranian Village. Washington: Smithsonian Institution Press.

Ghalem, Ali. 1984. A Wife for My Son. Chicago: Banner Press.

Guppy, Shusha. 1988. The Blindfold Horse: Memories of a Persian Childhood. Boston: Beacon Press.

Haeri, Shahla. 1983. The Institution of Mut'a Marriage in Iran: A Formal and Historical Perspective. *In* Women and Revolution in Iran. Guity Nashat, ed. Pp. 231—252. Boulder: Westview Press.

Hegland, Mary Elaine. 1982. "Traditional" Iranian Women: How They Cope. The Middle East Journal 36:483—501.

———. 1983. Aliabad Women: Revolution as Religious Activity. *In* Women and Revolution in Iran. Guity Nashat, ed. Pp. 171—194. Boulder, Colorado: Westview Press.

———. 1986a. Imam Khomaini's Village: Recruitment to Revolution. Ph.D. dissertation, Department of Anthropology, State University of New York, Binghamton.

———. 1986b. Political Roles of Iranian Village Women. Middle East Research and Information Project Reports 138:14—19, 46.

———. In press. Political Roles of Aliabad Women: The Public/Private Dichotomy Transcended. *In* Shifting Boundaries: Gender Roles in the Middle East, Past and Present. Nikki Keddie and Beth Baron, eds. New Haven, Conn.: Yale University Press.

Hooglund (Hegland), Mary. 1982. Religious Ritual and Political Struggle in an Iranian Village. Middle East Research and Information Project Reports 102:10—17, 23.

Levinson, David. 1988. Family Violence in Cross-Cultural Perspective. *In* Handbook of Family Violence. Vincent B. Van Hasselt, Randall L. Morrison, Alan S. Bellack, and Michel Hersen, eds. Pp. 435—455. New York: Plenum Press.

Masumura, Wilfred T. 1979. Wife Abuse and Other Forms of Aggression. Victimology: An International Journal 4:46—59.

Mernissi, Fatima. 1987. Beyond the Veil: Male-Female Dynamics in Modern Muslim Society. Bloomington: Indiana University Press.

el-Messiri, Sawsan. 1979. Self-Images of Traditional Urban Women in Cairo. *In* Women in the Muslim World. Lois Beck and Nikki Keddie, eds. Pp. 522—540. Cambridge: Harvard University Press.

Papanek, Hanna. 1973. Purdah: Separate Worlds and Symbolic Shelter. Comparative Studies in Society and History 15:289—325.

———. 1979. Family Status Production. The "Work" and "Non-Work" of Women. Signs 4:775—781.

———. 1984. False Specialization and the Purdah of Scholarship—A Review Article. Journal of Asian Studies 44:127—148.

Rassam, Amal. 1980. Women and Domestic Power in Morocco. International Journal of Middle East Studies 12:171—179.

El Saadawi, Nawal. 1983. Woman at Point Zero. London: Zed Books Ltd.

Sanday, Peggy Reeves. 1981. The Socio-Cultural Context of Rape: A Cross-Cultural Study. Journal of Social Issues 37:5—27.

Sharma, Ursula. 1983. Women, Work, and Property in North-West India. London: Tavistock Publications Ltd.

Vieille, Paul. 1979. Iranian Women in Family Alliance and Sexual Politics. *In* Women in the Muslim World. Lois Beck and Nikki Keddie, eds. Pp. 451—472. Cambridge: Harvard University Press.

Walker, Lenore E. 1979. The Battered Woman. New York: Harper and Row, Publishers.

———. 1984. The Battered Woman Syndrome. New York: Springer Publishing Company.

Yllo, Kersti and Michele Bograd, eds. 1988. Feminist Perspectives on Wife Abuse. Newbury Park California: Sage Publications, Inc.

Zenie-Ziegler, Wedad. 1988. In Search of Shadows: Conversations with Egyptian Women. London: Zed Books.

16

Wife Abuse in the Context of Development and Change: A Chinese (Taiwanese) Case

Rita S. Gallin

INTRODUCTION

References to both verbal and physical wife abuse are scattered through the literature on China. Most consist of a sentence or two noting that abuse does occur, but rarely are specific incidents or the related dynamics discussed (Cohen 1976:199; Lang 1946:201). My chapter both supports and challenges this tradition by discussing first the general phenomenon as well as a specific case of wife-beating, and second the reasons that underlie such abuse in a Taiwanese rural community.

The chapter is based on data collected in Hsin Hsing, a village that has changed over the past 30 years from an economic system based almost purely on agriculture to one founded predominantly on off-farm employment.[1] I begin by describing life in the traditional Chinese family and the socioeconomic transformation of the village, then discuss wife abuse there, and conclude with comments on the cause of violence in the hierarchically structured family.

THE TRADITIONAL CHINESE FAMILY

The "economic family," the *jia,* is the basic socioeconomic unit in China. Such a family can take one of three forms: conjugal, stem, or joint. The conjugal family consists of a husband, wife, and their unmarried children; the joint family adds two or more married sons and their wives and children to this core group. The stem family—a form that lies somewhere between the conjugal and joint family types—includes parents, their unmarried offspring, and one married son with his wife and children.

China's patrilineal kinship structure recognizes only male children as descent group members with rights to the family's property.[2] In the past, and to a large extent today, residence was patrilocal; when a woman married, she left her natal home to live as a member of her husband's family, severing her formal ties with her father's household. Parents considered daughters a liability—as household members who drained family resources when they were children and who withdrew their assets of domestic labor and earning power when they married. Sons, in contrast, steadily contributed to the family's economic security during its growth and expansion and provided a source of support in old age. Parents therefore strongly preferred male children.

Members of the older generation also strongly favored arranged marriages. Marriage brought a new member into the household, joined two people in order to produce children, and established an alliance between families. The needs of the family therefore took precedence over the desires of the individual in the selection of a mate. When parents arranged marriages, they attempted to recruit women who would be compliant, capable workers who were able to produce heirs for the group, and who came from families willing to forge bonds of cooperation and obligation.

Traditionally, then, an authoritarian hierarchy based on gender, generation, and age dominated life within the family. The oldest male had the highest status, and women's status, although it increased with the birth of sons and age, was lower than that of any man. The roots anchoring this hierarchy were the mores of the "three obediences," which required a woman to defer to father, husband, and sons, and the norms of piety (*xiao*), which obligated offspring to repay parents for nurturing them. Both principles served as forms of social control, perpetuating the family, the subordination of women to men, and the domination of the young by the old.

DEVELOPMENT IN HSIN HSING VILLAGE

Hsin Hsing is a nucleated village approximately 125 miles southwest of Taiwan's major city, Taipei, and located beside a road that runs between two market towns. Its people, like most in the area, are Hokkien (Minnan) speakers whose ancestors emigrated from Fujian, China several hundred years ago.

The registered population of the village in 1958 was 609 people grouped into 99 economic families. Conjugal families predominated, accounting for 66 percent of village families (56 percent of the population). In contrast, only 5 percent of village families (10 percent of the population) were of the joint type, while the remaining 29 percent of families (35 percent of the population) lived in stem families.

During the 1950s, no significant industries or job opportunities existed locally and land was the primary means of production. Almost all families were agriculturalists, deriving most of their livelihood from two crops of rice, marketable vegetables grown in a third crop, and, in some cases, from farm labor hired out for wages. Men, working outside the home in the fields, dominated the public domain. Women managed the house and children, raised poultry, contributed to farm production by weeding fields and drying rice, and, in their "spare time," wove fiber hats at home to supplement the family income.

As in most of Taiwan, the structure of marriage in Hsin Hsing during the 1950s was framed by Chinese tradition (see Freedman 1979:290; B. Gallin 1966:204–213). Yet, because Hsin Hsing was a village undergoing change, tradition had been modified so that a young woman and man were allowed to have some part in the decision about the desirability of their marriage. A brief meeting was arranged during which the couple could see each other, and each was then asked for an opinion about the tentatively chosen mate. Given the brevity of the meeting, the young couple could not really evaluate each other, except perhaps by appearance and, if they were at all filial, they were not likely to reject their parents' choices. Consequently, after this initial meeting, the young couple had no further contact with each other until their marriage. Given this traditionalism, one might ask how the villagers responded to the transformation of Hsin Hsing's economic system in the 1970s, when labor-intensive factories, service shops, retail stores, and construction outfits burgeoned in the area. During this period, seven small satellite factories, three artisan workshops, and twenty-six shops and small businesses were established in the village (Gallin and Gallin 1982).

A comparison of the village population in 1979 with the population in 1958 suggests one change. By 1979 only 383 people lived in Hsin Hsing, although the villagers considered the population to include 543 people in 73 households. Further, conjugal families no longer predominated in the village; only 45 percent of families (30 percent of the population) were of this simple type. Fully 18 percent of families (34 percent of the population) were of the joint type, while the remaining 39 percent of families (36 percent of the population) were of the stem type.

Further examination of the data suggests another way in which the villagers responded to economic change. By 1979, 85 percent of resident families' incomes were derived from off-farm employment, and almost half of the villagers 16 years or older no longer identified farming as either their primary or secondary activity. The movement of villagers off the land, however, was not limited only to men. In 1979 one-half of the married women and four-fifths of the single women in the village worked for remuneration (R. Gallin 1984a).

The wage employment of single women and men, not surprisingly, was accompanied by modifications in the way marriages were arranged. Parents' monopoly on mate selection disappeared, although the maintenance of family continuity required that parents still be involved in negotiations. Once negotiations between families were completed, however, dating in the Western sense usually occurred. Consequently, women and men married each other, frequently after having already developed an emotional commitment.

WIFE-BEATING IN HSIN HSING

The cruelty of a Chinese mother-in-law toward her daughter-in-law is common knowledge and, during the 1950s, an older woman's treatment of a younger woman in Hsin Hsing was no different.[3] Women today frequently speak of the bitterness of their early years of marriage, when they were saddled with work under the close supervision and scrutiny of their mothers-in-law.

Many describe the capricious ways in which the older woman exercised their authority, by cursing, harassing, and even beating them on occasion.[4] Such tyranny by a mother-in-law has been explained in terms of the need to break a newcomer to the ways of the home (Baker 1979:43). A young woman had to be socialized and integrated into the household and, in the division of labor, this task fell to her mother-in-law. To enforce obedience, and perhaps in retaliation for her own lifelong subjugation, and older woman might well resort to physical abuse of a daughter-in-law with whom she was dissatisfied.

Ten women reported, however, that men also had beaten their wives to keep them in line. And, these men had acted as agents of their mothers, who had demanded they bend their wives to the older women's will. One might ask why an older woman would find it necessary to impose her authority through her son. Enforcing compliance was considered to be the mother-in-law's prerogative; a daughter-in-law did not have sufficient power as an individual to defy her mother-in-law or disobey her commands.

The explanation for a mother-in-law's abrogation of authority to her son, then, must lie elsewhere. In Hsin Hsing, the reason for the transfer of authority most likely was rivalry for the affections of the son. An older woman had first come as a stranger to her husband's family and the birth of her son had improved her status within it and guaranteed her old age insurance. She had spent years nurturing her relationship with her son and tying him firmly to her (Wolf 1972:32–41). She saw the young wife as a competitor for claims on her son, someone who would deprive her of her son's loyalty and support.

Older women had witnessed cases in which, despite the mother's stratagems to protect the filial bond between her son and herself, a real compatibility or unity of interest had developed between the husband and wife, so that the husband had listened to his wife's views and had accepted her advice. From the perspective of the mother, such an alliance represented a powerful and significant threat to her relations with her son, because the younger woman could use her husband to remove the older woman from the family.

To counter this threat, then, the mother-in-law enlisted her son as an ally in the abuse of his wife. Because he had been taught that the goal of marriage was the continuation of the family, and because he had close emotional ties with his mother, the man sacrificed his personal feelings toward his wife and beat her. The effect was that his acquiescence to his mother's demand reaffirmed and strengthened his solidarity with her, while his wife's resentment toward him for the beating negated and weakened his solidarity with her. And, the invigoration of filial ties and erosion of marital bonds contributed to the family's longevity and the older woman's future economic and social security.

Undoubtedly, the ability of a mother-in-law to work her will so successfully reflected a young brides's lack of recourse. The husband was expected to, and as we saw did, side with his mother in dealings with his wife. Her neighbors were reluctant to interfere; "husband-wife violence . . . [was] regarded as something 'to shut the door and listen to' " (Harrell 1982:128). Nor could her father and brothers be counted on to intervene in her behalf (see Levy 1949:188; Wolf 1975:124).

The inaction of her relatives, in part, was due to the fact that they did not see her that often: marriage was usually village exogamous; people were poor; transportation facilities were not well developed; and visiting primarily revolved around village-based religious events. Thus, unless the abuse of a woman was extreme, her natal family probably was not aware of a beating until long after the incident had occurred.[5] In part, however, their inaction was also due to the fact that most affines were unwilling to jeopardize a meaningful and utilitarian relationship; ties of affinity served as an important foundation for economic activities and were a source of support which supplemented that which was derived from patrilineal kin (B. Gallin 1966:165–181; Gallin and Gallin 1985). It was therefor not in the family's interest to support a female relative who "belonged" to a unit from which it hoped to elicit assistance.

An abused wife, then, had but two alternatives available to relieve her misery. She could endure it and look to the time when she would assume the role of the wife of the head of the house. Or, she could escape it by committing suicide. I do not specifically know whether any woman from Hsin Hsing chose this alternative, but Margery Wolf has pointed out that "for peasant women suicide was . . . and still is . . . a socially acceptable solution to a variety of problems that offer no other solution" (1975:112).

Given this situation, did the pattern of wife abuse and the reasons that underlie it change with the transformation of the village's economy? One way to begin to answer this question is to look at the way brides were integrated into the households of their husbands in the 1970s. We saw above that, in the 1950s, young women had few resources with which to contend the authority of their mothers-in-law. In the 1970s, in contrast, young brides were not as helpless in dealing with their mothers-in-law as the older women had been with theirs, because they brought decided emotional and economic advantages to the relationship (R. Gallin 1984b, 1986).

First, the mutual affection that a young couple developed during the betrothal period represented in marriage a serious challenge to the mother-son bond on which an older woman depended to subjugate her daughter-in-law.

Second, the value of a young woman's *sia-khia* (private money) — funds which represented a sizeable portion of the seed money for the conjugal family she and her husband would eventually establish and which he would head — outweighed the resources a man's mother had at her command.[6] An older woman, then, was no longer assured of the loyalty and support of her son in confrontations with his wife.

Perhaps for this reason, a mother-in-law undertook with moderation the integration of a new bride into the household. Although older women frequently complained about their daughters-in-law's failings, they tended to avoid direct confrontations with them. It was better to side-step an issue than pit a son's ties to his mother against those to his wife, since at best, a son might remain neutral and withdraw from the fray, but at worst, he might defend his wife.

Ironically, it was the material resources which allowed young women to negotiate the new role relationship with their mothers-in-law that precipitated the 1979 beating described below. The couple involved in the incident had been married about seven years and the husband drank and gambled heavily. Although he and his wife were members of a joint family, the woman knew that division of the large unit was inevitable and that, when it occurred, she would not be able to depend on her husband, certainly not as a stable source of support for their conjugal family.

It was in her interest, therefore, to guard her *sai-khia* — to invest and cultivate it for future use. Consequently, when her husband demanded that she give him her private money she refused. He, unable to extract the money from her through verbal abuse, resorted to physical abuse and beat her. Despite this beating, the young woman remained uncowed. She had very practical reasons not to give up her *sai-khia:* the future prosperity of her family, and, more importantly, the future prosperity of her two sons — which would determine the nature of her life in old age — depended on this money.

Like her counterparts in the 1950s, however, the young woman had little recourse to escape her husband's abuse. Divorce was not really a viable option; customary law required that sons remain with their father upon dissolution of a marriage and, without sons, who would take responsibility for her in her old age? Her father and brothers also were unlikely to offer protection or a haven to which she could retreat. The increasing importance of affinal ties in the world of a cash economy meant they would place their family's interests before her needs.

Indeed, her natal family did not intercede in her behalf to demand that her husband stop his abuse. Rather, recognizing the importance and delicacy of affinal ties, her father acted as his son-in-law's agent and also beat her. To reinforce his own family's security, her father forced her to give her *sai-khia* — her bulwark against her future insecurity — to her husband.

SUMMARY AND CONCLUSION

To summarize, during the 1950s, wife abuse was triggered by a mother-in-law's fear that her son's wife would alienate him from her and would relegate her to an old age fraught with insecurity and loneliness. In 1979, in contrast, the abuse was provoked by a young woman's fear that her husband would squander her *sai-khia* and, therefore, jeopardize her chance to enjoy a secure old age. On face value, it would appear that, in the absence of a well-developed social security system, women's attempts to ensure the support of others in their old age underlie wife abuse in Hsin Hsing.

This explanation, however, masks the fundamental cause of wife abuse in the village and constitutes victim-blaming. The perceived coalition of a young woman with her husband and the refusal of a wife to relinquish her private money were not the cause of wife-beating, though they provided significant excuses for it. In the cases described, young women were considered to have stepped outside the bounds of the cultural definition of femininity by challenging the traditional authority of both the older women and the man. To strengthen and sustain the hierarchical structure of subordination within the family, therefore, beating them was believed to be justified. The abuse of women in Hsin Hsing, in short, was motivated by the need of the older women and the men to reaffirm their control over the women who, by cultural definition, were their subordinates.

NOTES

Research for this paper was carried out in collaboration with Bernard Gallin, whose insights have helped me immeasurably. We acknowledge with thanks the organizations that provided financial assistance over the years and made our field trips to Taiwan possible. Specifically, funding was provided by a Foreign Area Training Fellowship, Fulbright-Hays Research Grants, the Asian Studies Center of Michigan State University, the Midwest Universities Consortium for International Activities, the Social Science Research Council, and the Pacific Cultural Foundation.

1. The research covers the period from 1957 to 1982. The first field trip, in 1957—1958, involved a seventeen-month residence in the village of Hsin Hsing. This was followed by two separate studies, in 1965—1966 and 1969—1970, of out-migrants from the area. The most recent research spanned two months in 1977, six months in 1979, and one month in 1982. During these visits, we collected data using both anthropological and sociological techniques, including participant observation, in-depth interviews, surveys, censuses, and collection of official statistics contained in the local family, land, school, and economic records.

2. Laws in both Taiwan and the People's Republic of China have attempted to alter this traditional pattern of inheritance by providing women with institutionalized access to the property of their families of origin. Women, however, seldom claim their inheritance, but rather accept their dowries as their patrimony.

3. Wife abuse was never a focus of the research and we did not interview villagers directly about the phenomenon. Interviews with approximately 300 people as well as our observations suggest that mothers-in-law in Hsin Hsing treated their daughters-in-law harshly and that the relationship between older and younger women in the family was an unhappy one.

4. During the summer of 1982, I interviewed 25 women aged 47 and older about changes in family life. In comparing their early years of marriage with those of their daughters-in-law, only one woman reported that she had been treated well by her mother-in- law; the remaining 24 reported that their mothers-in-law had been cruel to them. Of these 24 women, fully half said the older women "beat" them, although only about six qualified their reports by indicating that their skin became "black and blue" as a result. Unfortunately, I did not pursue the subject in the interviews, and I do not know how frequently the beatings occurred.

5. I use the term "extreme" to describe cases of wife abuse in which a woman required medical treatment after she was beaten. No Hsin Hsing woman described such an occurrence but Wolf (1975) speaks to the issue.

6. Cash and jewelry are given to a young woman as part of her dowry, the amount varying with the economic condition of her natal family. In contrast to the other items a woman takes with her to her husband's home at marriage, this cash and jewelry is considered to belong to her and not the family as a whole. Taiwanese call this "private property" a woman's *sai-khia*. On family division, a woman's *sai-khia* is merged with the property inherited by her husband, and she loses control of her private fund. The practice of *sai-khia* was recognized in Hsin Hsing during the 1950s but was not prevalent because of the poverty of the local people.

REFERENCES CITED

Baker, Hugh D.R. 1979. Chinese Family and Kinship. New York, NY: Columbia University Press.

Cohen, Myron. 1976. House United House Divided. New York, NY: Columbia University Press.

Freedman, Maurice. 1979. Ritual Aspects of Chinese Kinship and Marriage. *In* The Study of Chinese Society: Essays by Maurice Freedman, G. William Skinner, ed. Pp. 273—295. Stanford, CA: Stanford University Press.

Gallin, Bernard. 1966. Hsin Hsing, Taiwan: A Chinese Village in Change. Berkeley, CA: University of California Press.

Gallin, Bernard and Rita S. Gallin. 1982. Socioeconomic Life in Rural Taiwan: Twenty Years of Development and Change. Modern China 8(2):205—246.

———. 1985. Matrilateral and Affinal Relationships in Changing Chinese Society. *In* The Chinese Family and Its Ritual Behavior. Hsieh Jin-chang and Chuang Ying-Chang, eds. Pp. 101—116. Taipei, Taiwan: Institute of Ethnology, Academia Sinica.

Gallin, Rita S. 1984a. The Entry of Chinese Women into the Rural Labor Force: A Case Study from Taiwan. Signs 9(3):383—398.

———. 1984b. Women, Family and the Political Economy of Taiwan. Journal of Peasant Studies 12(1):76—92.

———. 1986. Mothers-in-Law and Daughters-in-Law: Intergenerational Relations Within the Chinese Family in Taiwan. Journal of Cross-Cultural Gerontology 1(1):31—49.

Harrell, Stevan. 1982. Ploughshare Village. Seattle, WA: University of Washington Press.

Lang, Olga. 1946. Chinese Family and Society. New Haven, CT: Yale University Press.

Levy, Marion J., Jr. 1949. The Family Revolution in Modern China. Cambridge, MA: Harvard University Press.

Wolf, Margery. 1972. Women and the Family in Rural Taiwan. Stanford, CA: Stanford University Press.

———. 1975. Women and Suicide in China. *In* Women and Chinese Society. Margery Wolf and Roxane Witke, eds. Pp. 111—141. Stanford, CA: Stanford University Press.

17

Wife-Battering: Cultural Contexts Versus Western Social Sciences

Jacquelyn C. Campbell

The preceding chapters have examined fourteen human societies and studies of non-human primates in which males beat their female partners and one culture in which they do not. These chapters describe the whole continuum of amount and severity of violence. They demonstrate both the range of circumstances in which males beat their female partners and the contexts in which beating either escalates to battering or is circumscribed. This final chapter reviews current Western social science theories that attempt to explain wife-beating and then uses the evidence from this volume to evaluate hypotheses derived from the theories.[1] The analysis will be used to suggest ways to help prevent, or at least limit, wife-beating in all cultures.

The societies described in this volume are not a random sample. Neither were they systematically selected because they represent the full range of degrees of spousal violence. We include examples of a variety of points along a wife-beating continuum and from a variety of geographic areas and a range of levels of societal complexity. I used the evidence in this volume to roughly group these societies in comparison with each other into four levels of wife-beating. Using the criteria of frequency (number of times beating occurs) and ubiquity (approximate prevalence among couples), I found five to exhibit high levels of wife-beating (Iran, India, Indo-Fijian, Taiwan, Bun), five intermediate (Aborigine, Ecuadorian villagers, !Kung, Kaliai, and Marshall Islanders), three with low frequency of beatings (Garifuna, Nagovisi, Mayotte) and one negative case, the Wape, with almost none (see Table 17.1).

Our sample of societies is obviously too small to either validate or refute any hypothesis, but it does provide data from societies representing a range of complexity and it contributes important information about cultural influences on wife-battering. Discussion of the latter has unfortunately been omitted from much of the Western social sciences literature (Lockhart 1987; Torres 1987).

TABLE 17.1

FREQUENCY AND UBIQUITY OF WIFE BEATING, WIFE BATTERING, AND MUTUAL VIOLENCE IN 14 SOCIETIES

Society (Chapter #)	Wife Beating	Wife Battering	Mutual Violence
Iran (15)	3	3	0
India (13)	3	3	0
Indo-Fijian (14)	3	3	0
Taiwan (16)	3	2	0
Bun (6)	3	2	2
Kaliai (5)	2	1-2	0
Aborigine (3)	2	1	3
Ecuadorian Village (11)	2	1	0
!Kung (4)	2	1	0
Marshall Islanders (9)	2	1	1
Garifuna (10)	1	0	0
Nagovisi (8)	1	0	0
Mayotte (12)	1	0	0
Wape (7)	0	0	0

3 = High frequency and ubiquity
2 = Medium frequency and ubiquity
1 = Low frequency and ubiquity
0 = Essentially none

In an earlier paper (Campbell 1985), I argued that evidence from other societies used to explain wife-beating often relied on secondary sources based on evidence contributed by predominately male anthropologists using predominately male informants.[2] The evidence in this volume is largely primary data collected by anthropologists, a majority of whom are female, using direct observation and female as well as male informants. The data here can be presumed to be less androcentric and can, therefore, shed a different light on what exacerbates or discourages wife-beating.

WIFE-BATTERING; WIFE-BEATING

In this volume we attempt to distinguish between wife-beating and wife-battering. According to Counts (1990) wife-beating can be described as an act of physical aggression by a husband against his wife that at least some members of the society condone. It only happens occasionally and is not seriously or permanently injurious to the woman. Male beating of female partners apparently occurs in nearly all societies (but is by no means practiced by all individuals), thereby making it difficult to determine culturally specific causative factors. It is, therefore, more useful to concentrate on the societal factors that either facilitate or prevent the escalation of wife-beating to wife-battering. That is not to say that we find wife-beating acceptable. Rather, our purpose is to concentrate on what is theoretically and practically promising; to explain a variable rather than a constant.

It is proposed in this chapter that individual psychological factors within a context of cultural tolerance (differentiated from acceptance, see Greenblat 1985) predict the occurrence of an individual incident of wife-beating, while cultural, political, and economic factors may lead to wife-beating being more frequent and severe. Escalation is the usual pattern according to evidence from the most recent American national survey (Straus and Gelles 1990). It is a pattern found in some but not all the societies described in this volume (see especially descriptions of the Bun in Chapter 6, Ecuadorian villagers in Chapter 11, and the Indo-Fijians in Chapter 14). Furthermore, as pointed out by Kerns (Chapter 10), our evidence demonstrates that frequency and severity of wife-beating do not always vary together, contrary to the assumption usually made in Western social science literature.

Wife-Beating; Husband-Beating

In some societies, including the United States, women also commit acts of violence against male partners. If acts of self-defense and instances of mutual combat are not separated from those unilaterally initiated, American data suggest that there are nearly as many acts of violence by women against men as there are by men against women (see Saunders 1988; Steinmetz and Lucca 1988 for both sides of the ongoing debate). I assume in this chapter that violence between partners could be, and sometimes is, husband-beating or mutual beating rather than wife-beating.

Yet, cross-culturally wife-beating occurs far more frequently than does husband-beating. Levinson (1989) reports that husband-beating occurs in only 26.9 per cent of small-scale societies. It happens in a majority of households in only 6.7 percent of the cultures sampled for that study. This is in contrast to wife-beating which sometimes occurs in 84.5 percent of these societies and happens in all or a majority of households in 48.7 percent of his sample. Since Levinson asserts that husband-beating occurs only where there is also wife-beating, it is possible that all of the aggression termed husband-beating in his volume is in the context of a mutually violent relationship or in self-defense. These comparative data certainly support the contention that most spousal violence is violence against women.

Mutual Violence

In two societies in this volume (Bun and Aborigine) a high degree of mutual violence exists. I say mutual violence rather than husband-beating because in both societies the wife is also beaten and because there is little evidence of husband-battering in either. Even though the female may use weapons to fight when her mate is using "only" hands and feet (see McDowell in Chapter 6), this must be interpreted in the context of sexual dimorphism (superior male size and strength), and the socialization of males to use hands and feet as instruments of aggression. Therefore, although it may seem that a woman has raised the level of violence when she uses weapons in response to male fists, in fact a woman's use of weapons usually evens the exchange.

The Bun of Papua New Guinea and the Aborigines of Australia have few similarities other than the presence of mutual violence, and the Bun exhibit more wife-beating (and battering) than the Aborigines. It is possible, therefore, that mutual violence is influenced by different factors than are either beating or battering. This is a possibility taken into account only marginally in Western social science research.

Wife-Battering

Battering, in contrast to beating and mutual violence, is a phenomenon almost exclusively directed toward women. This assertion is supported by cross-cultural studies by Levinson (1989), Carroll (1980), and Masamura (1979) as well as by studies from Euro-American societies (Campbell 1989; Dobash and Dobash 1979; Saunders 1988). Wife-battering includes ongoing and severe acts of violence considered by others in the society to be unusual. It is often accompanied by other forms of coercive control as well. Most Western social science research on violence against women is in fact focused on wife-battering, but most studies often also include acts of wife-beating without differentiating between the two. For instance, Straus and Gelles (1990) distinguish between severe and minor violence but base their distinction on the seriousness of the violent tactic used, rather than on the outcome of the violence or the degree of injury. Parker and Schumacher (1977) separated battered woman's syndrome victims from "violence syndrome averters," but they did so in terms of the woman's behavioral responses to violence rather than according to the degree of violence used against her or the context in which the violence occurred.

Evidence in this volume suggests a correlation between wife-beating and wife-battering. However, while both wife-beating and battering are horrifyingly frequent in Iran and India, battering is not ubiquitous in the other three cultures where wife-beating abounds. Theory should help us to differentiate between these two types of societies and to isolate the factors contributing to the relative infrequency of spousal violence in the remaining societies. Some of those societies accept wife-beating in principle but have very little (Ecuadorian villagers, Aborigine, Marshall Islanders) or virtually no battering in practice (Garifuna).

It is not possible to identify simple linear causative factors of wife-battering that can be easily remedied once they are identified. As is true of most human behavior, the use of violence has complex causes that include an interplay of individual, contextual, and societal forces. However, our purpose in this volume is both to contribute to theory development in the area of violence against wives and to suggest some practical societal level interventions to limit wife-battering. The review of existing social science theories which follows demonstrates that these theories are inadequate in the face of cross-cultural evidence and suggest alternative avenues for theory development.

EXPLANATORY THEORIES

Western social sciences have developed a variety of hypotheses to explain the occurrence of wife-beating. These can be divided into the broad categories of psychological and socio-cultural. Various forms of stress theory, social learning theory, and exchange theory are currently receiving the most empirical support and attention in psychology (see Van Hasselt, Morrison, Bellack and Herson 1988). Researchers have also proposed psychoanalytic and neuropsychological reasons for wife-beating, but these explanations are only infrequently endorsed by current scholars and activists. They are less well accepted partly because their logical extension is to excuse the perpetrator and/or blame the victim (see Yllo and Bograd 1988) and partly because of a lack of consistent empirical support (see Campbell and Humphreys 1984; Ptacek 1988; and Tolman and Bennett 1990 for representative reviews). Scholars have also used sociobiological theory to explain female homicide (Daly and Wilson 1988) which can be conceptualized as the extreme end of the continuum of wife-beating (see Campbell 1992). This perspective has been reviewed in the chapters by Brown and

Draper. I will review the following theories which use a wider societal perspective: feminist theory, resource theory, subculture of violence theory, and systems theory. I will also examine the societal factors identified in social learning and exchange theories.

The Feminist Perspective

Feminist explanations of wife-battering were originally most fully explicated by Russell Dobash and Rebecca Dobash (1979) in their text *Violence Against Wives*. Their basic premise is that wife-battering is allowed and encouraged by patriarchal societal organizations which mandate women's dominance by men, by force if necessary. Feminist perspectives usually include wife-battering with other forms of violence against women (rather than other forms of "family violence") as measures that keep women dominated in patriarchal societies (Daly 1979; Hanmer and Maynard 1985). Evidence of historical precedents for wife-battering (e.g. Davidson 1978; Pleck 1987) and research demonstrating correlations between patriarchal social structures and rates of violence against women (e.g. Baron and Straus 1987; Yllo 1984) support these assertions.

However, both cross-cultural studies and research focusing on individual persons demonstrate that there is no simple linear correlation between female status and rates of wife assault (Campbell 1985; Levinson 1989; Straus and Gelles 1990; Yllo 1984). As anthropologists have long demonstrated, female status is not a single variable (e.g. Rosaldo and Lamphere 1974). Rates of wife assault variously operationalized have also confounded exploration of this relationship. Levinson (1989) found variables related to women's status in the family (economic factors, female decision making, and divorce restrictions) to be more predictive of wife-beating than were societal level variables (control of premarital sexual behavior, place of residence, property inheritance). An important exception to this generalization was female economic work groups. Their presence predicted an absence of wife-beating. Similarly, while the economic dependence of women and male decision making is associated with wife-battering in the United States (Kalmuss and Straus 1982; Straus and Gelles 1990), individual male attitudes toward women and sex role stereotypes do not differentiate abusive men from others (Dutton 1988; Hotaling and Sugarman 1986).

In the feminist view, male sexual jealousy is considered to be an expression of a societal norm that women are the property of men. This attitude is accompanied by other kinds of controlling behavior by men (e.g. economic coercion, social isolation). This approach better explains the wide range of male sexual jealousy found in the preceding chapters than does the notion that jealousy is motivated by parental certainty concerns, which would be expected to be more universal.

Primary Data Related to Feminist Theory

There is mixed support for feminist theory in the descriptions in this text. A general pattern of strong male sexual jealousy exists in the societies with severe wife-battering (e.g. Iran, India, Indo-Fijian), and there is very little jealousy among the Wape, Garifuna, Nagovisi and Mayotte, the four societies where there is little or no wife-battering or beating of wives. However, the cultures between the extremes show more variation in jealousy, and this does not seem to correlate with the variations in battering.

Other expressions of male ownership of women include female chastity before marriage as a critical criterion in evaluating a woman's worth (Iran, Indo-Fijian), dowry payments (India), forced sexual intercourse in marriage (Iran), and physical punishment by other male kin (Bun).[3] Without a feminist analysis, the dowry murders in India appear to be solely expressions of greed rather than also related to male jealousy. However, the Ecuadorian villagers described by McKee (Chapter 11) present an interesting exception to the pattern of male control and wife-battering. Although female chastity and other aspects of male control are the ideal, woman battering is relatively infrequent.

The role of mothers-in-law in wife-battering as described in the chapters on Iran, India, the Indo-Fijians and Taiwan would seem to counter feminist theory. Yet Daly (1979) has identified the role of women as "token torturers" in a variety of historical and current practices of violence against women. Daly cites Chinese mothers who bound their daughters' feet and African village women who circumcise young females as examples of women (usually older women) who were forced by patriarchal societies to inflict violence on other females. They did so both to gain some measure of personal power and to save their daughters and granddaughters from being socially unacceptable. This interpretation does allow the mother-in-law behavior described in this volume to support feminist theory, but the data describing the magical powers of Marshall Island women do not fit Daly's hypothesis. These powers are culturally perceived as forms of violence that are used against men at least as often as against other women.

In contrast, Brown (1982; Kerns and Brown in press) presents evidence that women universally enjoy an increase in power in middle age. This new role is by no means always accompanied by the use of violence. In Brown's review, the frequent bond between mother and adult son is more often characterized by attachment than by dominance. The relationship between dominance by mothers of their adult sons and the use by older women of violence toward younger females is a subject for further research.

When women have some significant power outside of the home — either economic (!Kung, Wape, Garifuna, Aborigine, Mayotte, and Ecuadorian villagers) or magical (Marshall Islanders, Garifuna) — there is less wife-battering. This supports feminist theory. However, in Taiwan and among the Indo-Fijians recent modernization affords economic possibilities for wives but battering continues. Possibly the persistent view of females as property combined with societal norms supporting wife-beating in those societies have prevented the development of sufficient female autonomy to significantly discourage battering.

The villagers in Ecuador offer an interesting contrast. Although they consider men and women to have different natures, with the ideal being female passivity and male dominance, Ecuadorian women traditionally have economic power and the authority to make decisions in the home. This combination of economic power and domestic authority protects women from being battered in spite of the society's machismo ethic. The Ecuadorian case challenges feminist theory and once again demonstrates the complexity of the phenomenon of wife-beating.

Feminist theory also seems, at first glance, to be challenged by the practices of the islanders of Mayotte. The people are Muslim, a religion that is strictly patriarchal, strongly believes in women as property, and approves of beating wives to correct them. Mayotte villagers do, indeed, strongly proscribe premarital sexual activity, but women otherwise wield a substantial amount of political power and personal freedom. They even have postmarital sexual autonomy. Feminist theory would consider the ritual defloration of young girls by their husbands in this society to be violence against women. Yet the act is often monitored by grandmothers and apparently is not experienced negatively. The contrast between the responses of Iranian and Mayotte brides to a similar act points out the fallacy of equating acts of "violence" toward women in different societies without taking account of the cultural context. The feminist perspective tends to make this equation, but it also provides the insight that the grandmother's monitoring could be interpreted as female solidarity and protection.

On Mayotte, divorce is easy for women, their kin actively intervene if the violence appears to be getting out of hand, and violence between marital partners is negatively sanctioned. Consequently, wife-beating is extremely infrequent and battering is unknown. All this is obviously in great contrast to Iran, although the basic religious premises are the same.

The feminist approach would see sanction and sanctuary as concomitant with female power and antithetical to a strictly patriarchal society. Our evidence shows a strong association between sanctions against battering, sanctuary for those severely beaten, and low levels or absence of battering. All four of the societies where battering is absent (Mayotte, Garifuna, Nagovisi, and Wape) have significant sanctions against it. These are clearly demonstrated by active intervention when beating escalates to battering, and there is provision of sanctuary for beaten women.

Among the Wape, as described in Chapter 7, female groups provide active community intervention against potential beating. They present a compelling image of women surrounding a home where there is marital conflict until the wife comes outside with them. Garifuna (Chapter 10) females also unite in opposition to violence against women. These examples, when taken in conjunction with Levinson's (1989) correlations, suggest that the existence of female solidarity groups, in addition to negative sanctions against battering, may protect women against severe violence. In contrast, Taiwanese, Bun, and Indo-Fijian women are divided and are often battered. This contrast is highly supportive of feminist theory.

In the majority of cultures examined in this volume, people respond differently to beating than they do to battering; the former is always more acceptable. For instance, on Mayotte and even more strikingly among the Garifuna, there is some acceptance for wife-beating but none for battering. The woman's kin also intervene to prevent battering but not to prevent beating. Ideas of male kin ownership of women in Mayotte combine a patriarchal premise with a sanction *against* battering. Community intervention to prevent battering but not beating also occurs among the Kaliai and the !Kung. This differentiation does not support feminist analysis which asserts that all instances of violence against women are associated with other manifestations of patriarchy.

Feminist theory is also challenged by data from the Australian Aborigines and the villagers of Ecuador. Although there are similar levels of wife-beating and battering in both areas, Aboriginal men beat women because they are angry whereas Ecuadorian men beat their wives to establish dominance. It is additionally challenged by the fact that societies with strong ethos of female passivity (Taiwanese, Indo-Fijian, Ecuadorian, Iranian, and Indian) exhibit different degrees of wife-battering, while Kaliai and Bun women — who are hardly passive — may be severely beaten. Absence of female passivity is more strongly associated with ~~absence~~ *presence* of mutual violence than with absence of battering.

Feminist scholars insist that data about individual couples are meaningless without societal and historical context (Dobash and Dobash 1989). There has, however, been only limited feminist analysis of the cultural context of battering from an anthropological perspective. The data in this volume support several of the premises of feminist analysis in their most basic form (e.g. there is a relationship between the degree to which women are battered and social attributes such as female solidarity, sanctions against battering, the premise that men own women, or the provision of sanctuary for battered women). Yet our data, which emphasize the influence of different social and cultural context, also challenge feminist ideas. Our distinctions between mutual violence, battering and beating could also contribute to the refinement of feminist theory.

Resource Theory and Status Inconsistency

The basic premise of resource theory as applied to family violence by Goode (1971) is that the family is a power system like any other; when a person does not have other resources, he or she will be more likely to use violence in order to maintain power. This proposition helps explain the correlation between poverty and spousal violence which has been found consistently in American research (Hotaling and Sugarman 1986).[4] Research in the United States has also supported a specific hypothesis of status inconsistency that is derived from resource theory. According to this hypothesis, a husband who perceives that his status relative to his wife is inconsistent with social norms is more likely to use violence in dealing with her. For example, the woman having more education or a better job than her male partner is at risk for wife-battering, especially if he strongly believes in the prerogatives of male dominance (Allen and Straus 1980; Hornung, Mc-Cullough, and Sugimoto 1981).

Where rapidly changing mores and societal developments lead to a relative decrease in traditional male resources, resource theory would predict an increase in wife-beating, but our data do not support this prediction. Although wife-battering is frequent and severe in both the Taiwanese village described in Chapter 16 and among the Indo-Fijians (Chapter 14), it seems to remain constant or decrease as women increase their economic resources, redefine their roles, and no longer accept abuse.

Among the !Kung, the relative status of young people is changing. Parents regard sons-in-law as less economically necessary while there is increasing autonomy for daughters. This change has apparently not resulted in increased wife-beating. In her chapter, Draper argues that changes accompanying the transformation of the !Kung from a nomadic existence to a settled one have resulted in increased protective measures for women (e.g. later marriage) and continued intervention of kin against battering. These are probably balanced by increased vulnerability resulting from increased alcohol consumption and jealousy on the part of men. This balance has resulted in a net lack of change. An additional challenge to resource theory is found among the violent Bun and the totally nonviolent Wape. Men in both societies have few economic resources and little power available to them.

In Iran, Westernization under the Shah apparently lead to a temporary decrease in wife-battering. When society returned to a strictly interpreted patriarchal Muslim structure, abuse increased again (see Chapter 15). Societal sanctions were apparently more important factors in the treatment of women than was status inconsistency. The increased relative power of women, even if temporary, seemed to accompany decreased violence against them. Thus, our evidence suggests that resource theory does not seem to explain changes in the frequency or severity of wife-battering or beating at the societal level in other cultures. However, it may be explanatory at the individual level. In several case studies in this volume, wives were beaten more frequently because they, as individuals, challenged the male role.

Culture/Subculture of Violence

Theorists seeking to explain causes of violence in a particular society have often examined the cultural norms surrounding violent practices. Thus, scholars have examined the relationship of various forms of violence (for example homicide and warfare) within individual societies, but anthropologists have been unable to consistently demonstrate what, if any, forms of violent behavior vary together.[5] For example, both Masamura (1979) and Lester (1980) sought to correlate other indices of violence with wife-beating in simple societies and found conflicting results (see Brown's chapter, for further analysis of these two studies). Levinson (1989) found wife-beating to be part of a pattern of violence within families and among acquaintances but different from aggression toward strangers.

The notion of a subculture of violence was originally developed by sociologists to explain differential rates of interpersonal violence (mainly homicide) among different ethnic and income groups in the United States (Wolfgang and Ferracuti 1981). They used social learning theory to explain the transmission of norms valuing qualities such as toughness, masculinity and honor, that support interpersonal violence within certain subcultures (mainly minority groups and the lower class). These definitive qualities include a willingness to use violence in certain specific situations even when it is not advantageous to do so.

Bowker (1983) extended the theoretical premise to wife-beating by identifying some male subcultures that justify wife abuse because of norms of male dominance. He proposed that men who are most involved with a peer group that supports dominance by the use of force would be most violent toward their female partners. Both Carroll's (1980) and Smith's (1989) research gave some support to Bowker's premises. Application of Bowker's ideas and supporting research extended the concept of a wife-beating subculture beyond the lower class, thereby providing a fuller explanation for the pattern of violence toward women which occurs among all classes in the United States. In addition, research findings suggest that batterers who are violent only towards their wives can be differentiated (by social class as well as by other factors) from wife abusers who are also violent toward non-family members (Gondolf 1988; Shields, McCall, and Hanneke 1988). These results support Bowker's (1983) suggestion that the subculture of violence theory applies to wife-beating.

The subculture of violence theory has been criticized for its class and ethnic biases and for its inconsistent support by research. For example, when data is controlled for poverty, the differences in homicide rates between ethnic groups in the United States virtually disappears (Hawkins 1986). Recently Bernard (1990) has suggested that the subculture premises be combined with cognitive aggression theories which emphasize cognitive interpretations of events and physiological arousal as well as intention. This integration has the potential to better explain data and could perhaps be applied to wife abuse.

When critically examining cross-cultural evidence about the treatment of women in a society, the following variables must be taken into account: (1) the degree of general violence in the society; (2) the presence or absence of active community intervention against wife-beating and battering (signaling general cultural norms regarding this violence); and (3) the degree of acceptance of definitions of masculinity that include the use of violence against women and/or their dominance by men (see Campbell and Humphreys 1984 for a further explanation of the integration of these variables). For instance, Iran (Chapter 15) has been characterized as a violent culture. There high levels of wife-beating and battering accompany extreme general violence and warfare. There is no community intervention against violence against wives, and definitions of masculinity promote both general aggressive behavior and dominance of women. The Wape (Chapter 7) represent the opposite extreme.

The other cultures in this volume provide variations on these patterns. High levels of both wife-beating and wife-battering are found among the Taiwanese, Indo-Fijians, and Bun. There are, however, disparate levels of other forms of interpersonal violence that seem to vary together. These include contemporary or historical warfare and support for aggressive masculinity. Although norms valuing aggressive masculinity outside the home have been thought to accompany norms valuing dominance over women (e.g. Campbell and Humphreys 1984), our data challenge this assumption. For example, both the Taiwanese and Indo-Fijians have strong norms of male dominance but are non-aggressive in other spheres. The Marshallese of Ujelang, on the other hand, do not have an ideal of male dominance but are violent in their non-domestic interpersonal relationships. There also seems to be more active community interference in wife-beating where norms of masculinity do not strongly encourage male dominance of women.

We find little reason to extend the premise of a general culture of violence to wife-beating, and only marginal support for a theory positing a subculture of violence. In the societies reported here, variations among men in levels of general aggression and in the degree of dominance of women are congruent with American research findings on typologies of batterers (e.g. Gondolf 1988). However, this does not necessarily support extending the theory of a subculture of violence to wife abuse. Our data might support the argument that there are cultures or subcultures of violence *against women*, rather than cultures of general violence. In fact, homicide epidemiologists are beginning to recognize strikingly different dynamics between homicides in the United States involving women (as either victims or perpetrators) and those among men (Campbell 1992; Mercy and Saltzman 1989).

Systems Theory

The use of systems theory to explain wife abuse has been most fully articulated and tested by Murray Straus and his associates in an extensive body of research spanning the last ten years. Straus incorporates the beating of wives within the category of "marital violence." This category is seen as a subcategory of family violence, rather than as a form of violence against women. While Straus recognizes that the most injurious violence in marriage is against wives, and that inequality in both individual marriages and societal structures influences wife-beating, he emphasizes other factors in the social system (Kalmuss and Straus 1990; Yllo and Straus 1990). The most recent formulation of the theory identifies six major causes of family violence: stress (stressful life events); intrafamily conflict; male dominance in the family and society; cultural norms permitting family violence; family socialization for violence; and the pervasiveness of violence in the society (Straus and Gelles 1990; Straus and Smith 1990). Systems theory also posits the presence of feedback mechanisms which serve to further encourage violence once it has begun (see Giles-Sims 1983 for a complete account of the systems feedback mechanism as applied to wife-battering).

Those who formulate theories of family violence systems assume the existence of an interrelationship between wife abuse and child abuse. In his latest American national random survey, Straus (1990) found the relationship to be most robust for those fathers who severely battered their wives. Straus also concluded that wives who were beaten were more likely to abuse children, although those who were severely battered were less likely to abuse a child than were those who were less abused. Straus also found that people who were physically punished in their childhood were more likely to engage in child abuse and marital violence as adults. The systems framework treats physical punishment as part of a continuum of physical violence toward children, with child abuse at the far end in terms of frequency and severity of the violent act.

The chapters in this book describe no definite association between physical violence toward children and the beating of wives. The chapter authors did not systematically address child rearing strategies including forms of violence against children. We, therefore, have incomplete data on this topic, and our conclusions are extremely tentative. Severe physical punishment of children was definitely noted in Iran and among the Bun. There are less severe examples of child beating among the descriptions of the Kaliai, Indo-Fijians and Taiwanese villagers. At least moderate wife-beating and battering occurs in all these societies. However, the Wape and Marshallese also use corporal punishment in disciplining children, but seldom batter women. Levinson (1989) also failed to find a clear relationship between violence toward children and violence toward wives. Generally, small scale societies do not exhibit the magnitude of incidence or severity of child abuse seen in Western, industrialized countries; the majority only infrequently use physical punishment (Levinson 1989; McGehee 1985). It is, therefore, difficult to support the proposal that violent childrearing socializes people for wife-battering and that this socialization occurs cross-culturally.

Our evidence does not allow us to estimate individual family stress, but we certainly see several entire societies under extreme stress as they experience massive change (Iran, Aborigine, Mayotte, !Kung, Taiwanese, and to a somewhat lesser extent, the Kaliai and Indo-Fijians) and/or extreme poverty (Aborigine and Wape). Yet the amount of wife-battering varies considerably among these societies. Furthermore, as discussed above, there is evidence of an increase in violence against wives in only one of the four societies for which we have longitudinal data.

In defense of systems theory, there is considerable evidence in this volume linking male dominance and cultural norms to wife-battering. Also, social feedback mechanisms support wife-beating in the majority of cultures where women are frequently beaten. An example of such feedback is found in Iran (Chapter 15) where the community encourages husbands to keep their wives submissive and disapproves of men who fail to do so. The negative feedback loops found in some of our societies add new insights to a systems approach. For instance, the Ecuadorian villagers described in Chapter 11, recognizing the potential for acceptable wife-beating to escalate to unacceptable battering, assign a *compadre* to each young couple. These persons are responsible for mediating conjugal quarrels. There is also a strong emphasis on balance and reciprocity in this society; it is important that persons do not feel beholden to each other and that actions are repaid in kind. Yet the ideal in a marriage (at least in the first few years) is for men to have more than women. Thus, an ideal of reciprocity is not the same as equality between the genders.

An ideal of balance also exists among the Bun, Marshallese, and Nagovisi. The Nagovisi also have several nonviolent, but serious and systematized, strategies for managing discord. Contrast these societies with the strict hierarchical relationships existing in Iran and India. Ideals of balance do not seem to protect women from being beaten. They, do however, serve to keep wife-battering in check, even where wife-beating is relatively frequent, especially if they are combined with other remedies specifically aimed at decreasing marital conflict.

Social Learning Theory

Social learning theory has consistently provided evidence to explain at least some family violence in general and wife abuse specifically. Battering husbands in the United States often come from homes where wife abuse and/or child abuse was practiced (Hotaling and Sugarman 1986; Straus and Gelles 1990). The behavior was modeled in childhood and reinforced by American media and peers. A parallel from a less complex society would be a boy who was beaten as a child and exposed to the beating of his mother. This experience would be reinforced by the idealization of the warrior-type male.

As previously noted, our chapters provide little data on child abuse, and we have found relatively little support for a connection between the ideals of male aggression and wife-battering. However, societies where wives are battered have apparently condoned violence against women over many generations. In small scale societies where nuclear families are not isolated, children certainly learn behavior from others in the community. Social learning theory is compatible with all of the major theories thus far advanced as to how individual batterers learn their behavior.

Exchange Theory

Gelles (1983) drew upon existing behavioral exchange theory and criminology's social control theory to advance his exchange theory of family violence. Its origins are in behavioral psychology and presume that human beings act in order to be rewarded and to avoid punishment. When applying exchange theory to family violence, Gelles posits that family members will be violent toward each other if the benefits of violence outweigh the costs. An assumption of social control theory is that all people will act violently if they are not controlled by their society. This premise is supported by American research documenting that batterers perceive an absence of negative sanctions (Carmody and Williams 1987). Gelles sees the inevitable lack of negative sanctions against violent family members as a defect in social control. According to Gelles, the isolation and privacy of the American nuclear family enables a family member to be violent without cost. Benefits of wife-beating include increased power and control and an enhanced "tough guy" image.

Nuclear families are not isolated in most of the cultures described in this volume. In fact, only India and (increasingly) Taiwan even approximate the degree of family privacy found in North America. Yet in Taiwan (Chapter 16), as extended family living arrangements are replaced by nuclear family residence patterns, wife-battering is decreasing if there is any change at all.

Furthermore, a range of violence against women is found in communal living situations.

Our findings, that negative sanctions against wife-battering are important factors in its prevention, support exchange theory. As our authors frequently note, there is little privacy in small villages, and homes are not soundproof. It is, therefore, much easier for community members to apply negative sanctions at the exact times they are needed. Few of these societies have indigenous formal sanctions such as laws or criminal proceedings against wife-beating. However, the women of some societies—for example the Kaliai—may now appeal to the imposed legal system if they are being battered. Among the Wape, the ancestors may punish abusive behavior. This system of sanctions is unusual, but it obviously increases the costs of violence. In this volume, the Ujelang, Garifuna, Ecuadorian villagers and Mayotte peoples illustrate the point that community sanctions against battering outweigh individual proclivities for beating and control expressions of dominance that well might escalate to battering.

CONCLUSIONS

Anthropology can contribute significantly to both the scholarly formulations explaining wife-battering and the practical solutions derived from them. The evidence from the societies presented in this volume does not clearly support any one of the theoretical models over the others. Instead it suggests that no Western social science theory explains all of the patterns of wife-beating and battering we describe. Specifically, I found only limited support for the culture/subculture of violence, resource, and social learning theories as they are now articulated. Data from our sample provide only mixed support for exchange theory, especially the social control premise. Feminist theory offered many important insights for understanding our evidence. However, feminist theory should distinguish between wife-beating, wife-battering and mutual violence (and admit the latter exists) and discriminate more carefully between the various forms of violence against women. Finally, systems theory needs either to treat wife and child abuse as separate phenomena or to differentiate between child beating and child battering if it is to have cross-cultural validity.

This review demonstrates the importance of societal level influence on violence, an insight that is significant for policy initiatives to prevent violence. One widespread if not universal phenomenon is the struggle of young men between 15 and 30 to define their roles and achieve manhood status, however it is defined. There are similarities between the young married Ujelang male who wishes he could play the role of an unmarried warrior and the young married American who yearns to be either Rambo or Donald Trump. Both go out to drink with the guys and envy their unmarried and apparently free counterparts. Both may go back home and attack their wives. We cannot explain the individual act, but the society's response to the beating is based in cultural differences. In the Ujelang village, the man will be chastised if he does more than hit; in the United States, usually only his female partner will rebuke him, and his violence will probably escalate. In Ujelang, political leaders scrutinize and evaluate the actions of both husband and wife; in the United States, probably no one will analyze the situation until it becomes severe. In both places the man blames the woman's behavior for his actions. His sexual jealousy and her failure to adhere to prescribed female role behavior are widespread reasons given for wife-beating. However, communities vary in their acceptance of these reasons (or excuses) for violence against wives.

Where negative sanctions against battering are combined with a sense of group honor based on nonviolence (as among the Ujelang) and the decent treatment of women (as the Kaliai are trying to establish), there is a chance to limit battering. If women are not to be battered it is essential that they have options including personal autonomy, economic opportunity, and the ability to form close linkages with other women. Among the Ujelang, Garifuna and Ecuadorian villagers, and in Mayotte, options for female power in at least one of these spheres, combined with community sanctions against violence, seem to override norms of male dominance and verbal bravado. In these societies wife-beating seldom escalates to wife-battering. Efforts to control wife-beating are also enhanced if the cultural (or subcultural) definition of a "real man" does not include the idea of controlling women by force. It is apparent, however, that social and cultural constraints against wife-beating can overcome individual propensities to violence.

The current calls from feminists and activists to change societal structures which allow or facilitate battering are supported by our anthropological data. Sanctuary for beaten women is necessary in all cultures and is provided by wife abuse shelters in most industrialized countries. Much more needs to be done in this regard in Iran, India, and Taiwan. There should also be strong sanctions against wife-beating and battering, but our data shows that community action can be more effective than official sanctions in preventing battering. Community action that is consistent with the society's level of industrialization and with established custom is a more realistic and effective strategy than expecting to change basic religious precepts or social practices such as marital exchanges or post marital residence.

In the United States and Canada we have publicized nationally the plight of battered women, passed laws prohibiting marital assault, and provided wife abuse shelters, and we are in the process of increasing the economic and political status of women. Although work in those areas must continue, perhaps it is time to start applying sanctions at the neighborhood level. Let us make individual batterers known to their communities, their churches, their schools, and their job sites for public censure. Let us work toward forming community and neighborhood level groups of women, both for economic solidarity and solidarity against men who batter. When a woman is being beaten, her neighbors can call the police for her if they are alerted to watch for danger signs before the violence begins. In this way, we can borrow ideas from Wape and Garifuna women and the *compadres* of Ecuador, imitate intercession by kin and community courts as among the Nagovisi, and pattern ourselves after the !Kung who help their neighbors. All these societies have mechanisms to limit the harm done by wife-beating and they all have much to teach us.

NOTES

I would like to thank Dorothy Counts and Judith Brown for their invitation to take part in the symposium from which this book has grown, for their insights into wife-beating which have changed my thinking on the subject, and for their extensive editorial and substantive contributions to this chapter.

1. The word theory will be used here as it is used in the most current social science literature on wife-beating. We recognize that these "theories" do not meet the most rigid scientific criteria, that these explanatory models are generally at the descriptive level with a few hypotheses at best.

2. Levinson (1989) thoughtfully countered this critique by statistically controlling for the gender of the anthropologist and found that the basic relationships between his quantified measures of wife-beating and other societal factors remained essentially the same. This strategy did not solve the issues of secondary data and gender of informants, but strengthens the case for considering his volume in conjunction with the data presented here.

3. See Young (1989) for an excellent discussion of an example of how, in less complex societies, enforcement of chastity before marriage has been translated into terms used in complex societies. Also see Collier and Rosaldo (1981) for discussion of the correlates of bridewealth societies which include those with dowry payments, also briefly discussed by Lambek in Chapter 12, this volume.

4. It has frequently been noted that the correlations between poverty and violence may be an artifact of increased visibility of violence among the poor and/or less reticence among poor people to admit violence when they are questioned by those conducting surveys.

5. Scholars have defined violent behavior and have distinguished between various aspects of violence in order to explain what appears to be paradoxical and contradictory behavior in other societies. See, for instance, Heider's (1979) distinction between aggression and acts of violence among the Dani of Irian Jaya, who are peaceful in their interpersonal relationships yet constantly engaged in warfare with their neighbors.

REFERENCES CITED

Allen, C. M., and Murray A. Straus. 1980. Resources, Power, and Husband-Wife Violence. *In* Social Causes of Husband-Wife Violence. Gerald T. Hotaling and Murray A. Straus, eds. Pp. 188—208. Minneapolis: University of Minnesota Press.

Baron, Larry, and Murray A. Straus. 1987. Legitimate Violence, Violent Attitudes, and Rape: A Test of the Cultural Spillover Theory. Annal of the New York Academy of Sciences 528:79—110.

Bernard, Thomas J. 1990. Angry Aggression Among the "Truly Disadvantaged." Criminology 28(1):73—96.

Bowker, Lee H. 1983. Beating Wife-beating. Lexington, MA: Lexington Books.

Brown, Judith K. 1982. Cross-Cultural Perspectives on Middle-Aged Women. Current Anthropology 23(2):143—156.

Campbell, Jacquelyn C. 1985. The Beating of Wives: A Cross-Cultural Perspective. Victimology 10:174—185.

———. 1989. A Test of Two Explanatory Models of Women's Responses to Battering. Nursing Research 38:1—24.

———. 1992. "If I Can't Have You, No One Can:" Issues of Power and Control in the Homicide of Women. *In* Femicide. J. Radford and Diana Russell, ed. London: Twayne.

Campbell, Jacquelyn C., and Janice Humphreys. 1984. Nursing Care of Victims of Family Violence. Norwalk, CT: Appleton.

Carmody, Dianne C., and Kirk Williams. 1987. Wife Assault and the Perceptions of Sanctions. Violence and Victims 2:25—38.

Carroll, James C. 1980. Cultural-Consistency Theory of Family Violence in Mexican-American and Jewish-American Ethnic groups. *In* Social Causes of Husband-Wife Violence. Gerald T. Hotaling and Murray A. Straus, eds. Minneapolis: University of Minnesota Press.

Collier, Jane F., and Michelle Rosaldo. 1981. Politics and Gender in Simple Societies. *In* Sexual Meanings. Sherry Ortner and Harriet Whitehead, eds. New York: Cambridge University Press.

Counts, Dorothy Ayers. 1990. Introduction. Pacific Studies 13(3):1—6. Special Issue: Domestic Violence in Oceania. Dorothy Ayers Counts, ed.

Daly, Martin, and Margo Wilson. 1988. Homicide. New York: Aldine de Gruyter.

Daly, Mary. 1979. Gyn/Ecology: The Metaethics of Radical Feminism. Boston: Beacon Press.

Davidson, Terry. 1978. Conjugal Crime: Understanding and Changing the Wifebeating Problem. New York: Hawthorn Books.

Dobash, Rebecca Emerson, and Russell Dobash. 1979. Violence Against Wives. New York: The Free Press.

Dutton, Donald G. 1988. The Domestic Assault of Women. Newton, MA: Allyn and Bacon, Inc.

Gelles, Richard J. 1983. An Exchange/social Theory. *In* The Dark Side of Families: Current Family Violence Research. David Finkelhor, Richard J. Gelles, Gerald T. Hotaling, and Murray J. Straus, eds. Pp. 151—165. Beverly Hills: Sage.

Giles-Sims, Jean. 1983. Wife-Battering: A Systems Theory Approach. New York: Guilford Press.

Gondolf, Edward. 1988. Who Are Those Guys? Toward a Behavioral Typology of Batterers. Violence and Victims 3(3):187—203.

Goode, William. 1971. Force and Violence in the Family. Journal of Marriage and the Family 33:624—636.

Greenblat, Cathy. 1985. "Don't Hit Your Wife . . . Unless . . .": Preliminary Findings on Normative Support for the Use of Physical Force by Husbands. Victimology 10:221—241.

Hanmer, Jalna and Mary Maynard, eds. 1985. Women, Violence and Social Control. Atlantic Highlands, NJ: Humanities Press.

Hawkins, Darnell F. 1986. Homicide Among Black Americans. Lanham, MD: University Press of America.

Heider, Karl. 1979. Grand Valley Dani: Peaceful Warriors. New York: Holt, Rinehart and Winston.

Hornung, Carlton A., B. Claire McCullough and Taichi Sugimoto. 1981. Status Relationships in Marriage: Risk Factors in Spouse Abuse. Journal of Marriage and the Family 43(3):675—692.

Hotaling, Gerald, and David Sugarman. 1986. An Analysis of Risk Markers in Husband to Wife Violence: The Current State of Knowledge. Violence and Victims 1:101—124.

Kalmuss, Debra S., and Murray A. Straus. 1982. Wife's Marital Dependency and Wife Abuse. Journal of Marriage and the Family 44:277—286.

Kalmuss, Debra S., and Murray A. Straus. 1990. Wife's Marital Dependency and Wife Abuse. In Straus, Murray and Richard Gelles, eds. Physical violence in American Families. Pp. 369—382. New Brunswick: Transaction Press.

Kerns, Virginia, and Judith K. Brown, eds. In press. In Her Prime: New Views of Middle-Aged Women. Second Edition. Urbana: University of Illinois Press.

Lester, David. 1980. A Cross-Culture Study of Wife Abuse. Aggressive Behavior 6:361—364.

Levinson, David. 1989. Family Violence in Cross-Cultural Perspectives. Newbury Park, CA: Sage Publications.

Lockhart, Lettie L. 1987. A Reexamination of the Effects of Race and Social Class on the Incidence of Marital Violence: A Search for Reliable Differences. Journal of Marriage and the Family 49:603—610.

Masamura, Wilfred T. 1979. Wife Abuse and Other Forms of Aggression. Victimology 2:479—485.

McGehee, Charles L. 1985. Responses to Child Abuse in World Perspective. Victimology 10:140—163.

Mercy, James A., and Linda Saltzman. 1989. Fatal Violence Among Spouses in the United States, 1976—85. American Journal of Public Health 79:595—599.

Parker, Barbara, and Dale Schumacher. 1977. The Battered Wife Syndrome and Violence in the Nuclear Family of Origin: A Controlled Pilot Study. American Journal of Public Health 67:760—761.

Pleck, Elizabeth. 1987. Domestic Tyranny: The Making of Social Policy Against Family Violence from Colonial Times to the Present. New York: Oxford University Press.

Ptacek, James. 1988. The Clinical Literature on Men Who Batter: A Review and Critique. In Family Abuse and Its Consequence. Gerald T. Hotaling, David Finkelhor, John Kirpatrick and Murray Straus, eds. Pp. 149—192. Newbury Park, CA: Sage.

Rosaldo, Michelle Zimbalist, and Louise Lamphere. 1974. Women in Politics. *In* Women, Culture and Society. Pp. 89—96. Stanford: Stanford University Press.

Saunders, Daniel. G. 1988. Wife Abuse, Husband Abuse, or Mutual Combat? A Feminist Perspective on the Empirical Findings. *In* Feminist Perspectives on Wife Abuse. Kersti Yllo and Michele Bograd, eds. Pp. 90—113. Newbury Park, CA: Sage.

Shields, Nancy, George J. McCall and Christine R. Hanneke. 1988. Patterns of Family and Nonfamily Violence: Violent Husbands and Violent Men. Violence and Victims 3:83—97.

Smith, Michael D. 1989. Is There a Patriarchal Subculture of Wife Abusers? Paper presented at the American Criminological Society Annual Meeting.

Steinmetz, Suzanne K., and Joseph H. Lucca. 1988. Husband Battering. *In* Vincent Van Hasselt, Randall L. Morrison, Alan S. Bellack, and Michel Hersen, eds. Pp. 233—246. Handbook of Family Violence. New York: Plenum Press.

Straus, Murray A. 1990. Ordinary Violence, Child Abuse, and Wife-Beating: What Do They Have in Common? *In* Physical Violence in American Families. Murray A. Straus and Richard Gelles, eds. Pp. 403—423. New Brunswick: Transaction.

Straus, Murray, and Richard Gelles. 1990. Physical Violence in American Families. New Brunswick: Transaction Press.

Straus, Murray, and Christine Smith. 1990. Violence in Hispanic Families in the United States: Incidence Rates and Structural Interpretations. *In* Physical Violence in American Families. Murray Straus and Richard Gelles, eds. Pp. 341—367. New Brunswick: Transaction Press.

Tolman, Richard, and Larry Bennett. 1990. A Review of Quantitative Research on Men Who Batter. Journal of Interpersonal Violence 5:87—118.

Torres, Sara. 1987. Hispanic-American Battered Women. Why Consider Cultural Differences? Response 10:20—21.

Van Hasselt, Vincent, Randall Morrison, Alan Bellack and Michel Hersen, eds. 1988. Handbook of Family Violence. New York: Plenum Press.

Wolfgang, Marvin E., and Franco Ferracuti. 1981 [1967]. The Subculture of Violence. Beverly Hills: Sage.

Yllo, Kersti. 1984. The Status of Women, Marital Equality, and Violence Against Wives. Journal of Family Issues 3:307—320.

Yllo, Kersti, and Michelle Bograd. 1988. Feminist Perspectives on Wife Abuse. Beverly Hills: Sage.

Yllo, Kersti, and Murray A. Straus. 1990. Patriarchy and Violence Against Wives: The Impact of Structural and Normative Factors. *In* Physical Violence in American Families. Murray Straus and Richard Gelles, eds. Pp. 383—399. New Brunswick: Transaction Press.

Young, Kathleen Z. 1989. The Imperishable Virginity of Saint Maria Goretti. Gender and Society 3(4):474—482.

About the Editors and Contributors

JUDITH K. BROWN is professor of anthropology at Oakland University in Rochester, Michigan. She has conducted cross-cultural research on initiation rites for girls, female economic roles, and middle-aged women.

VICTORIA K. BURBANK received her Ph.D. from Rutgers University in 1980 and did three years of post-doctoral study at Harvard University. She is currently research associate in the Department of Anthropology at the University of California at Davis.

JACQUELYN C. CAMPBELL is associate professor at Wayne State University College of Nursing, conducts longitudinal research on women's responses to battering, and has authored many articles and co-authored a book dealing with nursing care of battered women and violent families. She also provides health consultation and facilitates a support group at My Sister's Place battered women's shelter in Detroit, Michigan.

LAURENCE MARSHALL CARUCCI is associate professor in the Department of Sociology at Montana State University. He has conducted field research among the people of Enewetak, Ujelang, and Majuro Atolls of the Marshall Islands of Micronesia. His publications have focused on culture change, aging, kinship, and social organization.

DOROTHY AYERS COUNTS is professor of anthropology at the University of Waterloo. She has conducted research in West New Britain Province, Papua New Guinea since 1966. She is author, editor, or co-editor of five books as well as numerous journal articles and book chapters on subjects including mythology, cargo belief and activity, political and economic change, aging and dying, domestic violence, and female suicide.

CHARLES B. CRAWFORD is associate professor of psychology at Simon Fraser University. He has spent sabbatical leaves at the Institute of Behavior Genetics, University of Colorado, and at the Evolution and Human Behavior Program, University of Michigan. He is editor of a recent book on sociobiology and psychology and has published in journals such as the American Psychologist, Psychological Bulletin, and the Journal of Comparative

Psychology with the goal of integrating psychobiology with mainstream psychology.

PATRICIA DRAPER is associate professor in the Program for Individual and Family Studies, College of Human Development at Pennsylvania State University. She has done repeated field work among the !Kung, working with both traditional and acculturated communities. Her research has focused on !Kung women and children with a focus on the biocultural bases of sex roles, child development, and social and psychological anthropology.

RITA S. GALLIN is director of the Women and International Development Program and associate professor of sociology at Michigan State University. She has published extensively in journals and edited volumes on economic development and social change in Taiwan and is the founding editor of *The Women and International Development Annual*, Westview Press.

MARY ELAINE HEGLAND is assistant professor of social/cultural anthropology at Santa Clara University, where she teaches courses related to the Middle East and women's studies. She conducted her Ph.D. field research on religion, ritual, and revolution in an Iranian village during 1978 and 1979 and is presently working on a research project with Iranian women in the United States.

VIRGINIA KERNS is associate professor and chair of the Department of Anthropology at the College of William and Mary and is author of *Women and the Ancestors: Black Carib Kinship and Ritual* (1983), co-editor of *In Her Prime: New Views of Middle-Aged Women* (second edition in press), and a former associate editor of the *American Ethnologist*. She currently serves on the board of directors of the Williamsburg (Virginia) Task Force on Battered Women/Sexual Assault.

MICHAEL LAMBEK is professor of anthropology at the University of Toronto. He is author of *Human Spirits: A Cultural Account of Trance in Mayotte* (1981) as well as papers on various aspects of gender, personhood, ritual, and knowledge.

SHIREEN LATEEF is an Indo-Fijian anthropologist who teaches in the School of Early Childhood Studies at the University of Melbourne in Australia. She received her Ph.D. from the Department of Anthropology and Sociology, Monash University, Victoria, Australia. Her dissertation research was conducted among Indo-Fijian women in Suva, Fiji.

NANCY MCDOWELL received her B.A. degree from the University of Illinois and her Master's and Ph.D. degrees from Cornell University. She conducted field research in Bun, Papua New Guinea, in 1972–1973, 1977, and 1981. She is currently associate professor of anthropology and chairperson of the women's studies program at Franklin and Marshall College in Lancaster, Pennsylvania.

LAURIS MCKEE is assistant professor of anthropology at Franklin and Marshall College. Her work in Ecuador began in 1975 and has been funded by the National Institute of Mental Health, the National Science Foundation, and the Fulbright Foundation. She is the author of many publications, including work on children's health and gender issues.

BARBARA DIANE MILLER has studied several aspects of women's status in India, especially the neglect of daughters and public health interventions. She has analyzed the relationship between internal migration and suicide in Sri Lanka and has also done research in Jamaica on household budgeting and food security. Her books on these subjects include *The Endangered Sex: Neglect of Female Children in Rural North India* (1981) and *Internal Migration and Its Social Consequences in Sri Lanka* (1985) plus an edited collection of essays entitled *Sex And Gender Hierarchies*. (She has a new book on India in preparation.)

WILLIAM E. MITCHELL, professor of anthropology at the University of Vermont, received his Ph.D. from Columbia University. He has done field work among the Lujere, Iatmul, and Wape peoples of Papua New Guinea, the Chinese and Jewish people of New York City, and child patients of a mental institution. His research interests center on problems of family and kinship, psychological anthropology, exchange theory, and ethnotherapy.

JILL NASH is professor and chair of anthropology at the State University College at Buffalo, Buffalo, New York. Her major research interests are Melanesia, gender, and kinship. She is the author of a monograph and numerous papers focusing on the Nagovisi of North Solomons Province, Papua New Guinea.

KAREN KELJO TRACY is associate professor of psychology at Marygrove College. Her research interests are in the areas of sex roles, intimate relationships, and cross-cultural psychology. Her dissertation research was on sex roles and moral development.

Index